For Reference

Not to be taken from this room

AFRICAN AMERICAN ALMANAC

African American Almanac

**Volume I
History**

Jay P. Pederson and Kenneth Estell, Editors

SOUTH HUNTINGTON
PUBLIC LIBRARY
2 MELVILLE ROAD
HUNTINGTON STATION, N.Y. 11746

An Imprint of Gale Research Inc.

AFRICAN AMERICAN ALMANAC

Jay P. Pederson and Kenneth Estell, *Editors*

Staff

Carol DeKane Nagel, *U·X·L Developmental Editor*
Thomas L. Romig, *U·X·L Publisher*

Amy Marcaccio, *Acquisitions Editor*

Barbara A. Wallace, *Permissions Associate (Pictures)*
Margaret A. Chamberlain, *Permissions Supervisor (Pictures)*

Mary Kelley, *Production Associate*
Evi Seoud, *Assistant Production Manager*
Mary Beth Trimper, *Production Director*

Mary Krzewinski, *Cover Designer*
Cynthia Baldwin, *Art Director*

The Graphix Group, *Typesetter*

This publication is a creative work fully protected by all applicable copyright laws, as well as by misappropriation, trade secret, unfair competition, and other applicable laws. The editors of this work have added value to the underlying factual material herein through one or more of the following: unique and original selection, coordination, expression, arrangement, and classification of the information. All rights to this publication will be vigorously defended.

Copyright © 1994
U·X·L
An Imprint of Gale Research Inc.

All rights reserved, including the right of reproduction in whole or in part in any form.

™ This book is printed on acid-free paper that meets the minimum requirements of American National Standard for Information Sciences—Permanence Paper for Printed Library Materials, ANSI Z39.48-1984.

ISBN 0-8103-9239-9 (Set)
ISBN 0-8103-9240-2 (Volume 1)
ISBN 0-8103-9241-0 (Volume 2)
ISBN 0-8103-9242-9 (Volume 3)

Printed in the United States of America

Published simultaneously in the United Kingdom
by Gale Research International Limited
(An affiliated company of Gale Research Inc.)

I(T)P™

The trademark **ITP** is used under license.

ADVISORY BOARD

Alton Hornsby, Jr.
Professor of History
Morehouse College

Jean Blackwell Hutson
Former Curator and Director
Schomburg Center for Research in Black Culture

William C. Matney, Jr.
Public Affairs Coordinator
U.S. Bureau of the Census

Carole McCullough
Professor of Library Science
Wayne State University

Brenda Mitchell-Powell
Editor
Multicultural Review

Jessie Carney Smith
University Librarian
Fisk University

READER'S GUIDE

African American Almanac features a comprehensive range of historical and current information on African American life and culture. Organized into 26 subject chapters, including Civil Rights, The Family and Health, and Science, Medicine, and Invention, the volumes contain more than three hundred black-and-white photographs and maps, a glossary of terms used in the text, a selected bibliography, and a cumulative subject index.

Other titles of interest:

African American Biography profiles three hundred African Americans, both living and deceased, prominent in fields ranging from civil rights to athletics, politics to literature, entertainment to science, religion to the military. A black-and-white portrait accompanies each entry, and a cumulative subject index lists all individuals by field of endeavor.

African American Breakthroughs: Five Hundred Years of Black Firsts provides fascinating details on hundreds of "firsts" involving African Americans. The volume is arranged in subject categories, and entries summarize events and include brief biographies of the people involved. *African American Breakthroughs* features illustrations, a timeline of firsts, and a thorough index.

African American Chronology explores significant social, political, economic, cultural, and educational milestones in black history. Arranged by year and then by month and day, the chronology spans from 1492 to modern times and contains more than one hundred illustrations, extensive cross references, and a cumulative subject index.

Comments and Suggestions

We welcome your comments on *African American Almanac* as well as your suggestions for topics to be featured in future editions. Please write: Editors, *African American Almanac*, U·X·L, 835 Penobscot Building, Detroit, Michigan 48226-4094; call toll-free: 1-800-877-4253; or fax: 313-961-6348.

CONTENTS

Advisory Board v
Reader's Guide vi
Picture Credits xv
Words to Know xvii

Volume 1: History

1 **Flashbacks: The Birth and Rise of the African American, 1492-1993** 1
   Columbus's Great Discovery to the Beginnings of Colonial America 1
   The Pilgrim Landing to the American Revolution 2
   The Independence of a Nation to the Emancipation of a Race 4
   The Death of Lincoln to the Birth of King 4
   The Depths of the Depression to the Dawn of the Civil Rights Movement 8
   The Montgomery Boycott to the Death of King 11
   The Newton Trial to the Miami Riots 15
   The Rise of the Black Middle Class to Jackson's Second Running 16
   New Heights, New Lows 19

2 **Motherland: A Survey of African South of the Sahara** 21
   A Brief History 21
   Africa Today 23
   Country Profiles
      West Africa 24
      West Central Africa 35
      Northeast Africa 40

vii

CONTENTS

    East Africa 43
    Southeast Central Africa 46
    Southern Africa 49
    East African Island Nations 52

3 Neighbors: Blacks in the Western Hemisphere **55**
  A Brief History 55
  The Caribbean Today 55
  Country Profiles
    The Caribbean 56
    Central America 68
    South America 70
    North America 73

**4 Words: Letters, Laws, Speeches, Songs, and Other Chronicles of
African American History, 1661-1993** **75**

5 Places: African American Landmarks around the United States **124**
  The Midwest 125
  The Northeast 135
  South Central States 152
  The Southeast 159
  The West 170

Further Reading 183
Index 185

Volume 2: Society

6 Slavery: From the Beginnings of America to the End of the 19th Century **213**
  African Roots of Slavery 213
  The Growth of Slavery in Colonial America 217
  Slavery in the New Nation 218
  Expansion of Slavery 220
  Antislavery Movements 222
  The Abolition Movement 222
  The Underground Railroad 224
  Civil War 224
  Civil Rights at the End of the Civil War 225

CONTENTS

**7   Civil Rights: The Struggle That Shaped the Hearts and Minds of
    African Americans** 227
    Reconstruction and Civil Rights 227
    Civil Rights in the Twentieth Century 229
    Boycotts, Marches, Sit-ins, and Demonstrations: Civil Rights in the 1960s 232
    "Letter from Birmingham Jail" 232
    Urban Tension and Civil Disorder 235
    The Fading of Militancy and a New Civil Rights Era 241
    Racism in the 1980s 242
    1993 and Beyond 243

8   Black Nationalism: Nation Building 245
    Early Black Nationalism in the United States 246
    The Flowering of the Movement 249
    Black Nationalism in the Twentieth Century 250
    Black Nationalism Today 253

9   Law: The Legal Status of African Americans 255
    Thurgood Marshall: A Beacon of Black Hope 255
    The Rights of African Americans: The First Hundred Years 256
    Civil Rights Following the Civil War 258
    The Twentieth Century and Full Legal Status for African Americans 262
    Twentieth-Century Supreme Court Decisions 262
    Justice Wins Out: The Medgar Evers Murder Case 266

10 Politics: The Voter and Elected Officeholder 267
    Black Politics during the Years of Slavery 268
    The Convention Movement 269
    Reconstruction and Backlash 271
    The Twentieth Century and Jim Crow 273
    World War II and the Election of Adam Clayton Powell, Jr. 275
    The Civil Rights Movement Leads to Breakthrough Gains for African Americans 277
    Politics in the 1990s 280
    Blacks and the Clinton Administration 280

11 National Organizations: In Unity There Is Strength 282
    Early Black Organizations 283
    Twentieth-Century Organizations 284

ix

CONTENTS

12 Population: The Growth and Settlement of a Race 295
   A New Land, a New People 295
   Emancipation and Migration 297
   The Great Migration 298
   Population Growth Since 1980 300
   The Present and Future 300
   Current Demographics 301
   The Future of the Black Population 304

13 Jobs and Money: The African American Labor Force and Economic Outlook 305
   Middle Class and Underclass 305
   Family Structure and Family Income 307
   Poverty 309
   The Role of the Government 312
   Current Trends 314

14 Entrepreneurship: Risk-taking and the Creation of Wealth 315
   Entrepreneurship before the Civil War 316
   Entrepreneurship after the Civil War 318
   Black Agriculture: A Story of Decline 319
   Black Entrepreneurs in the Post-Civil Rights Era 324
   Growth Industries 324
   Recent Trends 326
   Modern-Day Milestones: A Look Back and a Look Forward 327

15 The Family and Health: The Backbone of the Community 329
   The Family
      Hopeful Appraisals 329
      Different Shapes, Different Sizes 333
      Families and Money 334
      Family Structure and Stability 336
      Violence and Other Problems of the Inner-City Family 336
      The Great Society: A Failure? 338
      Number and Size of Families 339
      Families in Poverty 341
      The Elderly 341

    Marriage and the Shortage of Black Men 341
    Fertility and Births 342

Health
    Birth 344
    Child Health 344
    Sickle Cell Anemia 345
    AIDS 345
    Cigarette, Alcohol, and Drug Use 346
    Life Expectancy 346
    Homicide and Death by Accident 347
    Suicide 347
    Health Care 348
    Solutions 348

16 Education: The Force That Liberates **349**
    Education through the Church 349
    African Free Schools in New York and Philadelphia 350
    Freedmen's Organizations and Agencies 351
    Independent Schools in the Late Nineteenth Century 353
    Early Black Institutions of Higher Education 354
    Early Promoters of African American Studies 356
    The End of Segregation in Public Education 356
    Black Colleges in the Twentieth Century 360
    Independent Schools in the Late Twentieth Century 360
    Current Problems, Needs, and Trends 361

17 Religion: The Tie That Binds **365**
    The Old and the New 365
    Christian Missionary Efforts 366
    Early Black Congregations 367
    Black Female Religious Leadership 371
    Black Churches during Reconstruction 372
    Black Churches in the Twentieth Century 374
    Current Trends 375
    Black Denominations 379

Further Reading 387
Index 389

CONTENTS

Volume 3: Culture

18 Literature: African American Writers, Scholars, and Poets **417**
- The Oral Tradition 419
- Early African American Writers 419
- The Harlem Renaissance 423
- African American Writers after the Harlem Renaissance 425
- The Black Arts Movement 425
- Post-1960s Literature and the Rise of Black Women Writers 427

19 Performing Arts: The African American in the Performing Arts **429**
- African Americans and the Performing Arts 429
- The Earliest Plays with African American Actors 430
- Minstrel Shows 431
- Reclaiming the Black Image: 1890 to 1920 432
- The Development of Black Performers from the Harlem Renaissance
  through the 1950s 434
- Dramatic Theater in the 1950s 436
- Black Dance 437
- The Black Comedian 438
- The Civil Rights Movement and Its Affect on Black Performers 438
- Modern Black Musicals 440
- Modern Black Dance 441
- Modern Black Comedy 444

20 Film and Television **446**
Film
- The Silent Era 448
- Oscar Micheaux and Early Independent Filmmaking 449
- The 1930s and the Dawn of Musicals 450
- World War II and the 1940s 452
- Dorothy Dandridge and the 1950s 453
- The Reign of Sidney Poitier 453
- Black Power, Black Direction, and Blaxploitation 455
- Comedy: The Hottest Trend of the 1980s 456
- Spike Lee and a New Era of Filmmaking 459

Television
- *I Spy* 464
- The 1970s and the Rise of Programs for Blacks 466
- The 1980s 470
- Current Programming 472

21 Media: The African American Press and Broadcast Media 473
- Newspaper and Magazine Publishers 473
- **Broadcasting**
  - Radio 478
  - Television 481
  - Public Television 484
  - Public Radio 485
  - Cable Television 485
- **Book Publishers**
  - Religious Publishers 485
  - Institutional Publishers 487
  - Commercial Publishers 489

22 Music: Popular, Jazz, and Classical 490
- **Popular Music**
  - Gospel: The Root of Popular Music 490
  - The Rise of Rhythm and Blues 493
  - Rock and Roll 496
  - Blacks and Country Music 497
  - Soul: The Mirror of a Decade 498
  - Motown: The Capital of Northern Soul 499
  - Funk 501
  - Rap: A Voice from the Streets 502
- **Blues and Jazz**
  - Ragtime and Blues 504
  - New Orleans Jazz 504
  - Early Recordings and Improvisation 505
  - The Jazz Tradition 507
- **Classical**
  - Slave Music 511
  - Art Music in the Nineteenth Century 511
  - Classical Music in the Twentieth Century 512

CONTENTS

23 Fine and Applied Arts: The African American Artist 518
  Black Artists in Early America 519
  African American Artists in the Harlem Renaissance 521
  African American Artists since the Depression 522
  The Search for an African American Identity 524
  Architecture and the Applied Arts 524
  Museums and Galleries since the 1960s 526
  Black Milestones and Major Black Exhibits 529

24 Science, Medicine, and Invention: African American Contributions to Science .. 533
  Early Scientists and Inventors 534
  Scientists and Inventors in the 20th Century 535
  Highlights in Medicine 539

25 Sports: The African American Amateur and Professional Athlete 542
  Baseball 543
  Basketball 546
  Football 547
  Boxing 549
  Women in Sports 551
  Current Issues in Sports for African Americans 552

26 Military: African American Servicemen and the Military Establishment 556
  The American Revolution and the Revolutionary War (1775-83) 556
  The War of 1812 557
  The Civil War (1861-65) 557
  United States Colored Troops (USCT) 558
  The Indian Campaigns (1866-90) 560
  The Spanish-American War (1898) 561
  World War I 564
  The Interwar Years (1919-40) 565
  World War II 565
  The Move toward Equality in the Ranks 572
  The Korean War 573
  Vietnam 574
  The 1970s and 1980s 576
  The Persian Gulf War 577

Further Reading 581
Index 583

PICTURE CREDITS

The photographs and illustrations appearing in *African American Almanac* were received from the following sources:

Courtesy of the Library of Congress: pp. 3 (upper left), 4, 7, 91, 97, 107, 181, 214, 215, 219, 220, 221, 224, 226, 233, 246, 258, 259, 270 (lower right), 273 (lower right), 283, 317, 319, 351, 353, 431, 534, 558; **AP/Wide World Photos:** pp. 10, 12, 14, 18, 19, 20, 51, 86, 94, 108, 113, 122, 140 (lower right), 144, 146, 153, 155, 157, 161, 171, 231, 235, 244, 254 (upper right), 260, 262 (upper left), 262 (upper right), 265, 269 (upper left), 270 (upper left), 275, 281, 286, 291 (lower right), 292, 293 (lower right), 312, 318, 324 (lower right), 326 (lower right), 328, 356, 359, 374, 377, 378, 382, 418, 419, 427, 428 (upper left), 434 (lower right), 437, 440 (upper left), 440 (lower right), 443, 444, 447, 450, 451, 457, 458, 460, 462, 463, 467, 470, 471, 482, 483, 484, 492, 495 (lower right), 497, 498, 499, 502, 503, 505, 508, 514, 516, 527, 538, 543 (upper right), 546 (upper left), 547, 548, 550 (lower right), 551 (upper left), 552, 553, 554, 555, 560, 576, 577, 578, 579; **UPI/Bettmann:** pp. 13, 28, 105, 112, 120, 230, 238, 254 (upper left), 256, 280, 288, 291 (upper left), 293 (upper left), 307, 428 (upper right), 452, 468, 469, 478, 506, 513, 525, 541, 544, 549, 551 (lower right); *Harper's Magazine:* pp. 22, 147; **United Nations:** pp. 27, 33, 36, 42, 44, 48, 59, 61, 63 (upper left), 63 (lower right), 65, 67, 71, 385; **National Museum of African Art:** pp. 31, 35, 39; **Courtesy of Fisk University:** pp. 77, 95, 247, 272, 354 (lower right), 371, 422 (lower right), 430; **Bettmann Archive:** pp. 89, 172, 229 (lower right), 357, 453, 504, 535 (lower right), 559; **Courtesy of the Consulate General of Jamaica:** p. 102; **NBC:** 110, 466, 500; **The Granger Collection, New York:** p. 138; **The Schomburg Center for Research in Black Culture, the New York Public Library:** pp. 158, 512, 545; **Courtesy of the National Park Service:** p. 166, 168; **U.S. Navy:** 174, 572; **Denver Public Library, Western Collection:** pp. 176, 180; **Archive Photos/Lass:** p. 223; **Archive Photos:** pp. 252, 271, 384, 454, 455, 456, 459, 465, 515, 543 (upper left); **Courtesy of the NAACP:** pp. 264, 285, 290, 311, 320 (lower right), 331; **Courtesy of the New York Public Library:** pp. 269 (lower right), 434 (upper left), 495 (upper left); **Surlock Photographers:** p. 274; **Courtesy the National Archives:** pp. 284, 303, 521; **Reproduced by**

PICTURE CREDITS

permission of The Stanley B. Burns, M.D. Collection: pp. 299, 379; **NASA:** p. 306; **Photograph by Sue Stetler:** p. 309; **Photograph by Kenneth Estell:** pp. 310, 334, 336; **Photograph by Andy Roy:** pp. 314, 324 (upper left), 326 (upper left); **Courtesy of the Walker Collection of A'Lelia Bundles:** p. 320 (upper left); **Photograph by Brian V. Jones:** 330, 333, 341; **Courtesy of the Bethune Museum and Archive:** p. 354 (upper left); **Photograph by Bruce Giffin:** p. 362; **Photograph by Beverly Hardy:** p. 364; **The National Portrait Gallery, The Smithsonian Institution:** p. 370; **Archive Photos/American Stock Photos:** p. 373; **John Duprey/***NY Daily News:* p. 381; **Springer/Bettmann Film Archive:** pp. 423, 493; **Courtesy of the Arthur B. Spingarn Collection, Moorland-Spingarn Research Center, Howard University:** p. 424 (upper left); **Courtesy WABC-TV, New York:** p. 442; **Courtesy of The Associated Publishers:** p. 475; **Archive Photos/Frank Driggs Collection:** p. 494; **Courtesy of Columbia Records:** p. 496; **Courtesy of the William Morris Agency:** p. 509; **Courtesy of** *Downbeat:* p. 510; **National Museum of American Art, Washington D.C./Art Resource, N.Y.:** pp. 520 (upper left), 523, 531; **General Motors, Public Relations Department:** p. 526; **Reuters/Bettmann:** p. 546 (lower right); **Photograph by Carl Nesfield:** p. 550 (upper left); **U.S. War Department/National Archives:** p. 563, 564; **U.S. Army:** p. 567, 569, 573.

WORDS TO KNOW

A

abolition: the destruction or ending of slavery; an *abolitionist* is a person or a group in favor of putting an end to slavery, or the principles behind such a person or group

abstain: to refrain from doing; *abstinence* is the act of voluntary avoiding a certain behavior

acquittal: a court decision freeing one of charges; to be *acquitted* is to be cleared of all charges, to be declared not guilty

aesthetics: the study or theory of beauty as it relates to art

affiliates: those businesses or persons associated or connected with an organization

affirmative action: a policy designed to correct the effects of racial and sexual discrimination through hiring quotas and other measures; sometimes negatively referred to as "reverse discrimination"

agrarian: relating to farming, agriculture, or agribusiness

alliance: a close partnership or association

alma mater: (Latin for *fostering mother*) the particular school or college a person attended

alumni: persons who have attended or graduated from a particular school or college

American Dream: the concept that all Americans, given equal opportunities, may strive for personal and financial success

anchor: in broadcasting, to serve as chief reporter of a newscast

annex: to add or attach

anthropology: the study of humans, including their characteristics, culture, and customs

anti-Semitism: discrimination or prejudice against Jews

apartheid: a policy of racial separation

applied arts: fields in which art serves a dual function, such as graphic or fashion design

apprehension: an understanding of an issue; fear that something bad will occur; capture or arrest

appropriations: funds set aside for a specific purpose

arbiter: one who judges or decides

archaeologists: scientists who study past civilizations, especially by a process of careful digging called excavation

WORDS TO KNOW

archipelago: a group of islands

archives: a place where important papers, documents, and other memorabilia are kept; the papers, documents, and memorabilia that are kept in such a place

arias: melodies in an opera, oratorio, or cantata created especially for a solo voice

Armageddon: the place referred to in the Biblical Book of Revelation where the last battle is to be fought between the forces of good and evil; the time of the last battle; also referred to as the *apocalypse*

aspirations: ambitions

assimilate: to become like or similar to, to join

attaché: a person with special duties, particularly in connection with international relations

autonomous: independent or self-governing

avant-garde: new and nontraditional

B

bequest: money or other personal property that is awarded by means of a will; the act of giving money or personal property

Black Muslim movement: also called the Nation of Islam; a religious movement, begun by W. D. Fard and furthered by Elijah Muhammad, that preached black self-sufficiency and worship of Allah. Among the most famous converts to the Black Muslims were Malcolm X and Muhammad Ali

Black codes: unfair rules and laws directed at African Americans following emancipation

Bohemianism: living outside the conventions of society

bourgeoisie: a social class between the wealthy and the working class; the middle class

boycott: a refusal by an individual or group to buy, sell, or use products or services

C

capital: money, property, and other valuable assets that are used to start and sustain a business

cardiovascular: the system that links the heart and blood vessels

catafalque: a wooden framework used to hold a coffin during elaborate funerals

catalysts: persons or objects that bring about events or results

caucus: a group of politicians or a meeting of political party leaders

ceded: formally transferred or surrendered

census: an official count of the population that also includes information about age, sex, race, economic status, etc.

CEO: *C*hief *E*xecutive *O*fficer; the highest executive of a company or organization

charter: a document that outlines the goals of a group

chattel: persons regarded as fixed items of personal property

choreography: the arrangement or step-by-step planning of a dance

civil disobedience: nonviolent resistance to a policy or law; first popularized by Indian leader Mohandas (Mahatma) Gandhi

clichés: unoriginal statements or ideas

coalition: a group united in purpose

collateral: a form of security that is offered to a lender until a loan is repaid

commercialism: business focused purely on profit

compromise: something blending qualities of two different things

compulsory: necessary or required

confrontations: bold face-to-face meetings

conglomerate: a large corporation that owns several smaller businesses in a number of different industries

WORDS TO KNOW

connoisseurs: those who take keen enjoyment in their field of expertise

conscientious: ruled by what one thinks to be right

consecrated: made or *ordained* a bishop through a religious ceremony; made or declared sacred

consensus: general agreement

conservatism: a political movement or philosophy that stresses less government and more private enterprise

conspiracy: a plot to work together in secret, especially for harmful or unlawful purposes

constituency: the group of voters an elected official serves

constitutionality: legality in relationship to the laws and principles set forth in the Constitution

controversial: subject to argument or debate

conversion: the change from lack of faith to religious faith; the change from one religion to another

corporations: businesses, formed with permission of the state or federal government, that have the power to own property and make contracts

coup: (short for the French *coup d'état*) a quick seizure of power, often by military force

crossover: the ability to please or appeal to more than one group

curators: heads of museums or special collections

curriculum: the standard information, teaching plan, and testing for a course or major field of study; the entire teaching program of a given school or college

D

defected: left because of disagreement

demographics: the census characteristics of a population, broken down by geographic regions

denigrated: belittled

denomination: a specific religious body or organization (for example, Baptist, Methodist, or Catholic); *denominational* means having to do with a specific religious group, the opposite of *nondenominational*

deportation: the sending away, by official order, of an undesirable alien

deposed: removed from office

derive: come from

dialect: a spoken language specific to a region or group

diaspora: a scattering or dispersion of people who share a common background

dictatorships: governments ruled by absolute power; the opposite of democracies

dilemma: a serious problem, usually one for which there are two equally difficult choices

dioceses: a religious district presided over by a bishop; large or prominent religious districts are called *archdioceses*

disenfranchised: the poor or disadvantaged

dissenting: in legal matters, a *dissenting* opinion is one that differs from the majority, or ruling, opinion; dissenting opinions are offered by justices who think their fellow members on the bench have made an error in their ruling

documentary: a nonfiction (true-to-life) film

dominion: the power to rule; a territory that is ruled

downsizing: trimming, through plant closings, layoffs, etc., to make a business healthier and more profitable

E

ecumenical: anything promoting the unity of Christian churches

WORDS TO KNOW

effigy (to burn in): to publicly burn an image of a person in protest

emancipation: to be freed from the control of another

enact: to pass into law

enclave: a territory or group that is surrounded by a larger territory or group

endowment: a gift, generally money, to an institution or person; a natural talent or ability

entrepreneurship: the business quality of undertaking risk for the sake of earning a profit

equatorial: near or of the equator, the imaginary line equidistant from the North and South Poles

equity: value or worth, as in money, property, stocks, etc.

eulogized: praised after death

Eurocentric: concerned primarily with European or Western culture

evangelists: literally, bringers of good news; those fervently devoted to spreading the gospel

execution: the act of legally putting to death; carrying out of a task

exile: a person who by force or choice lives outside his country; the condition of living outside a country

exodus: literally, a going out; a massive migration or departure of a people

exonerated: declared not guilty

exploitation: unfair use of an individual or group

F

fascism: government by a one-party dictatorship

fertility: the state of being able to produce children, determined by age and other factors

feudal: a system popular in Europe during the Middle Ages in which serfs were bound for life to work the land and were, in turn, protected by overlords

fine arts: fields in which art stands alone, such as painting or sculpture

flamboyant: flashy and exciting

franchise: in sports, a team that is granted membership in a league

fugitive: a person who flees from danger or from the law

G

generative: capable of continuing, through reproduction, etc.

genocide: the destruction or killing of an entire race

genre: a type of literary form, such as a poem, story, novel, essay, or autobiography

glaucoma: an eye-related disorder that can, if untreated, cause a total loss of vision

Gothic: a style of architecture that stresses pointed arches and steep roofs; a style of fiction that suggests horror, mystery, and gloom; anything ornate

H

Harlem Renaissance: a flowering of black literature and performing arts during the 1920s in which Harlem served as the artistic capital

heptathlon: a track and field contest consisting of seven separate events

I

illiterate: a person who cannot read or write; the phrase *functional illiterate* refers to those whose reading and writing abilities are less than adequate

impeached: brought before a hearing on charges of wrongdoing

importation: to bring into a new region goods that are then usually sold

WORDS TO KNOW

inauguration: the formal ceremony by which a person is placed in office; to be *inaugurated* is to be formally sworn into office

incumbent: the current office-holder

indemnity: protection

indentured servant: a person bound by contract to work for another for a certain length of time; during the early period of American history, both black and white indentured servants were commonly used and were usually forced to work for seven years before they gained their freedom

indigo: a plant of the pea family; the blue dye obtained from such a plant

inducted: enrolled or entered into

inevitably: predictably

infringement: the act of overstepping boundaries and intruding on another's

injunction: an order from the court either prohibiting or demanding a certain action

innovators: in the performing arts, those who introduce new methods and styles and thereby change the direction of the field

inoculation: an injection, aimed at disease prevention, that causes a mild form of the disease; the injection forces the body to build up an immunity to a later attack of the actual disease

institution: a person, thing, idea, or practice that has taken root or settled into habit

insurmountable: not able to be overcome

integration: the bringing together of races, classes, or ethnic groups that were previously separated; bringing a group into equal membership in society

interpretive: bringing out the meaning or importance of

intimidation: to scare or make timid by means of threats or violence

intravenous: directly into a vein

involuntary servitude: the institution of forcing people to work for their freedom; also called indentured servitude

ironically: in a manner opposite of what is expected

J

Jim Crow: a reference (taken from a minstrel song) to laws and practices supporting the segregation of blacks and whites

jurisdiction: legal territory

L

laypersons: nonordained church members; also referred to as the *laity*

leveraged buyout: the purchase of a company in which most of the sale price is financed using borrowed money

liable: responsible by law

liberal arts: a course of study that provides a broad background in literature, philosophy, languages, history, and abstract sciences; the opposite of a vocational or technical course of study

literacy: the ability to read and write

litigation: the process of filing and pursuing a lawsuit

liturgical: having to do with the order and nature of public worship, including the songs, rituals, readings, prayers, and sermon that form a religious service

lynching: murder without trial, frequently by hanging

M

maligned: spoken ill of

manumission: liberation from slavery; to be *manumitted* is to be freed from slavery

WORDS TO KNOW

Maroons: black slaves who escaped and formed communities in the mountains, swamps, and forests of the southern colonies

Mason-Dixon line: generally thought of as the line that divides the North and the South; named after surveyors Charles Mason and Jeremiah Dixon, who in 1767 settled a dispute over the east-west boundary between Pennsylvania and Maryland and the north-south boundary between Maryland and Delaware

Masonic: having to do with Masons or Freemasons, an international organization dedicated to universal brotherhood, charity, and mutual aid

media: a plural noun signifying all types of communication (radio, television, newspapers, etc.)

median: the midway point in a series of numbers (half of the numbers being above and half below); not to be confused with average

metaphor: a figure of speech in which one thing is identified with another

Middle Passage: the trade route from West Africa across the Atlantic Ocean to the West Indies and the East Coast of America

militant: aggressive; prepared to fight

minstrel: an entertainer typically associated with a traveling comic variety show, such as the Christy Minstrels (from which the word comes)

misogyny: hatred of women

monarchy: a government ruled by a king or queen or other person of royal birthright. Constitutional monarchies are limited in power, but absolute monarchies are essentially dictatorships

monographs: scholarly books or articles on a single subject

Monroe Doctrine: the policy established by President James Monroe that said the United States would not allow European interference in the affairs of America or her neighbors

mosaics: pictures composed of small bits of stone, glass, tile, etc.

mulatto: a person who has one black and one white parent; any person of black-white ancestry

multicultural: concerned with minority as well as majority cultures

N

nationalism: a movement to achieve independence; patriotism; a *nationalist,* in black studies, is one who believes in the creation of black power through a politically and economically strong black nation

negritude: the awareness among blacks of their cultural heritage

neoclassical: art or literature dating from the mid-seventeenth to mid-eighteenth century that revived the classic forms and styles of ancient Greece and Rome

niche: a desirable place; in business terms, typically a safe market not threatened by competitors

O

odyssey: epic journey

ordained: established or invested with the title of minister, priest, rabbi, and so forth

orthodox: traditional; conforming to established doctrine

ostracized: banished

P

pacify: to satisfy or calm

Pan-Africanism: a theory or movement embracing cooperation and unity among African nations and among all African peoples

WORDS TO KNOW

parodied: poked fun at through imitation

patents: legal and exclusive rights to produce, use, and sell what one has invented

pathology: the condition and results of a disease

patois: a differing form of a standard language

patron: a person, usually wealthy, who finances and supports another person, cause, or institution; *patronage* is that support given

pending: not yet decided or determined

per capita: per person

petition: a formal, signed request

philanthropists: those who share their wealth with various humanitarian, or charitable, causes

plaintiffs: those filing a lawsuit (*defendants* are those being accused or sued by the plaintiffs)

plasma: the fluid part of blood

plebiscite: an expression of the people's will, by ballot, on a political issue

posthumous: after death

poverty: the condition of being poor; the government determines poverty according to a poverty index based on monetary income alone; in 1990 a family of four was considered to be in poverty if the household income was less than $13,359

predecessors: those who have gone before, usually said of influential persons

prenatal: taking place before birth

proclamation: an official announcement

prohibit: to forbid or make illegal; something *prohibited* is not allowed by law

prolific: highly energetic and productive

propaganda: ideas and information used to further or to hinder a movement or cause

propagation: expansion from person to person, place to place; reproduction or multiplication

prosperity: wealth

protectorate: a weaker state that is governed by a stronger state

proteges: persons guided, taught, or shaped by generally older and more influential persons

provision: something set aside for the future; a section in a legal document that outlines a special condition or requirement

psychedelic: causing intense stimulation of the mind

pueblo: a close-knit village of sun-dried bricks and stone built by Native Americans in the southwestern United States; Pueblo Indian cultures include the Hopi and Zuni

pundits: experts or authorities on given topics

R

ratify: to approve or pass

ratio: the relationship of one quantity to another, expressed in a fraction or percentage

recession: a general decline in business activity that translates into more layoffs, fewer new jobs, and decreases in household spending power

referendum: a direct vote by the people

repatriationist: one who believes in returning to the country of origin

repeal: to cancel

repertoire: songs or pieces within a musician's or group of musicians' typical performance program

repertory: a group that alternates the works (from their *repertoire*) that they perform

repression: the act of keeping back, putting down, or holding down

resolutions: statements of intent

retaliation: to respond in kind, as in "an eye for an eye"

retrospective: an exhibit that looks back at an artist's development

rhetoric: especially effective speaking or writing; alternately, language that is flashy but insincere

WORDS TO KNOW

rigorous: very strict or challenging

S

savanna: a grassland

schism: a split or break within an organization, usually as a result of serious disagreement

secession: withdrawal from an organization

secular: relating to worldly things, as opposed to religious or spiritual things

segregation: the separation or isolation of a race, class, or ethnic group into a restricted area

seminary: a school where one is trained to become a minister, priest, or rabbi

separatism: a policy of keeping the races apart in all matters

seriocomic: mixing serious and comic elements

servitude: slavery

sociologist: one who studies human society

sole proprietorships: businesses in which the owner is also the chief operator

sovereignty: having dominion status or control over a nation

speaking in tongues: a gift of the Holy Spirit described in the New Testament (see Acts 2:4 and 1 Corinthians 12-14)

stereotypes: simple and inaccurate images of a person, group, etc.

stigmatizes: marks or brands unfavorably

subservient: inferior or subject to rule by another

suppression: keeping from happening or being known

supremacy: the state of having the most power or authority; a *supremacist* is one who believes in the superiority of a certain group

surveillance: continual observation

syncopated: shifted in beat from what is regularly accented to what is regularly unaccented

syndicated: sold and presented through many *media* outlets

syphilis: a venereal, or sexually transmitted, disease that can lead to a weakening of the bones, nerve tissue, and heart

T

temperance: in general, the quality of self-restraint; historically, movements promoting moderation, total avoidance, or prohibition of alcoholic liquor

tenure: a permanent right to a position, as in teaching

thesis: in education, a long, formal research paper

timpanist: a player of kettledrums (timpani)

tumultuous: troubled or characterized by upheaval

U

ultimatum: a final offer that, if rejected, will leads to a specific consequence

unalienable: secure from being transferred or taken away

unanimously: in total agreement

uncompromising: unwilling to change one's principles or alter one's behavior

unconstitutional: not permitted or spelled out in the United States Constitution; one of the primary duties of the Supreme Court is to determine whether laws or customs are constitutional or unconstitutional

Underground Railroad: a secret network of safe places, such as houses or barns, where runaway slaves could hide on their way north; these safe places were called "stations," and the people who operated them were called "conductors"

V

v.: an abbreviation for versus, a term used to separate opposing forces, such as the plaintiff and the defendant in a lawsuit

valets: personal servants who take care of clothes, help one dress, etc.

vaudeville: a form of entertainment consisting of skits, dances, songs, and other performances

versatile: multitalented

viability: ability to grow and prosper

Victorian: a nineteenth-century style of architecture characterized by largeness and ornamentation; anything dating from the reign of Queen Victoria (1837-1901)

virtuoso: someone with extraordinary skill in a given field

vulnerable: open to attack or injury

W

West Indies: a large group of islands, including the Bahamas, Puerto Rico, Jamaica, Cuba, Haiti, and the Virgin Islands, that lies between North and South America and to the east of Central America

Western Hemisphere: that half of the world containing the continents of North and South America; also called the New World

women's suffrage: a movement for the right of women to vote

African American Almanac

1
Flashbacks

The Birth and Rise of the African American, 1492-1993

"If there is no struggle, there is no progress."—Frederick Douglass

Just when does the history of the African American begin? One likely answer is that it began when Europeans first came to the Americas. In this opening chapter, we invite you to "flash back" in time to this important period. It was then that African Americans began to shape their own story, a history different though not separate from that of their ancestors in Africa.

This chapter is about dates: 1492, 1619, 1776, 1863, 1955, 1968, 1988, 1993. But it is also about individuals: Pedro Alonzo Niño, Estevanico, William Tucker, and several others you may be encountering for the first time.

Niño, Estevanico, and Tucker came very early in the history of African Americans. Without them, it's quite possible that there may not have been a Rosa Parks, a Martin Luther King, Jr., or a Jesse Jackson in our own century.

If you love to learn about how both dates and people *connect* to important places, events, and developments, read on! This is only the beginning.

FLASHBACKS

Stories and movies sometimes contain "flashbacks" to earlier events. These flashbacks help give a better understanding of what is happening now in the lives of the story or movie characters. In books of history, almost all of what you read is really a series of flashbacks. Somehow, these flashbacks all connect. Somehow, they all tell a story. Somehow, they all help to explain what is going on today, in the lives of real people.

Columbus's Great Discovery to the Beginnings of Colonial America

Before there was an America, blacks were here. They may have been present in the **Western Hemisphere** even before the time of Christopher Columbus. But there is

FLASHBACKS

no doubt that blacks were among the first explorers to visit the New World, from the time of Columbus onward.

On October 12, 1492, Pedro Alonzo Niño, who some historians think was black, arrived with Christopher Columbus on San Salvador (sometimes called Watlings Island) in the Bahamas. Columbus believed that he was the first European to discover an island in the East Indies, somewhere between China and Japan (the island is part of the *West* Indies; no one knew then that the **West Indies** also existed). Columbus was actually the first European to discover the New World.

Other blacks followed in Niño's footsteps. Sailing with such explorers as Núñez de Balboa, Juan Ponce de Leon, and Hernán Cortes, they too shared in the discovery and settlement of North and South America, Latin America, and the West Indies.

On August 20, 1619, more than one hundred years after Columbus's death, twenty blacks arrived in the colony of Virginia. Captured in Africa, they came against their will as **indentured servants** and settled with their masters in Jamestown. Unlike those who came to the New World before them, these Africans became the first blacks to settle permanently in what would one day become the United States.

The Pilgrim Landing to the American Revolution

In 1621, a year after the Pilgrims arrived at Plymouth, Massachusetts, the first African American child in the colonies was born. His name was William Tucker. A native of Jamestown, Virginia, Tucker enjoyed the same freedoms as his white neighbors.

Sadly, slavery was then on the rise in the New World, especially in the West Indies. After 1650, as the use of indentured servants

---

1492 Pedro Alonzo Niño sails with Christopher Columbus to the New World.

1502 Portugal sends black slaves to the New World.

1526 The first group of Africans sets foot on what is now the United States. Led by a Spanish explorer, they arrive in South Carolina.

1538 Estevanico, also known as Esteban, is the first European to come to what is now Arizona and New Mexico.

1619 A Dutch ship carries twenty blacks to Jamestown, Virginia.

1620 The *Mayflower* arrives at Plymouth, Massachusetts.

1641 Massachusetts becomes the first colony to legalize slavery.

1700 Approximately 28,000 slaves inhabit the English colonies.

1750 Over 236,000 slaves now live in colonial America.

1775 The first abolitionist society is organized in Philadelphia, Pennsylvania.

1776 The Continental Congress approves the Declaration of Independence, minus a paragraph against slavery written by Thomas Jefferson.

Slaves arrive in America

became less and less common in the colonies, slavery became more popular.

By 1700, slavery was a firmly established **institution. Fugitive** slave laws, bounty hunts for **Maroons,** and the demand for cheap labor were just some of the reasons why this happened. However, from the start there were efforts to stop slavery, or at least prevent its spread.

These efforts sometimes took the form of bloody slave revolts. (One of the most famous during this period was led by Cato, near Charleston, South Carolina, in 1739.) At other times they took the form of written or oral protests by both blacks and whites. Two white religious groups, the Mennonites and the Quakers, were among the first to join with black people in adopting **abolitionist,** or antislavery, principles.

Gradually laws began to reflect the colonists' growing desire to end slavery. In 1749, Georgia **prohibited** the **importation** of African slaves and protected existing slaves against cruel treatment. These laws, however, were often ignored and did little to assure justice for blacks in America.

In 1770 a black man named Crispus Attucks was shot and killed during the Boston Massacre. He thus became one of the first casualties of the American Revolution. When the Revolutionary War began in 1775, blacks fought on both the American and British sides.

Many escaped slaves joined Maroon camps deep in the southern wilderness

FLASHBACKS

Cripus Attucks, a runaway slave who gave his life for the American Revolution

The Independence of a Nation to the Emancipation of a Race

The signing of the Declaration of Independence was a bright moment in American history. Yet it was clouded by the decision not to include Thomas Jefferson's passage against slavery. In 1787 the adoption of the Constitution of the United States marked another landmark moment. Like the Declaration, the Constitution also fell short in its attempt to secure justice for all.

The same year, however, Congress passed a law to keep slavery out of the Northwest Territory (a region now comprised of Ohio, Indiana, Illinois, Michigan, Wisconsin, and a portion of Minnesota). Many slave owners found ways around this law and brought slavery with them to the region. One black man who was able to remain free and fulfill his dreams in the Northwest was Jean Baptiste Pointe Du Sable. The son of a slave and a French businessman, Du Sable became the first settler of what is now the city of Chicago, Illinois, when he established a fur trading post there in 1790.

Another development favorable to black people came in 1804. By passing its own emancipation law, New Jersey joined the rest of the North in opposing slavery. The South, or the region below the **Mason-Dixon line,** was now the sole region in the United States where slavery was permitted.

The years leading up to the Civil War were filled with suffering for blacks in the South. Still, there was hope. There were the inspiring stories of Harriet Tubman and Frederick Douglass, runaway slaves who had gone on to help awaken the country to the evils of slavery. There was the **Underground Railroad,** in which Tubman participated. And there was *Uncle Tom's Cabin* (1852), by white author Harriet Beecher Stowe. The most widely read novel of the nineteenth century, *Uncle Tom's Cabin* was equaled only by the speeches of Douglass in forcing Northerners to realize that slavery must end.

The Death of Lincoln to the Birth of King

The Civil War was fought to preserve the Union, to keep all the states united as one country. On April 9, 1865, generals Ulysses S. Grant and Robert E. Lee met at Appomattox Courthouse, Virginia, to end the war. The

The United States and neighboring territories, c. 1820

North had won and the Union was preserved. During the war, Lincoln had signed the Emancipation Proclamation, which freed southern but not northern slaves. Now *all* slaves were to be freed by the passage of the Thirteenth Amendment in December 1865.

At least three more critical events marked this turbulent year: the assassination of Lincoln, the beginning of Reconstruction, and the formation of the Ku Klux Klan. The wounds the country suffered from the war and Lincoln's death began to heal during Reconstruction. But it was a slow process and the North and the South remained deeply divided, as did President Andrew Johnson and the Republicans who ruled

FLASHBACKS

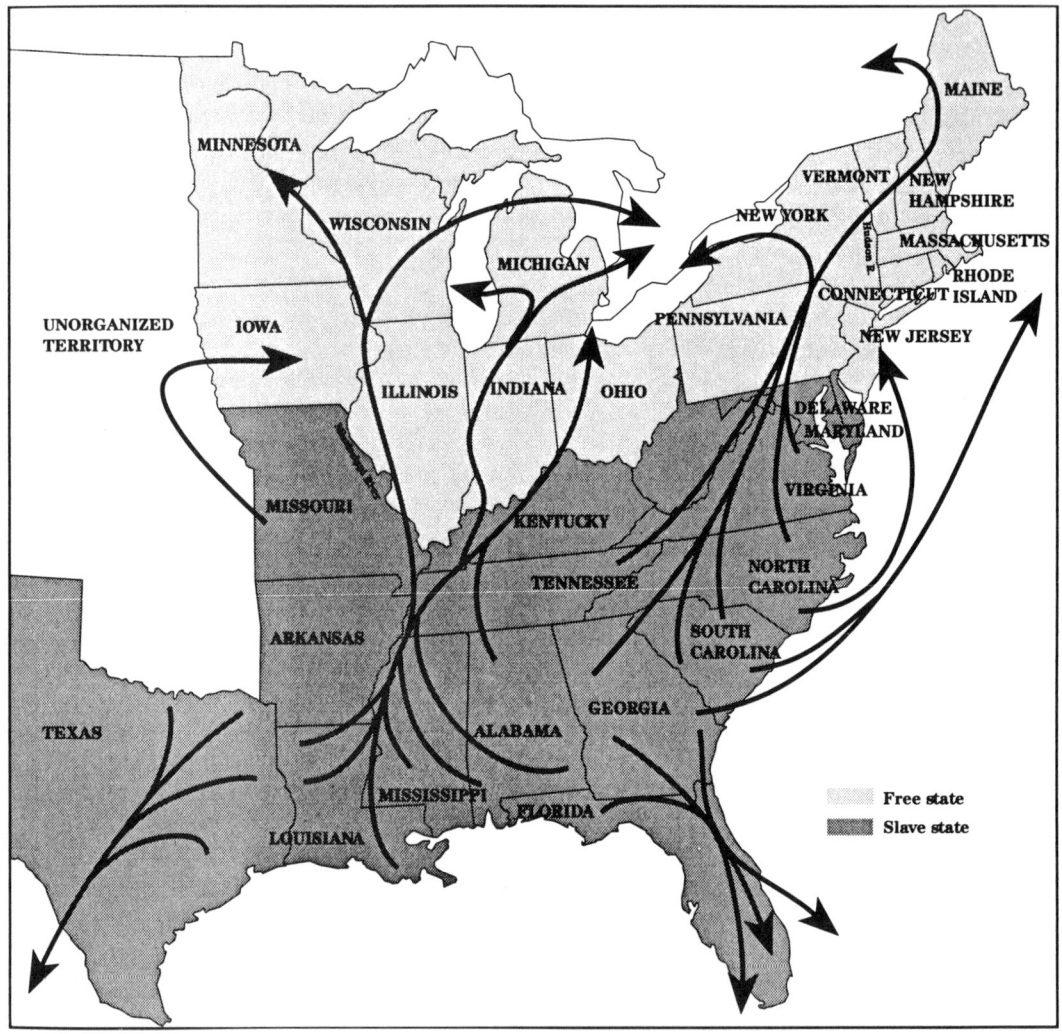

Underground Railroad routes

Congress. The Ku Klux Klan, formed in Pulaski, Tennessee, was a symptom of this division and of the desire of many whites in both the North and the South to withhold equal rights from blacks.

Despite the Klan's influence and the politics of the Old South, a large number of black Americans made rapid progress during this era. One person to do so was Hiram R. Revels, who in 1870 became the first black elected to the U.S. Senate. Another was Booker T. Washington, who in 1881 established the Tuskegee Institute in Alabama as the first school for the training of black teachers. (Both Washington and Tuskegee would later be identified with

FLASHBACKS

The lynching victim in the deep South

self-help programs for blacks choosing agricultural and labor-related careers.)

When federal troops completely withdrew from the South in 1877, Reconstruction officially failed. This meant that the federal government would no longer interfere in southern politics and southern society. As a consequence, black **repression** appeared everywhere. The regular **lynching** of blacks was one of the most horrifying examples of this repression.

During the first decades of the twentieth century, the prospects for black Americans

WORDS TO KNOW

abolitionist: a person or a group in favor of putting an end to slavery; the principles behind such a person or group

acquitted: cleared of all charges; declared not guilty

affirmative action: a policy designed to correct the effects of racial and sexual discrimination through hiring quotas and other measures; sometimes negatively referred to as "reverse discrimination"

Black Muslim movement: also called the Nation of Islam; a religious movement, begun by W. D. Fard and furthered by Elijah Muhammad, that preached black self-sufficiency and worship of Allah. Among the most famous converts to the Black Muslims were Malcolm X and Muhammad Ali

boycott: a refusal by an individual or group to buy, sell, or use products or services

caucus: a group of politicians or a meeting of political party leaders

civil disobedience: nonviolent resistance to a policy or law; first popularized by Indian leader Mohandas (Mahatma) Gandhi

coalition: a group united in purpose

conservatism: a political movement or philosophy that stresses less government and more private enterprise

conspiracy: a plot to work together in secret, especially for harmful or unlawful purposes

brightened somewhat. In 1909, the National Association for the Advancement of Colored People (NAACP) was formed. Then, with the advent of World War I, new industrial jobs opened to blacks in the North. From 1910 to 1930, a massive population shift occurred. Some 1.6 million southern blacks migrated to the North in the hope of a better life.

Soon, however, the Great Depression would cast a shadow over the dreams of Americans everywhere. Black America was advancing economically and educationally, but it still had many battles to fight on the civil rights front. Early in 1929 the greatest civil rights leader in American history was born in Atlanta, Georgia. Born Michael Luther King, he would eventually be known as Martin Luther King, Jr.

The Depths of the Depression to the Dawn of the Civil Rights Movement

The Great Depression began following the crash of the stock market in 1929. Many Americans who once thought themselves well off, if not rich, now found themselves poor, if not penniless. Jobs were scarce. Hunger was widespread. Misery was everywhere.

In 1932, Franklin Delano Roosevelt was elected president. He promised a New Deal, a number of programs designed to fix the

---

1777 Vermont becomes the first state to abolish slavery altogether.

1790 The first census records 757,000 blacks in the Unites States. This number represents close to one-fifth of the total population. Less than one-tenth of all blacks are free.

1793 Eli Whitney, a white inventor from Massachusetts, obtains a patent for his cotton gin. Whitney's machine makes cotton growing a very profitable business; as a result, the slave system expands, especially in the South.

1841 Frederick Douglass, a runaway slave, begins his career as a popular speaker and writer.

1863 President Abraham Lincoln signs the Emancipation Proclamation, freeing all slaves in the South.

1865 The Civil War between the North and the South ends.

1865 Lincoln is assassinated and Andrew Johnson becomes the country's new president. Johnson announces his program of Reconstruction, which is mild compared to the Reconstruction program put forth by the Radical Republicans in Congress two years later.

1870 Hiram R. Revels, of Mississippi, becomes the first black American to be elected to the U.S. Senate.

1881 Booker T. Washington establishes the Tuskegee Institute at Tuskegee, Alabama.

1894 W. E. B. Du Bois becomes the first black to receive a Ph.D. from Harvard University.

1916 Marcus Garvey brings the **black nationalism** movement to the United States.

1929 Martin Luther King, Jr., is born.

RECONSTRUCTION

During the Reconstruction period, from approximately 1867 to 1877, great efforts were made to rebuild and reform the antiblack Democratic South with the backing of the pro-black Republican North. In a political sense, Reconstruction failed after Rutherford B. Hayes, who became president of the United States in 1876, pulled the last federal troops out of the South the following year.

WORDS TO KNOW

fugitive: a person who flees from danger or from the law

importation: to bring into a new region goods that are then usually sold

indentured servant: a person bound by contract to work for another for a certain length of time; during the early period of American history, both black and white indentured servants were commonly used and were usually forced to work for seven years before they gained their freedom

institution: a person, thing, idea, or practice that has taken root or settled into habit

Jim Crow: a reference (taken from a minstrel song) to laws and practices supporting the segregation of blacks and whites

lynching: murder without trial, frequently by hanging

Maroons: black slaves who escaped and formed communities in the mountains, swamps, and forests of the southern colonies

Mason-Dixon line: generally thought of as the line that divides the North and the South; named after surveyors Charles Mason and Jeremiah Dixon, who in 1767 settled a dispute over the east-west boundary between Pennsylvania and Maryland and the north-south boundary between Maryland and Delaware

crippled economy, in part by creating new jobs for Americans. The country began a long process of rebuilding under Roosevelt. Roosevelt's specially selected "Black Cabinet," which included educator Mary McCleod Bethune, political scientist Ralph Bunche, lawyer William Hastie, and economist Robert Weaver, attended to the needs of black people.

The depression continued through much of the 1930s despite the New Deal, but signs of an improving economy increased. During this time, large numbers of blacks from the South continued to travel to the industrial centers of the North. Jobs were more plentiful in the North and racism was not as widespread.

Like World War I, World War II accelerated this population shift. The war itself was supported by most black civilians, despite the fact that the armed services were still largely segregated. Interestingly, by October 1940, a black man named Benjamin O.

FLASHBACKS

In 1948 America's new president, Harry S Truman, signed an executive order that once and for all ended **segregation** in the Armed Forces. Six years later the Supreme Court ruled that segregation in public schools was unconstitutional. Finally, the rights of African Americans guaranteed in the Declaration of Independence, the Constitution, and the Bill of Rights were beginning to be firmly upheld by the country's legal system.

Of course, one stubborn obstacle remained. This was the **Jim Crow** culture of the South. Fear, bigotry, and ignorance

A. Philip Randolph

Davis, Sr., had risen to the elite rank of brigadier general. Blacks in the military, though treated under the longstanding racial policy of "separate but equal," were highly valued and rewarded for their service.

As the possibility of American involvement in the war increased, blacks raised the issue of fairness in the military. A leading spokesperson of black labor in general, A. Philip Randolph, took up the cause and pledged a march to Washington, D.C., on July 1, 1941. A week before the proposed march, President Roosevelt signed a special order that banned discrimination in defense industries and government training programs.

BLACK NATIONALISM

In its original sense, the black nationalism movement sought to form a new black nation by transporting black Americans back to Africa. First seriously championed during the second decade of the twentieth century by Jamaican-born Marcus Garvey, black nationalism nonetheless stems back to the late 1700s and early 1800s, when Prince Hall and Paul Cuffe each attempted to advance the cause. Other early black nationalists included writer and Civil War veteran Martin R. Delany and pastor Henry H. Garnet. Black nationalists who came after Garvey included Malcolm X, who was less interested in forming a separate black nation than in building black pride (see Vol. 2, Ch. 8: "Black Nationalism").

among many whites in the South had kept Jim Crow laws in effect ever since the end of the Civil War. A black seamstress from Montgomery, Alabama, was about to set the stage to end this last relic of slavery.

The Montgomery Boycott to the Death of King

On December 1, 1955, a Montgomery woman named Rosa Parks refused to give up her bus seat to a white passenger. She was arrested. Within four days a city-wide **boycott** of the bus system had been organized. Martin Luther King, Jr., a 26-year-old Baptist preacher, was chosen to lead the boycott and the newly formed Montgomery Improvement Association. Twelve months later, the Montgomery bus system was integrated. This first battle, like the others that followed, was one of daily struggle.

1929 The New York stock market crashes on October 29.

1931 The Scottsboro trial begins when nine black youths are falsely accused of raping two white women.

1934 Elijah Muhammad becomes head of the **Black Muslim movement** in the United States.

1937 Joe Louis, "The Brown Bomber," becomes the heavyweight champion of the world.

1940 Hattie McDaniel receives an Academy Award for her performance in the supporting role of Mammy in *Gone with the Wind*. She is the first black ever to win an Oscar.

1941 On December 7, the Japanese attack the U.S. naval base at Pearl Harbor, Hawaii, bringing the United States into World War II.

1954 The Supreme Court rules, in *Brown* v. *Board of Education of Topeka, Kansas*, that segregation in public schools in **unconstitutional.**

1955 In Montgomery, Alabama, Rosa Parks refuses to give up her seat to a white person.

1963 Martin Luther King, Jr., delivers his "I Have a Dream" speech before a crowd of 250,000 at the Lincoln Memorial in Washington, D.C.

President John F. Kennedy is assassinated in Dallas, Texas.

1964 Black Muslim minister Malcolm X separates from Elijah Muhammad to start his own movement.

President Lyndon B. Johnson signs the Civil Rights Act.

1965 Malcolm X is assassinated in New York City.

1966 The Black Panther Party for Self-Defense is organized.

1967 Thurgood Marshall is appointed an associate justice of the U.S. Supreme Court, becoming the first black to serve on the nation's highest court.

1968 Shirley Chisholm of New York becomes the first black woman to serve in Congress.

King is assassinated in Memphis, Tennessee.

FLASHBACKS

Martin Luther King, Jr., shares his dream at the 1963 March on Washington

Thus began one of the richest and most troubled periods in African American history. In 1957 the Southern Christian Leadership Conference (SCLC) was formed, with King as its president. The SCLC was the main organization through which King, Ralph Abernathy, and numerous others led the fight for civil rights.

One of the loftiest moments of this fight—which quickly gained national and international attention for its many acts of **civil disobedience**—was the march on Washington, D.C., on August 28, 1963. The march consisted of 250,000 blacks and whites who gathered at the Lincoln Memorial to demand that Congress pass long-awaited civil rights laws.

King's "I Have a Dream" speech went far beyond the discussion of law and cut to the heart of the American racial problem. He knew that certain laws and customs needed to be changed, but he also knew that the conscience of America needed to change. While it was necessary to change the law immediately, the process of eliminating racism in the hearts and minds of all Americans would take years and years. This reality did not destroy his vision, for he said: "I have a dream my four little children will one day live in a nation where they will not be judged by the color of their skin but by the content of their character."

A partial fulfillment of King's dream came with the passage of the Civil Rights Act of 1964. This act banned discrimination in public accommodations, employment, and several other areas as well.

Just prior to this, Black Muslim minister Malcolm X announced his separation from Elijah Muhammad, leader of the Nation of

Malcolm X

Islam. As head of the Muslim Mosque, Inc., and the Organization of Afro-American Unity, Malcolm X became the central figure of a new black nationalist movement that emphasized pride, unity, self-reliance, and self-defense.

Following Malcolm's death by assassination, the movement survived in the work of the Black Panthers and the Stokely Carmichael-led Student Non-Violent Coordinating Committee (SNCC). Carmichael was the first to popularize the phrase "black power." His **militant** views eventually caused him to leave the SNCC and to join the Black Panthers, which had been found-

Stokely Carmichael at a rally at the University of California at Berkeley in 1966

ed by Huey P. Newton and Bobby Seale in October 1966.

The rise of the Panthers and similar organizations was a sign that the nonviolent civil rights movement had failed to connect with poor blacks in the violent inner city, especially ghetto youth. The anger expressed through the riots in Harlem, New York (1964), Watts, Los Angeles (1965), and then Detroit, Michigan, and dozens of other cities (1967) confirmed the belief of the Panthers and their followers that the time for nonviolence was over.

King's death at the hands of a white assassin, which caused further riots and enraged millions, thrust the Panthers into the national spotlight. Although always a small organization in terms of membership, the gun-toting Black Panthers became, in the eyes of many, the best alternative to King's philosophy. They were admired especially for their willingness to stand up to police. Indeed, one of their primary purposes was to "police" the actions of police. Consequently, it is not surprising that Federal Bureau of Investigation (FBI) director J. Edgar Hoover took drastic measures to stop the Panthers, believing them to be possibly "the greatest threat to the internal security of the country." Later evidence would show that FBI and police involvement in repressing the Panthers may have included **conspiracy** to murder Panther leaders.

FLASHBACKS

The Newton Trial to the Miami Riots

If Americans were still unfamiliar with the Black Panthers, they instantly became aware of them during the eight-week trial of Huey P. Newton. In the summer of 1968, Newton took the stand to defend himself against the charge that he had shot and killed an Oakland, California, police officer the previous year.

Fellow Panthers, wearing berets and leather jackets, turned out in large numbers to support Newton. Their slogan was "Free Huey." Newton was convicted and spent nearly two years in prison. He was later freed when a court of appeals ruled in his favor. By this time, however, Newton had decided that the Panthers were overly militant and did not serve the interests of black people well. Unfortunately, the number of Panthers killed in police raids could not be erased.

Panther operations all but ceased by the end of the 1970s. Black power alone was not enough to sustain a movement; power through politics became the newest sign of the times. In March 1972, 8,000 blacks were welcomed to the city of Gary, Indiana, by Mayor Richard Hatcher. They had come to attend the first National Black Political Convention, which was to be chaired by writer and activist Imamu Amiri Baraka (formerly Leroi Jones). The Congressional Black **Caucus,** formed in 1971, was further molded at the convention and has since become the most important black political group in the country.

In 1973 the Vietnam War ended with the signing of a peace treaty. The same year, blacks were elected as mayors of several large cities around the country, including Los Angeles, Detroit, and Atlanta. Although inner-city problems continued, blacks had gathered a far greater voice in how these problems were to be solved.

WORDS TO KNOW

militant: aggressive; prepared to fight

prohibited: not allowed by law

repression: the act of keeping back, putting down, or holding down

segregation: the separation or isolation of a race, class, or ethnic group into a restricted area

unconstitutional: not permitted or spelled out in the United States Constitution; one of the primary duties of the Supreme Court is to determine whether laws or customs are constitutional or unconstitutional

Underground Railroad: a secret network of safe places, such as houses or barns, where runaway slaves could hide on their way north; these safe places were called "stations," and the people who operated them were called "conductors"

Western Hemisphere: that half of the world containing the continents of North and South America; also called the New World

West Indies: a large group of islands, including the Bahamas, Puerto Rico, Jamaica, Cuba, Haiti, and the Virgin Islands, that lies between North and South America and to the east of Central America

Just as the era of modern racial violence seemed to be over, another major series of riots shook the nation. This time Miami, Florida, was the scene of unrest. On December 17, 1979, a black insurance executive named Arthur McDuffie failed to stop at a red light and was then pulled over by police after a high-speed chase. Although unarmed, he was severely beaten and died four days later. The black neighborhoods of Miami refrained from violent protest and instead waited for the outcome of the trial.

On May 17, 1980, an all-white jury found the four officers who were charged in McDuffie's death not guilty. The nation's worst riots since 1967 began within hours of the announcement of the jury's verdict. Five days later, ten blacks and seven whites were dead.

The Rise of the Black Middle Class to Jackson's Second Running

For most civil rights leaders, the 1980s were a time of extreme **conservatism,** particularly under the two-term presidency of Republican Ronald Reagan. **Affirmative action** programs appeared in danger of being weakened, if not eliminated. Reagan's appointment of Clarence M. Pendleton, Jr., a black conservative, as chairman of the U.S. Civil Rights Commission was perhaps most frustrating to liberal black leaders. Pendleton promised a "color-blind" approach to civil rights, was opposed to busing and the forced integration of schools, and called affirmative action a "bankrupt policy."

Several notable African Americans outside the civil rights movement shared Pendleton's views, stressing that the fight for civil rights was over, that racism was no longer a major cause of black social problems, and that blacks were more harmed than helped by liberal government programs. Economists Thomas Sowell and Walter Williams, sociologist Robert Woodson, Sr., and writer Shelby Steele numbered among this emerging group.

By end of the 1980s, at least one-third of

1968 Black Panther leader Huey P. Newton is convicted of manslaughter.

Shirley Chisholm becomes the first black woman to serve in Congress.

1972 Shirley Chisholm announces her intention to seek the Democratic presidential nomination. She is the first black and the first woman to do so.

1973 Thomas Bradley becomes mayor of Los Angeles.

1974 Frank Robinson is named the first black manager in major league baseball.

1977 The *Roots* television miniseries, based on Alex Haley's novel of the same title, attracts more than 130 million viewers. The final episode receives the highest single rating of any program in television history.

1980 A not guilty verdict in the trial of four white police officers accused in the beating death of a black insurance executive sparks riots in Miami, Florida.

African American families were solidly within the middle class. They, too, found themselves shifting away from the traditional black leadership, at least on such issues as school busing and affirmative action. This is not to say that black people either embraced the Republican Party or that black social problems suddenly disappeared. The vast majority of African Americans continued to vote the Democratic ticket. And rising poverty, dropout, unemployment, and other rates among segments of the African Ameri-

1980 Ronald Reagan is elected the fortieth president of the United States.

1983 Vanessa Williams becomes the first African American Miss America in the 62–year history of the pageant. The first runner–up is Suzette Charles, who is also African American. When Williams is forced to surrender her title after *Penthouse* magazine printed old nude photographs of her, Charles is crowned Miss America.

1984 A "Black Family Summit" is held at Fisk University in Nashville, Tennessee.

Reagan, in a landslide victory, captures a second term but only 10 percent of the African American vote.

1986 Martin Luther King, Jr.'s birthday is observed as a national holiday for the first time.

1988 Jesse Jackson finishes second, behind Michael Dukakis, in his bid for the Democratic presidential nomination.

1989 Ronald H. Brown becomes the first African American to head a major American political party when he is elected chairman of the Democratic party's national committee.

General Colin L. Powell becomes the first African American to serve as chairman of the Joint Chiefs of Staff.

1990 David Dinkins becomes the first African American mayor of New York City.

1990 L. Douglas Wilder, of Virginia, becomes the first African American elected governor.

1991 Clarence Thomas is confirmed as a Supreme Court justice.

1992 Carol Moseley Braun of Illinois is elected to the United States Senate, becoming the first African American female senator.

The most severe riot in U.S. history takes place in south central Los Angeles after a jury acquits four white police officers of charges of using excessive force in the beating of motorist Rodney King.

1993 All fifty states observe Martin Luther King Day for the first time.

Joycelyn Elders, Arkansas health director, is named surgeon general of the United States. Elders is the first African American and second woman to hold this position.

Forbes magazine names Oprah Winfrey as the highest–paid entertainer in America. The talk show host netted $98 million in earnings over a two-year period.

Jesse Jackson with his family as he prepares to speak at the 1988 Democratic National Convention

FLASHBACKS

Carol Moseley Braun

can population were nothing short of frightening. (By 1989, for example, 43 percent of all black children were living in poverty.)

For most African Americans looking for solutions within the political arena, Jesse Jackson offered the brightest ray of hope. Jackson, a minister and veteran civil rights activist, became the most popular national black leader since Martin Luther King, Jr. His bids for the presidency in 1984 and 1988, and his creation of a Rainbow **Coalition,** helped heighten awareness of pressing social problems throughout American society. In addition, his candidacy proved that it was possible for an African American to seek the nomination of a major political party.

New Heights, New Lows

During the brief period from 1989 to 1993, African Americans made significant strides in a number of areas, perhaps most notably in the political arena. In 1989 Ronald H. Brown was elected chairman of the Democratic Party's national committee. Three years later Americans elected Bill Clinton—the first Democratic president since 1981—and the African American presence in Congress increased by fourteen seats. The most surprising political success of an African American was that of Carol Moseley Braun, who won an upset victory to become the first black in the U.S. Senate since 1979 and the first black female senator ever.

FLASHBACKS

Rodney King meets with reporters to plead for calm during the Los Angeles riots

Clouding such accomplishments, however, was the aftermath of the Rodney King beating and the Los Angeles riots.

In March 1991 black motorist Rodney King was severely beaten by several white police officers after being stopped for a speeding violation and resisting arrest. A videotape of the incident that appeared on network news programs prompted an international uproar. Although King suffered no permanent injuries, the situation recalled the fatal beating of Arthur McDuffie in Miami a decade earlier.

In May 1992 a jury **acquitted** four white police officers of criminal charges of using excessive force. Widespread rioting in Los Angeles and other cities ensued. By the time the L.A. rioting ceased, 53 people were dead and billions of dollars in property had been destroyed.

The Rodney King story continued to attract national attention as late as August 4, 1993. On this day, the judge in a federal trial handed down his sentences for the officers who were this time charged with violating King's civil rights. Two of the officers were found guilty and sentenced to thirty months in prison.

2
Motherland

A Survey of Africa South of the Sahara

FACT FOCUS

- Africa is the second largest continent in the world.
- Africa is home to the world's largest desert, the Sahara, and the world's longest river, the Nile.
- In 1847 Liberia became Africa's first independent republic.
- By the year 2020, the population of sub-Saharan Africa alone is expected to reach 1.2 billion.
- Until recently, almost 90 percent of Africa's population lived in rural areas.
- At least 2,000 languages and **dialects** are spoken in Africa. Of these, about 50 are considered major and are spoken by one million or more people.
- The average life span for an African is 52 years. The world average is 63 years. The U.S. average is 75.
- The average yearly income in sub-Saharan Africa is less than $200.

"We're a special people. We're the best and the brightest our ancestors ever produced!"—James Weldon Johnson

Okra, gumbo, deep-fat frying, the banjo, jazz, blues, spirituals—these and countless other pieces of American culture may be traced back to Africa. The continent of Africa has been called the motherland of all African Americans. One could go even further and say that it is the motherland of all peoples of all nations.

A Brief History

Archaeologists believe that early humans arose in Africa some two to three million years ago. From Africa, these humans migrated to all the other continents. Advanced societies developed in early Africa between 700 B.C. and 200 A.D. These included the ancient Ghana, Mali, and Songhai kingdoms.

Trade with the Arabs, Indians, and Chinese may have begun as early as the first

MOTHERLAND

Arab slavers enter a West African village

century A.D. Coastal trade with Europeans definitely began by the fifteenth century, though perhaps much earlier. Gold, ivory, leather, and salt were among the goods that Africans had to offer. (Much later, Africa was found to contain such riches as diamonds, uranium, platinum, manganese, lead, tin, zinc, rubber, and petroleum, not to mention a number of food resources.)

Gradually, the slave trade became an especially important, if corrupt, part of Africa's development. An estimated 10 to 30 million people were sold into slavery by the mid nineteenth century. The interior of Africa was first exposed to Europeans in the eighteenth century by missionaries, traders, and adventurers. Reports of the continent's vast resources eventually led to European conquest, and soon nearly all of Africa was directly controlled. By 1900 only Ethiopia and Liberia were free of European control.

In 1910 the British granted **dominion** to the Union of South Africa. However, independence for the black dominated regions of Africa did not come until some forty years later. In 1957 independence movements sprang up in Kenya, Ghana, and Guinea. By the late 1960s most of Africa had achieved independence.

Africa

Africa Today

Thirty-five years after the independence movement began, many of Africa's problems remained. In fact, in many cases independence brought on new problems. For example, some African leaders began to run their countries as **dictatorships** in order to unite the many religious and tribal groups that were separated by different languages, cultures, and goals. Such situations often led to coups, clan fighting, or even civil wars, and always left citizens worse rather than better off. War-torn Angola and Somalia are prime examples of this tragedy.

In numerous other cases, democratic leaders attempted to improve their nations'

> **SPECIAL FOCUS**
>
> African cities with populations exceeding one million include:
>
> Abidjan, Ivory Coast
> Accra, Ghana
> Addis Ababa, Ethiopia
> Antananarivo, Madagascar
> Cape Town, South Africa
> Conakry, Guinea
> Dakar, Senegal
> Dar es Salaam, Tanzania
> Ibadan, Nigeria
> Johannesburg, South Africa
> Kampala, Uganda
> Khartoum, Sudan
> Kinshasa, Zaire
> Lagos, Nigeria
> Maputo, Mozambique
> Nairobi, Kenya

economies and living standards, but lacked both the massive funds and expert assistance required to succeed.

Most startling to Americans are the health conditions in sub-Saharan Africa. Numbers of commonly treated diseases (including measles, polio, and tuberculosis) persist due to lack of basic medical care. Diarrhea and tuberculosis alone account for one-half of all deaths in children. Almost two-thirds of Africans do not have access to safe drinking water. In addition, the emergence of Acquired Immune Deficiency Syndrome (AIDS) has had a disastrous effect on the continent. There are currently no signs that the AIDS epidemic will end.

Nonetheless, there is good news. One of the brightest success stories is that of Namibia, which in 1990 became the last of the African nations to gain independence. Namibia was able to learn from the mistakes of its neighbors and, because it had waited so long for independence, was determined not to repeat them. Although its **per capita** income ($1,400) and **literacy** rates (30 percent among blacks) are still low by American standards, this southern African country is considered very stable and endowed with a number of natural resources it has yet to take full advantage of.

Despite its long history, Africa is part of the developing world. That means its struggle to create a healthy, vibrant, and self-supporting network of nations is far from complete. Perhaps Africa will one day be linked politically and economically, just as is the United States of America. Many groups, including the Organization of African Unity (OAU), hope this will happen. Only time will tell.

COUNTRY PROFILES

West Africa

People's Republic of Benin

Independence: August 1, 1960

Area: 43,483 sq. mi. (a little larger than Tennessee)

Capital: Porto Novo

Population: (1991 estimate) 4.8 million

Official language: French

Before it became a colony, Benin was a collection of small dominions, the most powerful of which was the Fon Kingdom of Dahomey. By the seventeenth and eighteenth centuries, first the Portuguese and later other Europeans established trading posts along the coast. From here thousands of slaves were shipped to the New World, primarily to Brazil and the Caribbean. This part of West Africa soon became known as the Slave Coast.

In 1892 the country was organized as the French **protectorate** of Dahomey. It remained a French colony until it gained independence in 1960, when its name was changed to the Republic of Dahomey. In 1975 the country's name was finally changed to the People's Republic of Benin.

Following a series of coups and major economic troubles, Benin passed a new constitution in late 1990 and then elected economist Nicephore Soglo the following year as its president.

Burkina Faso (formerly Upper Volta)

Independence: August 5, 1960

Area: 105,868 sq. mi. (a little larger than Colorado)

Capital: Ouagadougou

Population: (1991 estimate) 9.3 million

Official language: French

Until the end of the nineteenth century, the history of Burkina Faso was dominated by the Mossi people, who probably came from central or eastern Africa in the eleventh century. When the French arrived and claimed the area in 1896, the Mossi resisted but were defeated when their capital at Ouagadougou was captured.

After World War II, the Mossi renewed their quest for separate territorial status. Upper Volta became a republic in the French Community on December 11, 1958, and achieved independence on August 5, 1960.

WORDS TO KNOW

abstained: refrained from doing

annex: to add or attach

apartheid: a policy of racial separation

archaeologists: scientists who study past civilizations, especially by a process of careful digging called excavation

archipelago: a group of islands

deposed: removed from office

dialects: spoken languages that are specific to regions or groups

dictatorships: governments ruled by absolute power; the opposite of democracies

dominion: the power to rule; a territory that is ruled

enclave: a territory or group that is surrounded by a larger territory or group

equatorial: near or of the equator, the imaginary line equidistant from the North and South Poles

exile: a person who by force or choice lives outside his country; the condition of living outside a country

feudal: a system popular in Europe during the Middle Ages in which serfs were bound for life to work the land and were, in turn, protected by overlords

literacy: the ability to read and write

monarchy: a government ruled by a king or queen or other person of royal birthright. Constitutional monarchies are limited in power, but absolute monarchies are essentially dictatorships

The Republic of Cameroon

Independence: January 1, 1960

Area: 183,568 sq. mi. (roughly the size of North Dakota and Arizona combined)

Capital: Yaoundé

Population: (1991 estimate) 11.7 million

Official languages: English and French

The earliest dwellers of Cameroon were probably Pygmies, who still inhabit the southern forests. However, Bantu-speaking people were among the first to invade Cameroon from **equatorial** Africa.

Europeans first encountered the area in the 1500s. For the next three centuries, Spanish, Dutch, and British traders visited the region. In July 1884 Germany, the United Kingdom, and France each attempted to **annex** the area. A 1919 declaration divided Cameroon between the United Kingdom and France, with France receiving the bulk of the territory. In December 1958 French ownership ended and French Cameroon became the Republic of Cameroon on January 1, 1960.

The Republic of Cape Verde

Independence: July 5, 1975

Area: 1,557 sq. mi. (a little larger than Rhode Island)

Capital: Praia

Population: (1991 estimate) 386,501

Official language: Portuguese

Cape Verde consists of ten islands off the coast of Senegal in the north Atlantic Ocean. This **archipelago** remained uninhabited until the Portuguese landed in 1456. They soon brought African slaves to work the plantations they established. As a result, Cape Verdeans have mixed African and Portuguese origins.

In 1951 Portugal changed Cape Verde's status from a colony to an overseas province. In 1956 the African Party for the Indepen-

---

West Africa
Benin • Burkina Faso • Cameroon • Cape Verde Islands • Ivory Coast • Gambia • Ghana • Guinea • Guinea-Bissau • Liberia • Mali • Mauritania • Niger • Nigeria • Senegal • Sierra Leone • Togo

West Central Africa
Angola • Central African Republic • Chad • Congo • Equatorial Guinea • Gabon • São Tomé and Príncipe • Zaire

Northeast Africa
Djibouti • Eritrea • Ethiopia • Somalia • Sudan

East Africa
Burundi • Kenya • Rwanda • Tanzania • Uganda

Southeast Central Africa
Malawi • Mozambique • Zambia • Zimbabwe

Southern Africa
Botswana • Lesotho • Namibia • South Africa • Swaziland

East African Island Nations
Comoros • Mayotte • Madagascar • Mauritius • Réunion • Seychelles

MOTHERLAND

Gambian President Dauda Jawara speaks to local authorities

dence of Guinea-Bissau and Cape Verde (PAIGC) was organized. The PAIGC began an armed rebellion against Portugal in 1961.

In December 1974 the PAIGC and Portugal signed an agreement providing for a transitional government. On June 30, 1975, Cape Verdeans elected a National Assembly and on July 5, 1975, the Republic of Cape Verde was formed.

Ivory Coast (Côte d'Ivoire)

Independence: August 7, 1960

Area: 124,502 sq. mi. (a little larger than New Mexico)

Capital: Yamoussoukro; before 1983: Abidjan

Population: (1991 estimate) 12.9 million

Official language: French

In 1637 French missionaries landed at Assinie, near the Gold Coast (now Ghana) border. During the 1840s France signed treaties with the kings of the regions, placing their territories under a French protectorate. French explorers, missionaries, trading companies, and soldiers gradually extended the area under French control. In 1893 Côte d'Ivoire was officially made a French colony.

In December 1958 the Ivory Coast

became a republic within the French community and then gained its independence on August 7, 1960.

The Republic of the Gambia

Independence: February 18, 1965

Area: 4,361 sq. mi. (smaller than Connecticut)

Capital: Banjul

Population: (1991 estimate) 874,553

Official language: English

Gambia was once part of the Empire of Ghana and the Kingdom of Songhai. When the Portuguese visited in the fifteenth century, it was part of the Kingdom of Mali.

By the sixteenth century, Portuguese slave traders and gold-seekers had settled in the area. In 1588 the Portuguese sold exclusive trade rights on the Gambia River to English merchants. During the late seventeenth and throughout the eighteenth century, England and France struggled continuously for control of the regions of the Senegal and Gambia Rivers.

In 1807 slave trading was banned throughout the British Empire. However, the British were unsuccessful in stopping the slave traffic in Gambia. An 1889 agreement with France established the present boundaries and Gambia became a British Crown Colony. Gambia achieved independence on February 18, 1965, as a constitutional **monarchy** within the British Commonwealth. In 1970 Gambia became a republic.

The Republic of Ghana

Independence: March 6, 1957

Area: 92,100 sq. mi. (somewhat smaller than Oregon)

Kwame Nkrumah, founder of modern-day Ghana

Capital: Accra

Population: (1991 estimate) 15.6 million

Official language: English

The first contact between Europe and the Gold Coast dates from 1470, when a party of Portuguese landed there. For the next three centuries, the English, Danes, Dutch, Germans, and Portuguese controlled various parts of the coastal areas.

In 1821 the British government took control of the trading forts on the Gold Coast.

In 1844 Fanti chiefs in the area signed an agreement with the British. Between 1826 and 1900 the British fought a series of campaigns against the Ashantis, whose kingdom was located inland. By 1902 the British had succeeded in colonizing the Ashanti region.

On March 6, 1957, the United Kingdom surrendered its control over the Colony of the Gold Coast and Ashanti, the Northern Territories Protectorate, and British Togoland. The Gold Coast and the former British Togoland merged to form what is now Ghana.

The Republic of Guinea

Independence: October 2, 1958

Area: 94,927 sq. mi. (slightly smaller than Oregon)

Capital: Conakry

Population: (1991 estimate) 7.4 million

Official language: French

French involvement in the area began in the mid-nineteenth century. By signing treaties with the French in the 1880s, Guinea's Malinke leader, Samory Toure, secured a free hand to expand eastward. In 1890 he allied himself with the Toucouleur Empire and Kingdom of Sikasso and tried to expel the French from the area. However, he was defeated in 1898 and France gained control of Guinea and the Ivory Coast. Guinea became an independent republic on October 2, 1958.

The Republic of Guinea-Bissau

Independence: September 24, 1973

Area: 13,946 sq. mi. (slightly smaller than Massachusetts, Connecticut, and Rhode Island combined)

> **WORDS TO KNOW**
>
> **nationalism:** a movement to achieve independence; patriotism
>
> **per capita:** per person
>
> **protectorate:** a weaker state that is governed by a stronger state
>
> **referendum:** a direct vote by the people
>
> **savanna:** a grassland
>
> **secession:** withdrawal from an organization
>
> **sovereignty:** having dominion status or control over a nation

Capital: Bissau

Population: (1991 estimate) 1 million

Official language: Portuguese

The rivers of Guinea and the islands of Cape Verde were the first areas in Africa to be explored by the Portuguese. Portugal claimed Portuguese Guinea in 1446. With the assistance of local tribes, the Portuguese entered the slave trade and exported large numbers of Africans to the New World via Cape Verde. The slave trade declined in the nineteenth century and Bissau, originally founded as a fort in 1765, became the major commercial center.

In 1956 the African Party for the Independence of Guinea and Cape Verde (PAIGC) was organized. The PAIGC declared the independence of Guinea-Bissau on December 24, 1973. Portugal granted independence on September 19, 1974, and Luis Cabral became president of Guinea-Bissau and

Cape Verde. In 1980 Cape Verde established its own independence from Guinea-Bissau.

The Republic of Liberia

Independence: July 26, 1847

Area: 43,000 sq. mi. (somewhat larger than Ohio)

Capital: Monrovia

Population: (1991 estimate) 2.7 million

Official language: English

The ancestors of many present-day Liberians probably migrated into the area from the north and east between the twelfth and seventeenth centuries. Portuguese explorers visited Liberia's coast in 1461 and European merchants and coastal Africans engaged in trade for the next 300 years.

The history of modern Liberia dates from 1816, when the American Colonization Society, a private organization, was given a charter by the United States Congress to send freed slaves to the west coast of Africa. Under President James Monroe, the U.S. government provided funds and assisted in talks with native chiefs for the transfer of land for this purpose. The first settlers landed at the site of Monrovia in 1822. In 1838 the settlers united to form the Commonwealth of Liberia, under a governor appointed by the American Colonization Society.

In 1847 Liberia became Africa's first independent republic. The republic's first hundred years have been described as a "century of survival" due to attempts by neighboring colonial powers (France and Britain) to take territory away from Liberia. Nonetheless, Liberia managed to remain independent.

The country also managed to remain relatively peaceful until 1979, when widespread unrest broke out after the government outlawed a popular demonstration against a proposed increase in prices. The following year president W. R. Tolbert was assassinated in a military coup led by Samuel K. Doe. That Doe was formally elected president in 1985 in fraudulent elections was typical of his regime; it was well known for its corruption and brutality. Thousands fled the country while under his rule, and numerous rebel groups tried to overthrow his government.

Charles Taylor and the National Patriotic Front of Liberia (NPFL) finally succeeded in 1990, and Taylor proclaimed himself president. Later that year another rebel group, led by Prince Yormie Johnson, assassinated Doe, and Johnson too sought the presidency. As peace was being negotiated among the two rebel groups and the government in 1992, Taylor and his supporters began a siege of Monrovia in an attempt to seize power. Peace negotiations broke off.

The Republic of Mali

Independence: September 22, 1960

Area: 478,764 sq. mi. (the size of California, Louisiana, and Texas combined)

Capital: Bamako

Population: (1991 estimate) 8.3 million

Official language: French

The Malinke kingdom of Mali, from which the republic takes its name, had its origins on the upper Niger River in the eleventh century. French entry into the area began around 1880. A French governor of Soudan (the French name for the area) was

A Malian woman pounding grain

appointed in 1893. Resistance to French control continued until 1898, when Malinke warrior Samory Toure was defeated after seven years of war.

In January 1959 Soudan joined Senegal to form the Mali Federation, which became fully independent within the French Community on June 20, 1960. The federation collapsed on August 20, 1960, when Senegal withdrew. On September 22, Soudan also withdrew from the French Community, proclaiming itself the Republic of Mali.

The Islamic Republic of Mauritania

Independence: November 28, 1960

Area: 419,229 sq. mi. (roughly the size of Montana and Texas combined)

Capital: Nouakchott

Population: (1991 estimate) 1.9 million

Official language: Arabic

Archeological evidence suggests that Berber and Negroid Mauritanians lived side by side before the spread of the desert drove them southward. Migration of these people increased during the third and fourth centuries A.D., when Berber groups arrived seeking pasture for their herds and safety from war in the north. The Berbers established a loose confederation, called the Sanhadja, as well as towns for the trade of gold, ivory, and slaves.

In the tenth century, conquests by warriors of the Soudanese Kingdom of Ghana broke up the Berber confederation. In the eleventh century, a Berber tribe's conquest of the Western Sahara regions destroyed the Ghanaian kingdom and firmly established Islam religion and culture throughout Mauritania.

French entry into Mauritania began early in the twentieth century and the region became a French colony in 1920. The Islamic Republic of Mauritania was proclaimed in November 1958. Mauritania became independent on November 28, 1960, and withdrew from the French Community in 1966.

The Republic of Niger

Independence: August 3, 1960

Area: 490,000 sq. mi. (roughly the size of Arizona, California, and New Mexico)

Capital: Niamey

Population: (1991 estimate) 8.1 million

Official language: French

Before the formation of the Sahara Desert, Niger was an important economic crossroads. The first European explorers reached the area in the nineteenth century while searching for the mouth of the Niger River.

Although French efforts at colonization began before 1900, ethnic groups, especially the desert Taureg people, were not defeated until 1922. On December 4, 1958, Niger became a state within the French Community. The country received full independence on August 3, 1960.

The Federal Republic of Nigeria

Independence: October 1, 1960

Area: 356,700 sq. mi. (roughly the size of Texas and Wyoming)

Capital: Abuja; former capital was Lagos

Population: (1991 estimate) 122.5 million

Official language: English

Evidence shows that more than 2,000

Teenagers drawing water in a rural Nigerian village

years ago, the Nok people of the region worked iron and produced terra cotta sculpture. In the centuries that followed, the Hausa kingdom and the Bornu empire, near Lake Chad, prospered as important centers of north-south trade between North African Berbers and forest people. In the southwest, the Uoruba kingdom of Oyo, which was founded about 1400 and reached its height between the seventeenth and nineteenth centuries, reached a high level of organization and extended as far as modern Togo. In the south-central part of present-day Nigeria, as early as the fifteenth century the kingdom of Benin had developed an efficient army, an elaborate ceremonial court, and artisans whose works in ivory, wood, bronze, and brass are today prized throughout the world.

Between the seventeenth and nineteenth centuries, European traders established coastal ports for the increasing traffic in slaves destined for the Americas. In 1855 British claims to a sphere of influence in that area received international recognition, and, in the following year, the Royal Niger Company was chartered. In 1900 the company's territory came under the control of the British government. In 1914 the area was formally united as the Colony and Protectorate of Nigeria. Nigeria was granted full independence on October 1, 1960.

Nigeria's history since 1960 has been troubled, marked by vicious fighting between and within native groups, bloody coups and oppressive military regimes, government corruption and assassinations, drought and famine, student uprisings, even civil war when the region of Biafra seceded in 1967 (it surrendered in January 1970 after much bloodshed). A 1985 coup brought a new regime to power, led by Major-General Ibrahim Babangida, who promised a return to civilian rule. But when the elections scheduled for 1990 were eventually held in June 1993 and Babangida lost, he voided the ballots.

In November 1993 General Sani Abacha forced his way into power. The following June the leading vote-getter of the previous year's election, Moshood K. O. Abiola, declared himself president. He was forced into hiding, however, when Abacha ordered his arrest. Abacha has made criticizing his government an act of treason.

The most populous country in Africa,

Nigeria is home to one-fourth of all sub-Saharan Africans.

The Republic of Senegal

Independence: April 4, 1960

Area: 75,749 sq. mi. (slightly smaller than South Dakota)

Capital: Dakar

Population: (1991 estimate) 7.9 million

Official language: French

The Portuguese were the first Europeans to trade in Senegal, arriving in the fifteenth century. They were soon followed by the Dutch and French. During the nineteenth century, the French gradually established control over the interior regions and administered them as a protectorate until 1920 and as a colony thereafter.

In January 1959 Senegal and the French Soudan merged to form the Mali Federation, which became fully independent on June 20, 1960. The federation broke up on August 20, 1960, and Senegal and Soudan (renamed the Republic of Mali) each proclaimed separate independence. Leopold Sedar Senghor, a world-renowned poet, politician, and statesman, was elected Senegal's first president in August 1960.

The Republic of Sierra Leone

Independence: April 27, 1961

Area: 27,699 sq. mi. (somewhat larger than West Virginia)

Capital: Freetown

Population: (1991 estimate) 4.2 million

Official language: English

Sierra Leone was one of the first West African British colonies. The site of Freetown received the first 400 freedmen from Great Britain in 1787. Disease and attacks by natives almost eliminated this first group. Five years later, another group of settlers—1,000 freed slaves who had fled from the United States to Nova Scotia during the American Revolution—arrived under the support of the newly formed British Sierra Leone Company. In 1800 about 550 blacks arrived from Jamaica via Nova Scotia. These were the Maroons, escaped slaves who maintained their independence in the mountains of Jamaica.

The 1951 constitution provided the framework for independence, which came in April 1961. In April 1971 Sierra Leone adopted a republican constitution, cutting its link to the British monarchy but remaining with the Commonwealth.

The Republic of Togo

Independence: April 27, 1960

Area: 21,853 sq. mi. (about twice the size of Maryland)

Capital: Lomé

Population: (1991 estimate) 3.8 million

Official languages: French, Ewe, and Kabiye

The Ewe people first moved into the area from the Niger River Valley sometime between the twelfth and fourteenth centuries. During the fifteenth and sixteenth centuries, Portuguese explorers and traders visited the coast. For the next two hundred years, the coastal region was a major raiding center for Europeans in search of slaves, earning Togo and the surrounding region the name "the Slave Coast."

In an 1884 treaty signed at Togoville, Germany declared a protectorate over the area. In 1914 Togoland was invaded by French and British forces and fell after a brief resistance. In 1955 French Togo became a republic within the French Community. In 1957 the residents of British Togoland voted to join the Gold Coast as part of the new independent nation of Ghana. On April 27, 1960, Togo cut its ties with France and became fully independent.

West Central Africa

The People's Republic of Angola

Independence: November 11, 1975

Area: 481,351 sq. mi. (about twice the size of Texas)

Capital: Luanda

Population: (1991 estimate) 8.6 million

Official language: Portuguese

The first European to discover Angola was Diego Cao of Portugal, in 1482. By the seventeenth century, Angolan slaves were being shipped to Brazil to work the coffee plantations there.

Angola's boundaries were formally established beginning in the late nineteenth century. In the twentieth century, the Popular Movement for the Liberation of Angola (MPLA), the National Front for the Liberation of Angola (FNLA), and the National Union for the Total Independence of Angola (UNITA) were formed to end Portuguese rule.

In January 1975 the Portuguese and the three liberation movements worked out a complicated agreement that led to the republic's independence by the end of the year. Since 1976 Angola has been politically unstable because of civil war and repeated attacks by South African forces operating from Namibia to the south. The United States does not maintain diplomatic relations with Angola (who throughout the 1970s and 1980s received large amounts of aid from Cuba and the Soviet Union, whom the U.S. government viewed as enemies), but since 1978 the two countries have had frequent contact.

A small **enclave** named Cabinda, north of the Zaire River, is also part of Angola.

The Bakongo people of Angola live in the northwest part of the country, near the Congo and Zaire

MOTHERLAND

Children studying at a school in Chad

The Central African Republic

Independence: August 13, 1960

Area: 240,533 sq. mi. (roughly twice the size of New Mexico)

Capital: Bangui

Population: (1991 estimate) 2.9 million

Official language: French

The first Europeans to settle in the area were the French. In 1889 they established an outpost at Bangui. United with Chad in 1906, the outpost formed the Oubangui-Chari-Chad colony.

In 1910 the Central African Republic became one of the four territories of the Federation of French Equatorial Africa, along with Chad, Congo (Brazzaville), and Gabon. However, a constitutional **referendum** of September 1958 dissolved the federation. The nation became a republic within the newly established French Community on December 1, 1958, and completed its independence as the Central African Republic on August 13, 1960.

The Republic of Chad

Independence: August 11, 1960

Area: 495,753 sq. mi. (a little smaller than Arizona, New Mexico, and Texas combined)

Capital: N'Djamena
Population: (1991 estimate) 5.8 million
Official language: French

The region of Chad was known to Middle Eastern traders and geographers as far back as the late Middle Ages. Since then, Chad has served as a crossroads for the Muslim peoples of the desert and **savanna** regions as well as the Bantu tribes of the tropical forests.

The French first entered Chad in 1891. In 1900 the French fought a major battle with the African leader Rabah. Although the French won that battle, they did not claim the territory until 1911. Armed clashes between colonial troops and local bands continued for many years thereafter. Although Chad joined the French colonies of Gabon, Oubangui-Charo, and Moyen Congo to form the Federation of French Equatorial Africa in 1910, Chad did not have colonial status until 1920.

In 1959 the territory of French Equatorial Africa was dissolved, and four states—Gabon, the Central African Republic, Congo (Brazzaville), and Chad—became members of the French Community. In 1960 Chad became an independent nation under its first president, François Tombalbaye.

The Republic of the Congo

Independence: August 15, 1960
Area: 132,046 sq. mi. (a little less than twice the size of Washington)
Capital: Brazzaville
Population: (1991 estimate) 2.4 million
Official language: French

The early history of the Congo involves three tribal kingdoms—the Kongo, the Loango, and the Teke. Established in the fourth century A.D., the Kongo was a highly centralized kingdom that later developed a close commercial relationship with the Portuguese, the first Europeans to explore the area.

With the development of the slave trade, the Portuguese turned their attention from the Kongo Kingdom to the Loango. By the time the slave trade was abolished in the 1800s, the Loango Kingdom had been reduced to many small independent groups. The Teke Kingdom of the interior, which had sold slaves to the Loango Kingdom, ended its independence in 1883 when the Teke king concluded a treaty that placed Teke lands and people under French protection. Under the French, the area became known as the Middle Congo.

In 1910 the Middle Congo became part of French Equatorial Africa, which also included Gabon, the Central African Republic, and Chad. A constitutional referendum in September 1958 replaced the Federation of French Equatorial Africa with the French Community. The Middle Congo, under the name the Republic of the Congo, and the three other territories of French Equatorial Africa became members within the French Community. On April 15, 1960, it became an independent nation but retained close, formal bonds with the community.

The Republic of Equatorial Guinea

Independence: October 12, 1968
Area: 10,820 sq. mi. (a little larger than Maryland)
Capital: Malabo (on Bioko Island)

Population: (1991 estimate) 360,000

Official language: Spanish

Pygmies were probably the first people to live in the Equatorial Guinea region. Bantu migrations between the seventeenth and nineteenth centuries brought the coastal tribes and later the Fang people to the area.

The Portuguese, seeking a route to India, landed on the island of Bioko in 1471. They maintained control until 1778, when they surrendered the island and nearby islets to Spain. From 1827 to 1843 Britain established a base on the island to combat the slave trade. In 1900 the Treaty of Paris settled conflicting claims to the mainland.

In 1959 the Spanish territory of the Gulf of Guinea was established. The name of the country was changed to Equatorial Guinea in 1963. In March 1968 Spain announced that it would grant independence to Equatorial Guinea. In September 1968 Francisco Macias Nguema was elected the first president of Equatorial Guinea, and independence was granted in October.

The Republic of Gabon

Independence: August 17, 1960

Area: 102,317 sq. mi. (slightly smaller than Colorado)

Capital: Libreville

Population: (1990 estimate) 1.2 million

Official language: French

Gabon's first European visitors were Portuguese traders who arrived in the fifteenth century. The coast quickly became a center of the slave trade. Dutch, British, and French traders came in the sixteenth century. France assumed the status of protector by signing treaties with Gabonese coastal chiefs in 1839 and 1841. In 1910, Gabon became one of the four territories of French Equatorial Africa, a federation that survived until 1959. The territories became independent in 1960 as the Central African Republic, Chad, Congo (Brazzaville), and Gabon.

The Democratic Republic of São Tomé and Príncipe

Independence: July 12, 1975

Area: 372 sq. mi. (one-third the size of Rhode Island)

Capital: São Tomé

Population: (1991 estimate) 128,499

Languages spoken: Portuguese

These uninhabited islands were first visited by Portuguese navigators between 1469 and 1472. The first successful settlement of São Tomé was established in 1493. Príncipe was settled in 1500. By the mid-1500s, with the help of slave labor, the Portuguese settlers had turned the islands into Africa's foremost exporter of sugar. São Tomé was taken over and administered by the Portuguese crown in 1522 and Príncipe followed in 1573. By 1908 São Tomé had become the world's largest producer of cocoa, still the country's most important crop.

Although Portugal officially abolished slavery in 1876, the settlers continued to practice forced paid labor. In 1953 riots broke out, leaving several hundred African laborers dead.

By the late 1950s, a small group of São Toméans had formed the Movement for the Liberation of São Tomé and Príncipe (MLSTP). In 1974 Portuguese representatives met with the MLSTP in Algiers, Alge-

Mbuti people of the Ituri forest in Zaire

ria, and worked out an agreement for the transfer of **sovereignty.** After a period of transition, São Tomé and Príncipe achieved independence on July 12, 1975, choosing as its first president the MLSTP Secretary General Manuel Pinto da Costa.

The Republic of Zaire

Independence: June 30, 1960

Area: 905,063 sq. mi. (the size of Alaska, North Carolina, and Texas combined)

Capital: Kinshasa (formerly Leopoldville)

Population: (1991 estimate) 37.8 million

Official language: French

It is possible that the region of present-day Zaire was populated as early as 10,000 years ago. By the seventh and eighth centuries A.D., large numbers of people came to the area. These included the Bantu, who brought with them knowledge of the manufacture and use of metals.

In 1482 the Portuguese arrived at the mouth of the Congo River. They found an organized society—the Bakongo Kingdom—which included parts of present-day Congo, Zaire, and Angola. The Portuguese named the area Congo.

The Berlin Conference of 1885 recognized King Leopold's claim to the greater part of the Zaire River basin. The Congo Free

State remained his personal possession until he awarded it to the Belgian State in 1907, when it was renamed the Belgian Congo.

Following riots in Leopoldville in 1958, Belgian King Bedouin announced that the colony could look forward to independence. Roundtable conferences begun in Brussels in January 1960 led to independence on June 30, 1960.

There was much confusion after independence, with ethnic and personal rivalries raging. Colonel Mobutu Sese Seko, who had been head of the army, seized power on November 1965, proclaiming himself president. For the next 30 years Mobutu would rule Zaire with an iron first and pillage its treasury.

The 1970s brought economic decline and great political opposition, yet Mobutu handily won elections for president in 1970, 1977, and 1984—no one dared oppose him. He survived a string of unsuccessful coup attempts in the late 1970s, and finally, in 1990, announced that a multiparty system of government would be allowed (a political ploy, many observers believe, to keep Zaire's 260 opposition parties at odds with each other). As of 1994, Mobutu was still in power and gross corruption, political turmoil, and economic devastation continue to wreak havoc in the twelfth-poorest nation in the world.

Northeast Africa

The Republic of Djibouti

Independence: June 27, 1977
Area: 8,494 sq. mi. (slightly smaller than New Hampshire)
Capital: Djibouti
Population: (1991 estimate) 541,000

Official language: French

The Djibouti region was first settled by the French in 1862. In 1884 France expanded its protectorate, calling it French Somaliland. The boundaries of the protectorate were marked out in 1897 by France and Emperor Manelik II of Ethiopia. Emperor Haile Selassie I agreed to these boundaries in 1945 and again in 1954.

In July 1967 the name of the territory was formally changed to the French Territory of Afars and Issas. In 1975 the French government began to listen to increasing demands for independence. In a May 1977 referendum, the electorate voted for independence, and the Republic of Djibouti was born on June 27, 1977.

Eritrea

Independence: April 27, 1993

Eritrea is the newest African nation, though it has its origin in the oldest, Ethiopia. Nonetheless, the region of Eritrea was largely independent until the sixteenth century, when the Ottomans began their rule. During the 1880s the Italians began conquering Eritrea and claimed it as a colony on January 1, 1890. During World War II the British took control of all of Italy's African possessions, including Eritrea. Then, in 1952, the United Nations awarded control of the region to Ethiopia's Haile Selassie.

On November 14, 1962, Eritrea officially became part of Ethiopia. At this same time, the Eritrean People's Liberation Front (the EPLF, founded in 1958) began a long armed struggle for Eritrean independence. Following the May 1991 overthrow of the Ethiopian army by the EPLF (and the collapse of

Ethiopia's Marxist government under Mengistu Haile Mariam), the path to Eritrean independence was prepared. Although an agriculturally poor region, Eritrea is especially valuable to Ethiopia because it provides that country's only access to the Red Sea.

The People's Democratic Republic of Ethiopia

Independence: 1974

Area: 471,776 sq. mi. (roughly the size of California, Pennsylvania, and Texas combined)

Capital: Addis Ababa

Population: (1990 estimate) 51.3 million

Official languages: Amharic and English

Ethiopia is the oldest independent country in Africa and one of the oldest in the world. (Herodotus, a Greek historian of the fifth century B.C., described ancient Ethiopia in his writings. The Old Testament, too, records the Queen of Sheba's visit to Jerusalem to consult King Solomon.) Missionaries from Egypt and Syria introduced Christianity in the fourth century A.D. The Portuguese established contact with Ethiopia in 1493.

In 1930 Haile Selassie was crowned emperor. His reign was interrupted in 1936 when Italian forces invaded and occupied Ethiopia. The emperor was eventually forced into **exile** in England despite his plea to the League of Nations for help. Five years later, British and Ethiopian forces defeated the Italians and returned the emperor to the throne. After a period of civil unrest, which began in February 1974, the aging Haile Selassie I was **deposed** on September 13, 1974.

The Provisional Military Administrative Council (PMAC) then formally declared its intent to remake Ethiopia into a socialist state. The Council finally destroyed its opposition through a program of mass arrests and executions known as the "red terror," which lasted from November 1977 to March 1978. An estimated 10,000 people, mostly in Addis Ababa, were killed by government forces.

Throughout the 1980s droughts ravaged Ethiopia bringing devastating famine. Tens of thousands fled to nearby countries as the government blocked famine relief to the region of Eritrea, which was seeking independence from Ethiopia [see above].

The Somali Democratic Republic

Independence: July 1, 1960

Area: 246,200 sq. mi. (about twice the size of New Mexico)

Capital: Mogadishu

Population: (1991 estimate) 6.7 million

Official languages: Somali and Arabic

The British East India Company's desire for unrestricted harbor facilities led to the conclusion of treaties with the sultan of Tajura as early as 1840. It was not until 1886, however, that the British gained control over northern Somalia through treaties with various Somali chiefs. In 1897 treaties between the British and King Menellik established the boundary between Ethiopia and British Somaliland.

In 1855 Italy obtained commercial advantages in the area from the sultan of Zanzibar and in 1889 concluded agreements with the sultans of Obbia and Caluula, who placed their territories under Italy's protection.

An Ethiopian market

Between 1897 and 1908 Italy made agreements with the Ethiopians and the British that marked out the boundaries of Italian Somaliland. In June 1940 Italian troops overran British Somaliland and drove out the British forces. In 1941 British troops began operations against the Italian East African Empire and quickly brought the greater part of the Italian Somaliland under British control.

From 1941 to 1950, under British military administration, Somalia began to move toward self-government. Elections for the

Legislative Assembly were held in February 1960. The protectorate became independent on June 26, 1960. Five days later, on July 1, it joined Italian Somaliland to form the Somali Republic

In 1991 a rebel group in the north announced its secession from Somalia and proclaimed itself the Somaliland Republic. The ensuing civil war and the worst African drought of the century created devastating famine. It was estimated in September 1992 that up to one-third of the population was in danger of starvation and the number dead was already in the tens of thousands.

The United States and the United Nations deployed a massive 15-month relief effort, but the distribution of food was hampered by widespread looting and by heavily armed gangs hostile to the troops and other relief workers. As of early 1994 there was a fragile truce in the capital, but clan violence threatens to explode at any time.

The Republic of Sudan

Independence: January 1, 1956

Area: 967,494 sq. mi. (the size of Alaska, Arizona, and Texas combined)

Capital: Khartoum

Population: (1991 estimate) 27.2 million

Official language: Arabic

From the beginning of the Christian era until 1820, Sudan existed as a collection of small independent states. In 1881 a religious leader named Mohammed Ahmed ibn Abdalla proclaimed himself the Mahdi, or "expected one," and began to unify tribes in western and central Sudan. The Mahdi led a nationalist revolt that climaxed in the fall of Khartoum in 1855. He died shortly thereafter, but his state survived until it was overwhelmed by Anglo-Egyptian forces in 1898. In 1899 Sudan was placed under British-Egyptian administration. In February 1953 the United Kingdom and Egypt concluded an agreement providing for Sudanese self-government. Sudan achieved independence on January 1, 1956.

Since May 1983 Sudan has been embroiled in a bitter civil war that has left more than 1.5 people dead, most from starvation. The fighting began when mutinous soldiers rekindled deep-seeded hatred between Christians and Islamic fundamentalists; the fighting then spread along tribal lines. The Islamic-dominated government has used food as a weapon and both sides are guilty of massacres and setting villages afire. Seven rounds of peace talks have failed in the twelve years of unrest.

East Africa

The Republic of Burundi

Independence: July 1, 1962

Area: 10,747 sq. mi. (almost the same size as Maryland)

Capital: Bujumbura

Population: (1991 estimate) 5.8 million

Official languages: French and KiRundi

Prior to the arrival of Europeans, Burundi was a kingdom with a **feudal** social structure. Rulers were drawn from princely dynastic families (*ganwa*), from whom a king (*mwami*) was chosen.

European explorers and missionaries began making brief visits to the area as early as 1858. However, Burundi did not come under European administration until the 1890s, when it became part of German East

MOTHERLAND

A mother and father with their baby in a Kenya first-aid station

Africa. In 1916 Belgian troops occupied the country. The League of Nations mandated the area to Belgium in 1923 as part of the Territory of Ruanda-Urundi, now the nations of Rwanda and Burundi. Burundi became independent on July 1, 1962.

The Republic of Kenya

Independence: December 12, 1963
Area: 224,961 sq. mi. (more than twice the size of Nevada)
Capital: Nairobi
Population: (1991 estimate) 25.2 million
Languages spoken: Swahili and English

From 1000 B.C. through the first century A.D., the people of Kenya maintained contact with Arab traders. Arab and Persian settlements were founded along the coast as early as the eighth century A.D. By then Bantu and Nilotic peoples had moved into the area. The Arabs were followed by the Portuguese in 1498. The Imam of Oman established Islamic control in the 1600s, and the area submitted to British influence in the nineteenth century. In 1885 European powers first divided east Africa into spheres of influence. In 1895 the British government established the East African Protectorate.

From October 1952 to December 1959 Kenya was under a state of emergency, arising from the Mau Mau rebellion against British colonial rule. Kenya became fully independent on December 12, 1963. Jomo Kenyatta, a member of the predominant Kikuyu tribe and head of the Kenya African National Union, became Kenya's first president.

The Republic of Rwanda

Independence: July 1, 1962

Area: 10,169 sq. mi. (about the size of Maryland)

Capital: Kigali

Population: (1991 estimate) 7.9 million

Official languages: French and Ki-Nyarwanda

For centuries farmers and herders populated the area of Rwanda. In 1899 a German protectorate was established. During World War I Belgian troops from Zaire occupied Rwanda. After the war, the League of Nations awarded Rwanda and its southern neighbor, Burundi, to Belgium as the Territory of Ruanda-Urundi. Following World War II, Ruanda-Urundi became a United Nations trust territory with Belgium as the administering authority. The Party of the Hutu Emancipation Movement (PARMEHUTU) won an overwhelming victory in a United Nations-supervised referendum.

The PARMEHUTU government, formed as a result of the September 1961 election, was granted control by Belgium on January 1, 1962. A June 1962 United Nations resolution ended all Belgian involvement and granted full independence to Rwanda (and Burundi) effective July 1, 1962.

Rwanda was thrown into civil war on April 6, 1994, when a plane carrying the presidents of Rwanda and neighboring Burundi mysteriously crashed [see above]. Rwandan government officials—mainly of the Hutu tribe—blamed the rebel Tutsi minority for the killings (both presidents were Hutus). In the two months following the crash, as many as 200,000 civilians, mostly Tutsi, were slaughtered by machete-, spear-, and knife-wielding Hutu gang members and Hutu-dominated government forces. Two million people have fled the country and thousands have been displaced.

As numerous cease-fire agreements between the warring tribes have been ignored, some nations have suggested embargoes and military intervention to stop the chaos before it spreads into neighboring countries. The United Nations has considered sending in 5,500 peacekeeping troops to protect civilians and relief workers stationed there.

The United Republic of Tanzania

Independence: December 9, 1961

Area: 363,950 sq. mi. (about the size of Arizona and Mississippi)

Capital: Dar es Salaam

Population: (1991 estimate) 26.8 million

Official languages: Swahili and English

The coast of Tanzania was discovered by foreigners as early as the eighth century. By the twelfth century, traders and immigrants came from as far away as Persia (now Iran) and India. Portuguese navigator Vasco da Gama first visited the East African coast in 1498 on his voyage to India. By 1506 the Portuguese claimed control over the entire coast.

German and English colonial interests were first advanced in the 1880s. Following World War I, control of most of the territory (then called Tanganyika) passed to the United Kingdom under a League of Nations mandate.

In the following years, Tanganyika moved gradually toward self-government and independence. In 1954 Julius K. Nyerere, a schoolteacher educated abroad, organized the Tanganyika African Union (UANU). Full independence was achieved on December 9, 1961. On April 26, 1964, Tanganyika united with Zanzibar to form the United Republic of Tanganyika and Zanzibar, renamed the United Republic of Tanzania on October 29.

The Republic of Uganda

Independence: October 9, 1962

Area: 93,354 sq. mi. (somewhat smaller than Oregon)

Capital: Kampala

Population: (1991 estimate) 18.6 million

Official languages: English and Swahili

Arab traders moving inland from coastal enclaves reached the interior of Uganda in the 1830s and found several African kingdoms, including the Buganda kingdom, that had well-developed political institutions dating back several centuries.

In 1888 royal charter assigned control of the emerging British sphere of interest in East Africa to the Imperial British East Africa Company. In 1894 the Kingdom of Uganda was placed under a formal British protectorate. The British protectorate formally ended in 1955, when constitutional changes leading to Uganda's independence were adopted. The first general elections in Uganda were held in 1961, and the British government granted internal self-government to Uganda on March 1, 1962.

In February 1966 Prime Minister Milton Obote suspended the constitution, assumed all government powers, and removed the president and vice president. On January 25, 1971, Obote's government was ousted in a military coup led by armed forces commander Idi Amin Dada. Amin declared himself president, dissolved the parliament, and amended the constitution to give himself absolute power. Amin's eight-year reign produced economic and social decline—and massive human rights violations (it is estimated that as many as 250,000 Ugandans were killed during the 1970s). In 1978 Tanzanian forces pushed back an advance by Amin's troops. Backed by Ugandan exiles, Tanzanian forces waged a war of liberation against Amin. On April 11, 1979, the Ugandan capital was captured, and Amin and his remaining forces fled.

Following Amin's ouster, various groups vied for power. Many people were killed, and more than 200,000 fled the country. Finally in 1986 Yoweri Museveni became president, and the nation began the difficult process of rebuilding itself.

Southeast Central Africa

The Republic of Malawi

Independence: July 6, 1964

Area: 45,747 sq. mi. (the size of Pennsylvania)

Capital: Lilongwe
Population: (1991 estimate) 9.4 million
Official languages: Chicewa and English

The Portuguese first came to the area in the sixteenth century. White explorer David Livingston reached the shore of Lake Malawi in 1859. By 1878 a number of traders, mostly from Scotland, formed the African Lakes Company to supply goods and services to the missionaries. In 1891 the British established the Nyasaland Protectorate. Nyasaland joined with Northern and Southern Rhodesia in 1953 to form the Federation of Rhodesia and Nyasaland.

In July 1958 Dr. H. Kamazu Banda returned to the country after a long absence spent in the United States, the United Kingdom, and Ghana. He assumed leadership of the Nyasaland African Congress, which later became the Malawi Congress Party (MCP). In 1959 Banda was sent to Gwele Prison for his political activities but was released in 1960.

Banda became prime minister on February 1, 1963, although the British still controlled Malawi's economic and judicial systems. The Federation of Rhodesia and Nyasaland was dissolved on December 31, 1963, and Malawi became fully independent on July 6, 1964. Two years later, Malawi adopted a new constitution and became a republic with Banda as its first president.

The Republic of Mozambique

Independence: June 25, 1975
Area: 303,769 sq. mi. (the size of Indiana and Texas combined)
Population: (1991 estimate) 15.1 million
Official language: Portuguese

Mozambique's first inhabitants were Bushmanoid hunters and gatherers. During the first four centuries A.D., waves of Bantu-speaking peoples migrated from the north through the Zambezi River Valley and then gradually into the plateau and coastal areas. Portuguese explorers reached Mozambique in 1498. But by then Arab trading settlements had existed along the coast for several centuries. Later, traders and prospectors penetrated the interior seeking gold and slaves.

After World War II, while many European nations were granting independence to their colonies, Portugal clung to the idea that Mozambique and other Portuguese possessions were "overseas provinces." In 1962 several anti-Portuguese political groups formed the Front for Liberation of Mozambique (FRELIMO), which began an armed campaign against Portuguese colonial rule in September 1964. Mozambique became independent on June 25, 1975.

In the years since its independence the nation has been ravaged by international and civil war and, with the worst drought of the century in 1992, famine. Rebels have hampered food distribution efforts, and tens of thousands have starved to death while more than one million refugees have fled the country. It has been reported that many rebels have put down their guns—exhausted by the famine and the fight—and will make a bid for peace.

The Republic of Zambia

Independence: October 24, 1964
Area: 290,585 sq. mi. (roughly half the size of Alaska)

MOTHERLAND

A woman fighting for Mozambique independence

Capital: Lusaka
Population: (1991 estimate) 8.4 million
Official language: English

About 2,000 years ago, hunter-gatherers in Zambia began to be displaced or absorbed by more advanced migrating tribes. By the fifteenth century, the major waves of Bantu-speaking immigrants began. By the end of the nineteenth century, the various peoples of Zambia were largely established in the areas they now occupy.

The area lay untouched by Europeans—except for an occasional Portuguese explorer—until the mid-nineteenth century, when it was penetrated by European explorers, missionaries, and traders. In 1888 Northern and Southern Rhodesia (now Zambia and Zimbabwe) were proclaimed a British sphere of influence. In 1953 both Rhodesias were joined with Nyasaland (now Malawi) to form the Federation of Rhodesia and Nyasaland.

Northern Rhodesia was the center of much of the turmoil that characterized the federation in its last years. A two-stage election held in October and December 1962 resulted in an African majority in the Legislative Council. The council passed resolutions that called for Northern Rhodesia's **secession** from the federation and demanded full internal self-government. On December 31, 1963, the federation was dissolved and Northern Rhodesia became the Republic of Zambia on October 24, 1964.

Zimbabwe

Independence: April 18, 1980

Area: 150,803 sq. mi. (the size of Nevada and Ohio)

Capital: Harare

Population: (1991 estimate) 10.8 million

Official language: English

During the sixteenth century, the Portuguese were the first Europeans to attempt colonization of south-central Africa, but the interior lay virtually untouched by Europeans until the arrival of explorers, missionaries, and traders some three hundred years later. In 1888 the area that became Southern and Northern Rhodesia was proclaimed a British sphere of influence. The British South Africa Company was chartered in 1889, and the settlement of Salisbury (now Harare) was established in 1890.

The territory was formally named Rhodesia in 1895. In September 1953 Southern Rhodesia was joined with the British protectorates of Northern Rhodesia and Nyasaland. After much turmoil, the federation was dissolved at the end of 1963. Northern Rhodesia and Nyasaland became the independent states of Zambia and Malawi in 1964.

Although prepared to grant independence to Rhodesia, the United Kingdom insisted that the authorities at Salisbury first demonstrate their intention to move toward eventual majority rule. Desiring to keep their power, the white Rhodesians refused to bend. On November 11, 1965, after lengthy and unsuccessful negotiations with the British government, Prime Minister Ian Smith issued a Unilateral Declaration of Independence (UDI) from the United Kingdom.

In 1976 the Smith government agreed in principle to majority rule. In 1979 Bishop Muzorewa became Zimbabwe's first black prime minister. However, the installation of the new black majority government did not end the guerrilla conflict that had claimed more than 20,000 lives. The British government formally granted independence to Zimbabwe on April 18, 1980.

Southern Africa

The Republic of Botswana

Independence: September 30, 1966

Area: 224,710 sq. mi. (more than twice the size of Nevada)

Capital: Gaborone

Population: (1991 estimate) 1.3 million

Official language: English

Europeans first entered the area of Botswana in the early nineteenth century. In the last quarter of the century, fighting broke out between the Botswana and the Afrikaners from South Africa (Transvaal). Following appeals by the Botswana for help, the British government in 1885 proclaimed "Bechuanaland," as the colony was then known, to be under British protection.

In 1909, against the wishes of South Africa, the people of Bechuanaland, Basutoland (now Lesotho), and Swaziland demanded and received British agreement that they not be included in the proposed Union of South Africa.

In June 1964, the British government accepted proposals for a form of self-government for Botswana that would lead to independence. Botswana became independent on September 30, 1966.

The nation strongly opposed South Africa's policy of **apartheid** and maintain no formal diplomatic relations with that country while the system was in place. But, because of its geographic location and reliance on South African goods and transportation systems, Botswana maintained a working relationship and close economic ties with South Africa.

The Kingdom of Lesotho

Independence: October 4, 1966
Area: 11,718 sq. mi. (somewhat larger than Maryland)
Capital: Maseru
Population: (1991 estimate) 1.8 million
Official languages: English and Sesotho

Until the end of the sixteenth century, Basutoland (now Lesotho) was sparsely populated by bushmen. Between the sixteenth and nineteenth centuries, refugees from surrounding areas gradually formed the Basotho ethnic group.

Moshoeshoe I consolidated various Basotho groupings in 1818 and became king. During his reign from 1823 to 1870 a series of wars with South Africa resulted in the loss of extensive lands, now known as the "Lost Territory." Moshoeshoe appealed to Queen Victoria for assistance, and in 1868 the country was placed under British protection.

In 1959 a new constitution gave Basutoland its first elected legislature. On October 4, 1966, the new Kingdom of Lesotho attained full independence.

The Republic of Namibia

Independence: March 21, 1990
Area: 320,827 sq. mi. (the size of Arkansas and Texas combined)
Capital: Windhoek
Population: (1991 estimate) 1.5 million
Official language: English

In 1878 the United Kingdom annexed Walvis Bay on behalf of Cape Colony; the area was incorporated into the Cape of Good Hope in 1884. A German trader claimed the remainder of the coastal region after negotiations with a local chief. German administration ended during World War I, when the territory was occupied by South African forces in 1915.

On December 17, 1920, South Africa undertook the administration of South West Africa. During the 1960s, as other African nations gained independence, pressure mounted on South Africa to do so in South West Africa.

In 1966 the United Nations General Assembly canceled South Africa's mandate. Also in 1966, the South West Africa People's Organization (SWAPO) began guerrilla attacks on Namibia. In 1971 the International Court of Justice determined that South Africa's presence in Namibia was illegal and required the republic to withdraw its administration from Namibia immediately.

However, the Republic of South Africa did not agree to withdraw its troops until

1988. By February 9, 1990, the Namibian assembly had drafted and adopted a constitution, and the republic achieved independence that same year.

The Republic of South Africa

Independence: May 31, 1961

Area: 472,359 sq. mi. (about three times the size of California)

Capitals: Pretoria (administrative); Cape Town (legislative); Bloemfontein (judicial)

Population: (1991 estimate) 40.6 million

Official languages: English and Afrikaans

In 1488 the Portuguese became the first Europeans to reach the Cape of Good Hope (near the southernmost tip of South Africa). Permanent white settlement began when the Dutch East India Company established a supply station there in 1652. In later decades French, Dutch, and German settlers came to the Cape area to form the Afrikaner segment of the modern population.

Britain seized the Cape of Good Hope at the end of the eighteenth century. Partly to escape British rule, many Afrikaner farmers (Boers) undertook a northern migration called the "Great Trek" beginning in 1836. This movement brought them into contact with several African groups, the most powerful of whom were the Zulu. Under their leader Shaka, the Zulu conquered most of the territory between the Drakensberg Mountains and the sea (now Natal). The Zulu were defeated at the Battle of Blood River in 1838.

The independent Boer republics of the Transvaal (the South African Republic) and the Orange Free State were created in 1852 and 1854. Following the two Boer wars (1880-81 and 1899-1902), British forces conquered the Boer republics and added them to the British Empire. A strong revival of Afrikaner **nationalism** in the mid-twentieth century led to a 1960 referendum among whites to give up dominion status. The Union of South Africa became the Republic of South Africa on May 31, 1961.

Nelson Mandela, president of South Africa

South African laws, until 1993, were based on apartheid, a political and social system that assigns basic rights and obligations according to racial or ethnic origin. The country's black majority (75 percent of the population) suffered from discrimination in nearly all areas of life. Political participation of the black majority, for instance, was limited to tightly controlled urban councils in the country's black townships and in the ten so-called homelands.

The African National Congress (ANC) is a mostly black South African organization that was founded in 1912. It is the oldest group to have opposed racism and rule by whites (who represent 14 percent of the population) in South Africa. It was banned by the South African government from 1960 to 1990, but operated underground and in exile.

Upon his election as president of South Africa in 1989, F. W. DeKlerk took several steps to help end apartheid. One of the most important was the release of long-imprisoned ANC leader Nelson Mandela and the lifting of the ban on the ANC and other opposition groups.

The 1990s saw a remarkable series of reforms in South Africa. In 1991 legislators ended residential segregation and racial restrictions on land ownership. In 1993 Mandela and DeKlerk negotiated a new constitution that prohibited discrimination on the basis of race or gender. It also provided for democratic elections—elections that would end white minority rule in South Africa. For their efforts the two leaders were awarded the Nobel Peace Prize.

On May 10, 1994, after a landslide victory in the nation's first all-race elections, Mandela was sworn in as president of South Africa. DeKlerk was elected second deputy president. In his inaugural address, Mandela called for unity in a country that—after nearly 350 years—was finally ruled by its black majority.

The Kingdom of Swaziland

Independence: September 6, 1968

Area: 6,704 sq. mi. (about the size of Hawaii)

Capitals: Mbabane (administrative); Lobamba (legislative)

Population: (1991 estimate) 859,000

Official languages: English and SiSwazi

The people of the present Swazi nation migrated south sometime before the sixteenth century to what is now Mozambique. After a series of conflicts with people living in the area of Maputo, the Swazi settled in northern Zululand in about 1750. Unable to match the growing Zulu strength there, the Swazis moved gradually northward in the early 1800s and established themselves in the area of modern Swaziland. The Swazi consolidated their hold in this area under several able leaders. The most important of these was Mswati, from whom the Swazi derive their name. Under his leadership in the 1840s, the Swazi expanded their territory to the northwest and stabilized the southern frontier with the Zulus.

The first Swazi contact with the British came early in Mswati's reign when he asked the British agent general in South Africa for support against Zulu raids into Swaziland. Agreements between the British and the Transvaal (South Africa) governments in 1881 and 1884 provided that Swaziland be independent. In 1903 Britain formally took over the administration of Swaziland.

Sobhuza II became head of the Swazi Nation in 1921. By the 1960s, political activity intensified, partly in response to events elsewhere in Africa. Several political parties that sought independence were formed. The traditional Swazi leaders, including King Sobhuza and his council, formed the Imbokodvo National Movement. In 1966 the British agreed to hold talks on a new constitution. Swaziland became independent on September 6, 1968.

East African Island Nations

The Federal Islamic Republic of the Comoros

Independence: July 6, 1975

Area: 838 sq. mi. (about three-fourths the size of Rhode Island)

Capital: Moroni (on Grand Comore)

Population: (1991 estimate) 476,678

Languages spoken: Shikomoro (a Swahili-Arab dialect), Malagasy, French

Portuguese explorers visited this archipelago off the coast of Mozambique in 1505. The four Comoros islands are Anjouan, Grand Comore, Mayotte, and Moheli. In 1843 the French persuaded the sultan of Mayotte to surrender the island of Mayotte. By 1912 France had established colonial rule over the other three islands, placing them under the administration of the governor general of Madagascar.

After World War II the islands became a French overseas territory. On July 6, 1975, the Comorian Parliament passed a resolution declaring independence. However, the deputies of Mayotte **abstained;** as a result, the Comorian government has effective control over only Grande Comore, Anjouan, and Moheli. Mayotte remains under French administration.

Mayotte (Mahoré)

Status: Overseas territory of France

Area: 600 mi. (about half the size of Rhode Island)

Population: (1992 estimate) 86,628

Languages spoken: Mahorian (a Swahili dialect) and French

Part of the Comoros archipelago, Mayotte shares its history with the Comoros Federal Islamic Republic. When Comoros declared independence in 1975, Mayotte voted to remain an overseas territory of France. Although Comoros has since claimed Mayotte, the French have promised the islanders that they may remain French citizens for as long as they wish.

The Democratic Republic of Madagascar

Independence: June 26, 1960

Area: 228,880 sq. mi. (about twice the size of Arizona)

Capital: Antananarivo

Population: (1991 estimate) 12.1 million

Official languages: Malagasy and French

Located east of the African mainland in the Indian Ocean, Madagascar is home to people who arrived from Africa and Asia during the first five centuries A.D. Three major kingdoms—Betsimisaraka, Merina, and Sakalava—ruled the island. In the seventh century A.D., Arabs established trading posts in the coastal areas of what is now Madagascar. Portuguese sighted the island in the sixteenth century, and in the late seventeenth century the French established trading posts along the east coast.

In the 1790s the Merina rulers established control over the majority part of the island. The Merina ruler and the British governor of Mauritius concluded a treaty abolishing the slave trade, which had been important in Madagascar's economy, and the island received British military assistance in return.

British influence remained strong until the French established control by military force in 1895. On October 14, 1958, the

Malagasy Republic was proclaimed as a state within the French community. A period of provisional government ended when the republic adopted a constitution in 1959 and achieved full independence in 1960.

Madagascar's independent years have been marked by political and social unrest as a series of repressive regimes governed the nation. Price increases and food shortages of the mid 1980s forced the government to establish a multiparty political system and move toward a capitalist (rather than socialist) economic system in the 1990s.

The Republic of Mauritius

Independence: March 12, 1968

Area: 720 sq. mi. (a little more than half the size of Rhode Island)

Capital: Port Louis

Population: (1991 estimate) 1,000,000

Official language: English

Portuguese sailors first visited Mauritius in the early sixteenth century, though the island had been known to Arabs and Malays much earlier. Dutch sailors, who named the island in honor of Prince Maurice of Nassau, established a small colony in 1638 but abandoned it in 1710. The French claimed Mauritius in 1715, renaming it Ile de France. In 1810 Mauritius was captured by the British, whose possession of the island was confirmed four years later by the Treaty of Paris. After slavery was abolished in 1835, indentured laborers from India brought an additional cultural influence to the island. Mauritius achieved independence on March 12, 1968.

Réunion

Status: Overseas department of France

Area: 970 sq. mi. (somewhat smaller than Rhode Island)

Capital: Saint Denis

Population: (1992 estimate) 626,414

Official language: French

The island of Réunion, located in the Indian Ocean east of Madagascar, remained uninhabited until 1654, when the French East India Company established trading bases and brought in slaves from Africa and Madagascar. France governed the island as a colony until 1946, when it was granted department status.

The Republic of Seychelles

Independence: June 29, 1976

Area: 171 sq. mi. (about one-tenth the size of Rhode Island)

Capital: Victoria

Population: (1991 estimate) 68,932

Languages spoken: Creole, English, and French

In 1742 the French governor of Mauritius sent an expedition to the islands. A second expedition in 1756 led to formal French possession. The Seychelles islands were captured and freed several times during the French Revolution and the Napoleonic wars. They then passed officially to the British under the Treaty of Paris in 1814. Negotiations with the British resulted in an agreement by which Seychelles became independent on June 29, 1976.

Most Seychellois are descendants of early French settlers and the African slaves brought to the Seychelles in the nineteenth century by the British, who freed them from slave ships on the East African coast.

3
Neighbors

Blacks in the Western Hemisphere

"In spite of everything that was done to me and my race, in spite of the adversity and the bitter moments, again we rise!"—Maya Angelou

A Brief History

The black population of the Caribbean and much of South America, like that in North America, is descended from African slaves who were transported to the New World to work on European settlements. Blacks make up the majority on many islands of the Caribbean.

On Barbados and Jamaica, for example, persons of African descent comprise more than 90 percent of the population. In other areas, notably on the continental mainland from Mexico south to Argentina, Africans have been absorbed into the mainstream of the population. In South America, the black population consists of a mixture of Africans and Indians, known as *Zambos*. Those who are primarily a mixture of Caucasian and American Indian are known as *mestizos,* and those who are a mixture of Caucasian and black are referred to as *mulattoes.*

> **WORDS TO KNOW**
>
> **autonomous:** independent or self-governing
>
> **ceded:** formally transferred or surrendered
>
> **coup:** a quick seizure of power, often by military force; short for the French *coup d'état*
>
> **emancipation:** to be freed from the control of another
>
> **fugitive:** a person who flees from danger or from the law
>
> **pacify:** to satisfy or calm
>
> **patois:** a differing form of a standard language
>
> **referendum:** a direct vote by the people

The Caribbean Today

In recent years, the Caribbean basin has been a source of black immigration. Jamaicans and Haitians, especially, have entered the United States in search of work and a better quality of life. In 1980 the *Mariel* boatlift successfully brought Cuban refugees to the United States. Since the September 1991 **coup** that removed Jean-Bertrand Aristide from the Haitian presidency, thousands of Haitians have attempted to immigrate to the United States.

COUNTRY PROFILES

The Caribbean

Anguilla

Status: Dependent territory of the United Kingdom

Area: 60 sq. mi. (slightly smaller than Washington, D.C.)

Population: (1992 estimate) 6,963

Languages spoken: English

Beginning in 1816 the islands of Anguilla, the British Virgin Islands, Saint Christopher (Saint Kitts), and Nevis were governed by the British as a single colony. When Saint Christopher was granted statehood in 1967, Anguilla declared its own independence; however, it has remained a dependent territory of the United Kingdom.

Antigua and Barbuda

Independence: November 1, 1981

Area: 108 sq. mi. (slightly larger than one and one-half times the size of Washington, D.C.)

Capital: St. John's (on Antigua)

Population: (1991 estimate) 64,400

Official language: English

Christopher Columbus first visited the islands of Antigua and Barbuda in 1493. Missionaries attempted to settle the area but were hindered by the native Carib Indians and by the absence of natural freshwater

---

The Caribbean
Anguilla • Antigua and Barbuda • Aruba • Bahama Islands ·Barbados • Bermuda • British Virgin Islands • Cayman Islands • Cuba • Dominica • Dominican Republic • Grenada • Guadeloupe • Haiti • Jamaica • Martinique • Montserrat • Netherlands Antilles • Puerto Rico • Saint Kitts and Nevis • Saint Lucia • Saint Vincent and the Grenadines • Trinidad and Tobago • Turks and Caicos Islands • Virgin Islands of the United States

Central America
Belize • Costa Rica • Nicaragua • Panama

South America
Brazil • Colombia • French Guiana • Guyana • Suriname • Venezuela

North America
Canada • Mexico

---

springs. In 1632 the British finally succeeded in establishing a colony.

Sir Christopher Codrington organized the first large sugar estate in Antigua in 1674, bringing slaves from Africa's west coast to work the plantations. Although Antiguan slaves were freed in 1834, they remained bound to their plantation owners. Opportunities for the new freemen were limited because they had no access to credit, the only jobs available were agriculture-related, and there was no extra land to purchase.

NEIGHBORS

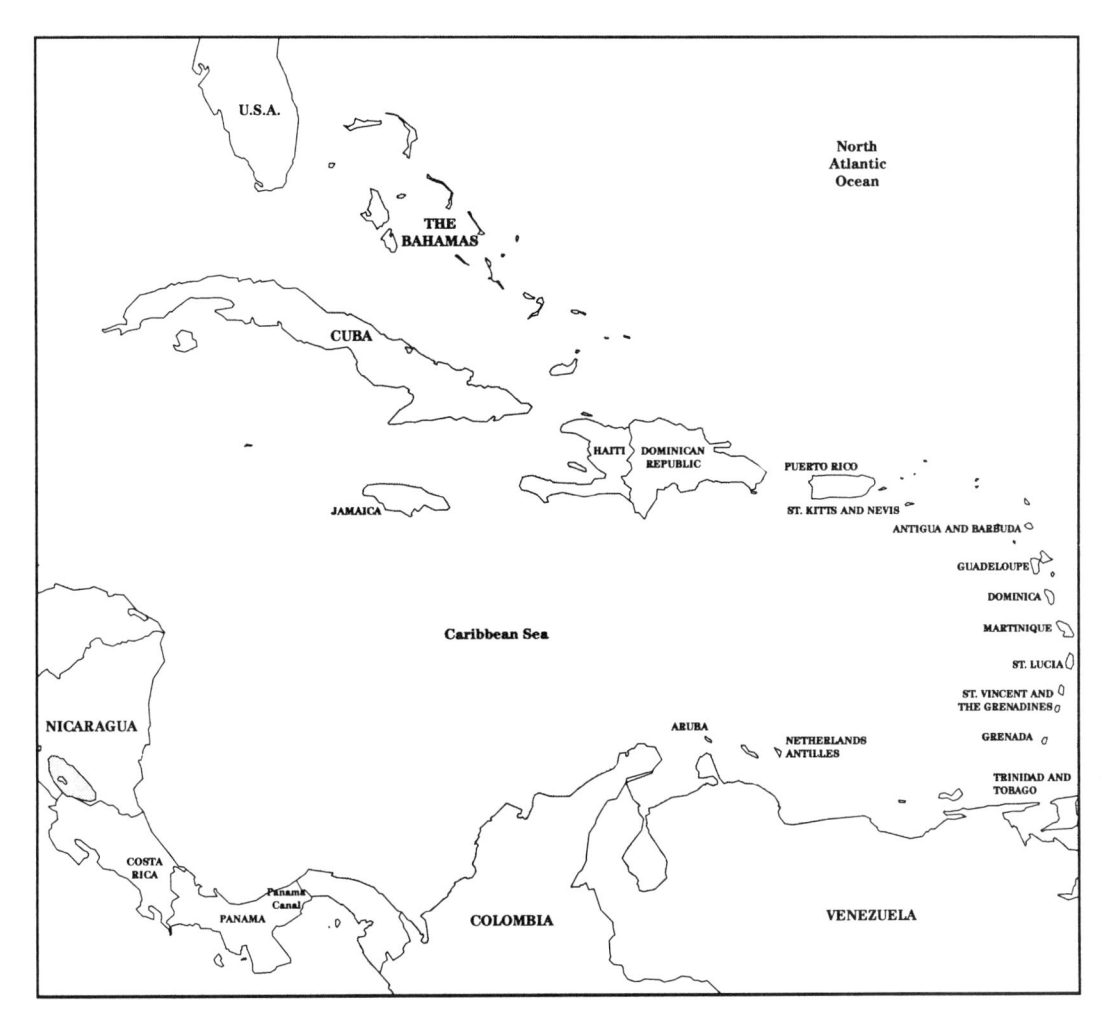

The Caribbean

Aruba

Status: Autonomous part of the Kingdom of the Netherlands
Area: 74 sq. mi. (slightly larger than Washington, D.C.)
Chief town: Oranjestad
Population: 60,000
Languages spoken: Papiamento, English, Dutch, Spanish

The Spanish landed in Curaçao (now the largest island of the Netherlands Antilles) in 1499 and in 1527 took possession of Curaçao, Bonaire, and Aruba. In 1634 ownership of the three islands passed to the Netherlands.

On December 15, 1954, the Netherlands Antilles became an autonomous part of the kingdom. In 1983 Aruba sought autonomy from the Netherlands Antilles. On January 1, 1986, it achieved separate status equal to that of the Antilles and is scheduled to become fully independent in 1996.

Bahama Islands

    Independence: July 10, 1973

    Area: 5,380 sq. mi (a little larger than Connecticut)

    Capital: Nassau (on New Providence Island)

    Population: (1991 estimate) 251,000

    Languages spoken: English, Creole

Columbus entered the New World via the Bahamas in 1492, when he first landed either on Samana Cay or San Salvador Island. The first permanent European settlement was founded in 1647. In 1717 the islands became a British crown colony. The Bahamas became independent on July 10, 1973.

Eighty-five percent of Bahamians are of African descent. Many of their ancestors arrived in the Bahamas when it was a staging area for the slave trade, or were brought there by the thousands of British loyalists who fled the American colonies during the Revolutionary War.

Barbados

    Independence: November 30, 1966

    Area: 166 sq. mi. (two and one-half times the size of Washington, D.C.)

    Capital: Bridgetown

    Population: (1991 estimate) 254,000

    Languages spoken: English

Barbados was under British control from the arrival of the first British settlers in 1627 until independence in 1966. As the sugar industry developed into the island's main commercial enterprise, Barbados was divided into large plantation estates. Slaves were brought from Africa to work on these plantations until slavery was abolished throughout the British Empire in 1834.

From 1958 to 1962 Barbados was one of ten members of the West Indies Federation. Barbados negotiated its own independence at a constitutional conference with the United Kingdom in June 1966. The country won self-rule on November 30, 1966.

Bermuda

    Status: Parliamentary British colony with internal government since 1620

    Area: 20.6 sq. mi. (less than one-third the size of Washington, D.C.)

    Capital: Hamilton

    Population: (1987 estimate) 57,619

    Languages spoken: English

Bermuda is located in the Atlantic Ocean about 650 miles east of North Carolina. The first Europeans to visit Bermuda were Spanish explorers in 1503. In 1609 a group of British explorers became stranded on the islands. Following their rescue, their favorable reports of the area aroused great interest back home. In 1612 British colonists arrived and founded the town of Saint George, the oldest surviving English-speaking settlement in the Western Hemisphere.

Slaves from Africa were brought to Bermuda soon after the colony began. By 1807 the slave trade was outlawed in Bermuda; all slaves were freed by 1834. Although Bermuda is a British colony, it has a great degree of internal autonomy, based on a 1968 constitution.

NEIGHBORS

An open-air market in the Caribbean

British Virgin Islands

Status: Dependent territory of United Kingdom

Area: 59 sq. mi. (slightly smaller than Washington, D.C.)

Capital: Road Town (on Tortola Island)

Population: (1992 estimate) 12,555

Official language: English

First visited by Columbus in 1493, the Virgin Islands is an archipelago consisting

59

of the British Virgin Islands (six main islands and nearly forty islets) and the Virgin Islands of the United States (three main islands and sixty-five islets). Great Britain obtained title to the islands and islets in 1666 and, until 1960, administered them as part of the Leeward Islands.

Cayman Islands

Status: Dependent territory of the United Kingdom

Area: 100 sq. mi. (one and one-half times the size of Washington, D.C.)

Capital: George Town (on Grand Cayman)

Population: (1992 estimate) 29,139

Languages spoken: English

The Cayman Islands—Grand Cayman, Little Cayman, and Cayman Brac—were discovered by Columbus in 1503 but were never occupied by the Spanish. The British colonized the islands in the mid-eighteenth century from Jamaica, and since 1962 the Caymans have been administered independently of Jamaica.

Cuba

Independence: May 20, 1902

Area: 44,200 sq. mi. (somewhat larger than Tennessee)

Capital: Havana

Population: (1991 estimate) 10.7 million

Languages spoken: Spanish

Cuba is a multiracial society with a population of mainly Spanish and African origins. As Spain developed its colonial empire in the New World following Columbus's arrival, Havana became an important commercial seaport. Settlers eventually moved inland, devoting themselves mainly to sugarcane and tobacco farming. As the native Indian population died out, African slaves were imported to work on the plantations. A 1774 census counted 96,000 whites, 31,000 free blacks, and 44,000 slaves in Cuba. Slavery was abolished in 1886.

Dominica

Independence: November 3, 1978

Area: 290 sq. mi. (one-quarter the size of Rhode Island)

Capital: Roseau

Population: (1991 estimate) 86,000

Official language: English

Europeans first visited Dominica on Columbus's second voyage in 1493. Spanish ships frequently landed on Dominica during the sixteenth century but had limited success at establishing settlements. In 1635 France claimed Dominica. Later, as part of the 1763 Treaty of Paris, the island became a British possession.

In 1763 the British established a legislative assembly that represented only the white population. But by 1831 nonwhites received equal political and social rights. Three blacks were elected to the Legislative Assembly the following year, and by 1838 blacks dominated that body. Most black legislators were smallholders or merchants, who held economic and social views opposed to the interests of the wealthy English planter class. Consequently, the planters lobbied for more direct British rule and black political power began to erode. All significant political rights for the black majority were eventually taken away.

NEIGHBORS

Makeshift homes (foreground) and public housing (background) in the Dominican Republic

On November 3, 1978, the Commonwealth of Dominica was granted independence by the United Kingdom. Almost all 81,000 Dominican blacks are descendants of African slaves imported by planters in the eighteenth century.

Dominican Republic

Independence: February 27, 1844

Area: 18,704 sq. mi. (about twice the size of New Hampshire)

Capital: Santo Domingo

Population: (1991 estimate) 7.3 million

Languages spoken: Spanish

The island of Hispaniola (of which the Dominican Republic forms the eastern two-thirds and Haiti the remainder) was originally occupied by members of the Taino tribe when Columbus and his companions landed there in 1492. Brutal colonial conditions reduced the Taino population from an estimated 1,000,000 to about 500 in only fifty years. To assure adequate labor for plantations, the Spanish began bringing African slaves to the island in 1503.

In the next century, French settlers occupied the western end of the island, which Spain **ceded** to France in 1697. In 1804 this became the Republic of Haiti. The Haitians conquered the whole island in 1822 and held it until 1844, when forces led by Juan

61

NEIGHBORS

Pablo Duarte, the hero of Dominican independence, drove the Haitians out and established the Dominican Republic as an independent state. In 1861 the Dominicans voluntarily returned to the Spanish Empire; independence was restored in 1865.

Grenada

Independence: February 7, 1974

Area: 133 sq. mi. (twice the size of Washington, D.C.)

Capital: St. George's

Population: (1991 estimate) 84,000

Official language: English

Like the rest of the West Indies, Grenada was originally settled by planters who wished to cultivate sugar using slave labor. Most of Grenada's population is of African descent; there is little trace of the early Arawak and Carib Indians.

Columbus first visited Grenada in 1498, but the region remained uncolonized for more than one hundred years. British efforts to settle the island were largely unsuccessful. In 1650 a French company purchased Grenada from the British and established a small settlement. The island remained under French control until captured by the British a century later. Slavery was outlawed in 1833, the same year in which Grenada was made part of the British Windward Islands Administration. In 1958 the Administration was dissolved. Grenada became an associated state on March 3, 1967, but sought full independence, which the British government granted on February 7, 1974.

Guadeloupe

Status: Overseas department of France

Area: 660 sq. mi. (somewhat smaller than one-half the size of Rhode Island)

Capital: Basse-Terre

Population: (1988 estimate) 337,524

Languages spoken: French, Creole

Columbus sighted Guadeloupe in 1493. The area was permanently settled by the French in the seventeenth century. The first slaves were brought from Africa to work the plantations around 1650, and the first slave rebellion occurred in 1656. Guadeloupe was poorly administered in its early days and was a dependency of Martinique until 1775.

Most Guadeloupeans are of mixed Afro-European and Afro-Indian ancestry (descendants of laborers brought over from India during the nineteenth century).

Haiti

Independence: January 1, 1804

Area: 10,714 sq. mi. (about the size of Maryland)

Capital: Port-au-Prince

Population: (1991 estimate) 6.2 million

Official language: French

Columbus first visited the island of Hispaniola in 1492. In 1697 Spain ceded the western third of Hispaniola to France. During this period, slaves were brought from Africa to work the sugar cane and coffee plantations. In 1791 the slave population, led by Toussaint L'Ouverture, Jean Jacques Dessalines, and Henri Christophe, revolted and gained control of the northern part of Santo Domingo (in what is now the Dominican Republic). The French were unable to regain control, though Toussaint was captured and sent to France, where he died in

NEIGHBORS

A student at a large ceramics center in Port-au-Prince, Haiti, molds an urn by hand

Jamaica

Independence: August 6, 1962

Area: 4,244 sq.mi. (about twice the size of Delaware)

Capital: Kingston

Population: (1991 estimate) 2.4 million.

Languages spoken: English, Creole

Columbus was the first European to visit Jamaica in 1494 and the area was settled by the Spanish early in the next century. In 1655 British forces seized the island and, in 1670, gained formal possession through the Treaty of Madrid.

In 1958 Jamaica joined nine other British territories in the West Indies Federation but withdrew when, in a 1961 **referendum,** Jamaican voters rejected membership.

1803 under inhumane conditions. In 1804 the slaves established an independent nation, renaming the area Haiti.

Haiti is the world's oldest black republic and the second oldest republic in the Western Hemisphere, after the United States. In September 1991 newly elected president Jean-Bertrand Aristide was ousted in a bloody military coup led by Brigadier General Raoul Cedras. Since Aristide's ouster, thousands of Haitians have been killed by the Haitian army and its allies and thousands more have attempted to immigrate to the United States. The United States government has forcibly returned Haitian refugees, maintaining that the majority of them have been economic, and not political, refugees. Haiti is the poorest country in the Western Hemisphere.

Two Jamaican children

63

NEIGHBORS

Jamaica gained independence from the United Kingdom in 1962 but has remained a member of the Commonwealth.

Sugar and slavery were important elements in Jamaica's history and development. With the abolition of slavery in 1834, the settlers resorted to importing East Indian and Chinese farm hands as cheap labor. As a result, Jamaica is a multiracial society.

Martinique

Status: Overseas region of France

Area: 425 sq. mi. (slightly smaller than one-third the size of Rhode Island)

Capital: Fort-de-France

Population: (1988 estimate) 351,105

Languages spoken: French

Columbus sighted Martinique in 1493 or 1502. The area was permanently settled by the French in the seventeenth century. Except for three short periods of British occupation, Martinique has been a French possession since 1635. About 95 percent of the people of Martinique are of Afro-European or Afro-European-Indian descent.

Montserrat

Status: Dependent territory of the United Kingdom

Area: 33 sq. mi. (one-half the size of Washington, D.C.)

Capital: Plymouth

Population: (1992 estimate) 12,617

Languages spoken: English

When Columbus first visited the Leeward Islands (Antigua, Anguilla, Barbuda, Montserrat, Nevis, and Saint Kitts) in 1493, they were inhabited by Carib Indians. Montserrat was first colonized in 1632. The French captured some of the islands in 1666 and again in 1782, but the islands were returned to the British under the Treaty of Versailles in 1783.

Most of the population is an intermixture of European settlers and the descendants of West African slaves.

Netherlands Antilles

Status: Autonomous part of the Kingdom of the Netherlands

Area: 324 sq. mi. (slightly smaller than five times the size of Washington, D.C.)

Capital: Willemstad

Population: 187,500

Languages spoken: Papiamento, English, Dutch, Spanish

The Spanish first landed in Curaçao in 1499, and in 1527 they took possession of Curaçao, Bonaire, and Aruba. In 1634 the three islands were passed to the Netherlands, where they have remained except for two short periods of British rule during the Napoleonic Wars.

Curaçao was the center of the Caribbean slave trade until **emancipation** in 1863. The Dutch Caribbean islands, which had been administered as Dutch colonies before the war, afterward entered negotiations to award a greater measure of self-government. On December 15, 1954, the Netherlands Antilles became an autonomous part of the kingdom.

Puerto Rico

Status: Commonwealth associated with the United States

NEIGHBORS

El Morro castle, at the northwest tip of old San Juan in Puerto Rico

Area: 3,425 sq. mi. (about half the size of Hawaii)

Capital: San Juan

Population: (1992 estimate) 3,776,654

Official language: Spanish

Visited by Columbus in 1493 on his second voyage to the New World, Puerto Rico was soon conquered by the Spaniard Ponce de León, who was appointed governor of the island in 1509. The native Carib Indians, almost all of whom were used by the Spaniards as plantation laborers, were eventually wiped out and replaced by African slaves. Puerto Rico was held by the English in 1598 and the Dutch besieged San Juan in 1625. Otherwise, Spanish control remained unchallenged until the Spanish American War.

The island was captured by United States forces during this conflict and ceded to the United States under the Treaty of Paris in 1898. Puerto Ricans were granted American citizenship in 1917. In 1950 an act of Congress enabled Puerto Rico to draft its own constitution and, in three years, it became a United States Commonwealth.

Many Puerto Ricans today are of mixed black and Spanish ancestry. For the most part, the original Indian inhabitants of the island were exterminated in the sixteenth century.

Saint Kitts and Nevis

Independence: September 19, 1983

Area: Saint Kitts, 68 sq. mi.; Nevis, 36 sq. mi. (combined, about one and one-half times the size of Washington, D.C.)

Capital: Basseterre

Population: (1991 estimate) 40,293

Languages spoken: English

Columbus visited these islands in 1493, on his second voyage to the area, naming the larger Saint Christopher, after his patron saint. In 1624 Saint Christopher became the first English settlement in the West Indies, and it was from here that colonists spread to other islands in the region. In 1624 the French colonized part of the island. However, it was ceded entirely to Britain by the Treaty of Utrecht in 1713. The Federation of Saint Kitts and Nevis gained full independence on September 19, 1983.

Saint Lucia

Independence: February 22, 1979

Area: 238 sq. mi. (about three and one-half times the size of Washington, D.C.)

Capital: Castries

Population: (1991 estimate) 163,075.

Official language: English

Europeans first visited the island in either 1492 or 1502. In the seventeenth century, the Dutch, English, and French all tried to establish trading outposts on Saint Lucia but faced opposition from native Carib Indians. The French, who had claimed the island, established a successful settlement in 1651 as an offshoot of the colony in neighboring Martinique. For the next century and a half, ownership was hotly disputed between France and England.

The English, with their headquarters in Barbados, and the French, centered on Martinique, found Saint Lucia even more attractive when the sugar industry developed in 1765. By 1780 almost fifty sugarcane estates had been established on the island. Heavy labor needs of the estates led to large-scale importation of slaves from West Africa.

A 1924 constitution gave the island its first form of representative government. As an associated state of the United Kingdom from 1967 to 1979, Saint Lucia was fully responsible for internal self-government but left its external affairs and defense to Great Britain. This arrangement ended on February 22, 1979, when Saint Lucia achieved full independence.

Saint Lucia is now inhabited mainly by people of African and mixed African-European descent, with small white and East Indian minorities.

Saint Vincent and the Grenadines

Independence: October 27, 1979

Area: 133 sq. mi. (twice the size of Washington, D.C.)

Capital: Kingstown

Population: (1991 estimate) 115,339

Languages spoken: English, French patois

NEIGHBORS

Christopher Columbus discovered Trinidad in 1498

Saint Vincent and the Grenadine islands began as a British territory during the eighteenth century. The islands were granted full autonomy in 1969 and won full independence in 1979.

Trinidad and Tobago

Independence: August 31, 1962.
Area: 1,980 sq. mi. (a little smaller than Delaware)
Capital: Port-of-Spain
Population: (1988 estimate) 1,279,920
Languages spoken: English

The island of Trinidad was visited by Columbus in 1498 on his third voyage to the New World. The Spanish made the first successful attempt to colonize Trinidad in 1592. Trinidad continued under Spanish rule until it was captured by the British in 1797.

Africans were brought to the islands during the eighteenth century to provide labor on the sugarcane plantations. Following the abolition of slavery, Indian and Chinese labor was brought in.

Trinidad was ceded formally to the United Kingdom in 1802; the island of Tobago was ceded to the United Kingdom in 1814. In 1888 Trinidad and Tobago merged to form a single colony. In 1958 the United Kingdom established the autonomous Federation of the West Indies. Jamaica withdrew in 1961 and, when Trinidad and Tobago followed, the federation collapsed. Trinidad and Tobago obtained full independence and joined the Commonwealth in 1962.

Turks and Caicos Islands

Status: Dependent territory of the United Kingdom

Area: 166 sq. mi. (two and one-half times the size of Washington, D.C.)

Capital: Grand Turk

Population: (1992 estimate) 12,697

Official language: English

Between 1874 and 1959, the Turks and Caicos Islands were administered as a dependency of Jamaica. In 1962 the islands became a separate colony.

Virgin Islands of the United States

Status: Territory of the United States

Area: 132 sq. mi. (slightly under twice the size of Washington, D.C.)

Capital: Charlotte Amalie

Population: (1992 estimate) 98,942

Official language: English

The Virgin Islands of the United States—the largest of which are the islands of Saint Croix, Saint John, and Saint Thomas—were originally settled by the Danish West India Company. Saint Thomas was the first to be colonized in 1672; in 1683 Saint John was colonized and by 1733 Saint Croix had been acquired from France. Some twenty years later, the holdings of this company were taken over by the Danish crown and the islands became known as the Danish West Indies.

The United States bought the territory from Denmark in 1917 for some $25 million and granted citizenship to the islanders ten years later. The first black governor, William H. Hastie, was appointed in 1946.

Under the terms of the constitution, the United States has the power to pass laws governing the territory. In 1972 the Virgin Islands were granted the right to send one nonvoting delegate to the House of Representatives. Island residents enjoy the same rights as mainlanders with the exception that they may not vote in a presidential election.

Central America

Belize

Independence: September 21, 1981

Area: 8,866 sq. mi. (a little larger than Massachusetts)

Capital: Belmopan

Population: (1991 estimate) 228,000

Official language: English

The Mayan civilization spread into the area of Belize between 1500 B.C. and 300 A.D. and flourished until about 1000 A.D. European contact began in 1502 when Columbus sailed along the coast. The first recorded European settlement was founded in 1638.

Over the next 150 years, more English settlements were established. Belize was named the Colony of British Honduras in 1840; it became a crown colony in 1862. Self-government was granted in January 1964. The official name of the territory was

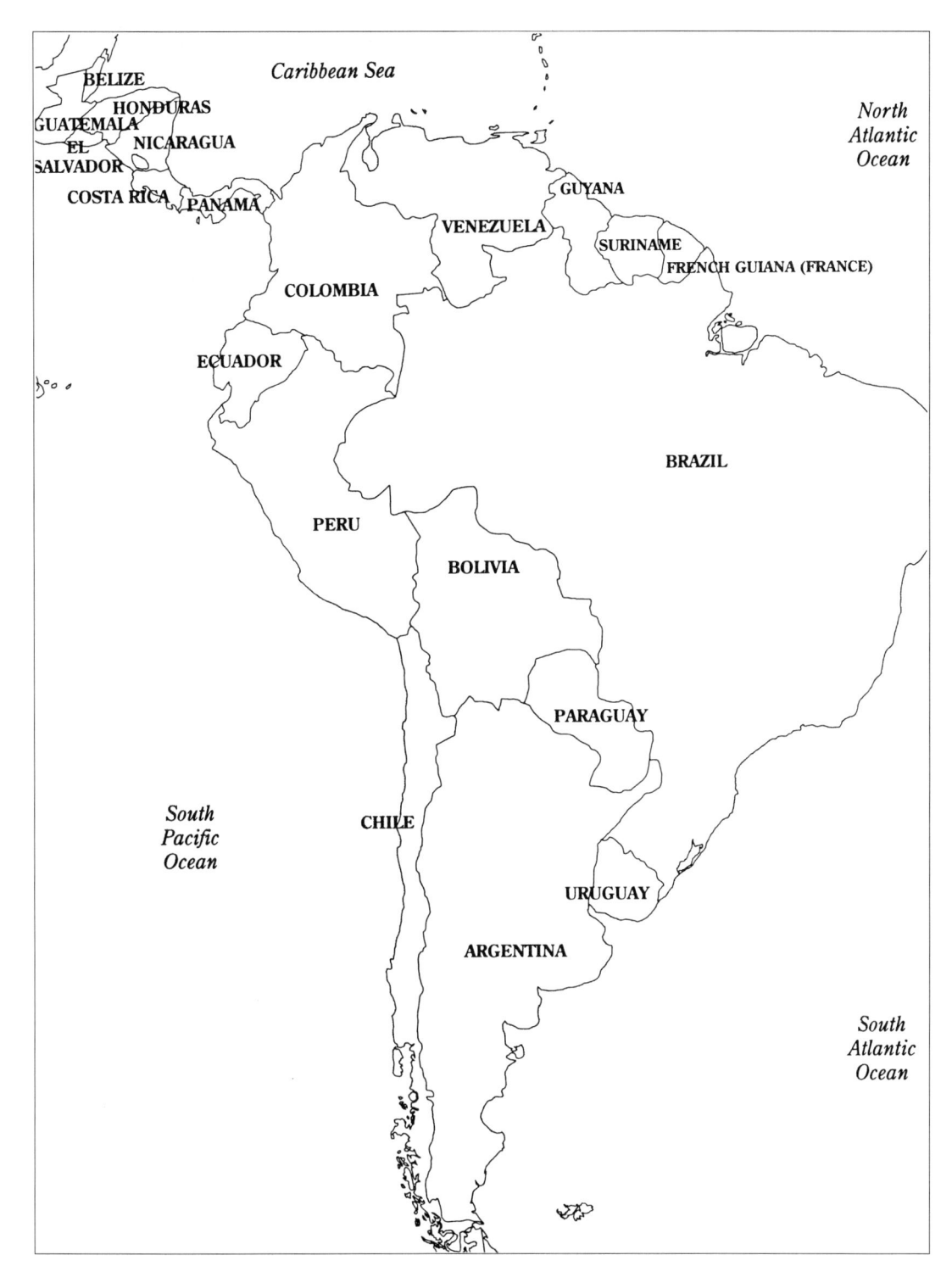

Central and South America

changed from British Honduras to Belize in June 1973 and full independence was granted on September 21, 1981.

Costa Rica

> **Independence:** September 15, 1821
>
> **Area 19,575 sq. mi. (about the size of Vermont and Maryland combined)**
>
> **Capital:** San José
>
> **Population:** (1991 estimate) 3.1 million
>
> **Languages spoken:** Spanish, Jamaican dialect

In 1502, on his fourth and last voyage to the New World, Columbus became the first European to set foot in the area. Settlement of Costa Rica began in 1522. In 1821 Costa Rica joined other Central American provinces in a joint declaration of independence from Spain. Unlike most of their Central American neighbors, Costa Ricans are largely of European rather than mestizo descent, and Spain is the primary country of origin. The native population today numbers no more than 25,000. Blacks, descendants of nineteenth-century Jamaican immigrant workers, constitute a significant English-speaking minority of about 30,000, concentrated around the Caribbean port city of Limon.

Nicaragua

> **Independence:** 1821
>
> **Area:** 54,342 sq. mi. (a little larger than Arkansas)
>
> **Capital:** Managua
>
> **Population:** 3.3 million
>
> **Languages spoken:** Spanish

Columbus sailed along the Nicaraguan coast on his last voyage in 1502. Wars with the Spanish in the Pacific and Indians and British on the Caribbean marked the colonial period. Guatemala declared its independence from Spain in 1821, but Nicaragua did not become an independent republic until 1838. British presence in the Caribbean continued until 1905.

Most Nicaraguans are a mix of European and Indian. Only the Indians of the Caribbean coast remain ethnically distinct and retain tribal customs and dialects. A substantial black minority of Jamaican origin is concentrated on the Caribbean coast.

Panama

> **Independence:** November 3, 1903
>
> **Area:** 29,762 sq. mi. (somewhat smaller than South Carolina)
>
> **Capital:** Panama City
>
> **Population:** (1991 estimate) 2.4 million
>
> **Official language:** Spanish

Prior to the arrival of Europeans, Panama was inhabited by native Indian groups. By 1519 the Spanish had established settlements, killing or enslaving much of the native population. Africans were brought in to replace the Indian slave population. Today, most Panamanians are of mixed Spanish, Indian, and African parentage.

South America

Brazil

> **Independence:** September 7, 1822
>
> **Area:** 3,286,540 sq. mi. (nearly the size of the United States)
>
> **Capital:** Brasília
>
> **Population:** (1991 estimate) 150.1 million
>
> **Official language:** Portuguese

Workers on a banana plantation in Central America

Brazil was claimed by the Portuguese in 1500 and was ruled from Lisbon, the Portuguese capital, as a colony until 1808. Brazil successfully declared independence on September 7, 1922. Four major groups make up the Brazilian population: native Indians, Portuguese, Africans brought to Brazil as slaves, and various European and Asian immigrant groups that have settled in Brazil since the mid-nineteenth century.

Slavery was introduced into Brazil in the 1530s. It expanded greatly after 1540 when sugar-growing became an important industry, and it grew most rapidly between 1580 and 1640, when Spain controlled the country. Estimates of the total number of slaves brought to Brazil vary from 6 to 20 million. Slavery did not end in Brazil until 1888. Though slavery in Brazil was often extremely brutal, and the death rate of blacks on sugar, coffee, and cotton plantations was very high, large numbers of Africans achieved freedom. About 25 percent of Brazil's blacks were free during the country's reign of slavery.

During the nineteenth century, free blacks

regularly intermarried; they enjoyed full legal equality both during the period of slavery and after it was abolished. Slaves who served masters in cities were often allowed to seek part-time and temporary employment elsewhere. They were able to read and write and develop employable skills. Blacks became important to the development and economy of the country and some became prominent in public life. Nilo Pecanha served as vice-president and briefly as president of Brazil in the first decade of the twentieth century. Blacks also achieved fame in Brazil's intellectual and artistic life.

Colombia

Independence: July 20, 1810

Area: 439,737 sq. mi. (about three-fourths the size of Alaska)

Capital: Bogotá

Population: (1991 estimate) 33.7 million

Languages spoken: Spanish

The diversity of ethnic origins in Columbia can be traced to the interrelationships among native Indians, Spanish colonists, and African slaves. In 1549 the area was established as a Spanish colony with the capital at Bogotá. In 1717 Bogota became the capital of the viceroyalty of New Granada, which included what is now Venezuela, Ecuador, and Panama. On July 20, 1810, the citizens of Bogota created the first representative council to defy Spanish authority. Total independence was proclaimed in 1813, and in 1819 the Republic of Greater Colombia was formed.

French Guiana

Status: Overseas department of France

Area: 43,740 sq. mi. (somewhat larger than Tennessee)

Capital: Cayenne

Population: (1988 estimate) 90,240

Languages spoken: French

The first French settlement in French Guiana was established in 1604. The first permanent settlement began in 1634, and, in 1664, the town of Cayenne was established. Following the abolition of slavery in 1848, the fragile plantation economy quickly declined.

Since 1946 French Guiana has functioned as an overseas department of France. About two-thirds of the population of French Guiana are Afro-European Creoles or Guianese.

Guyana

Independence: May 26, 1966

Area: 83,000 sq. mi. (a little smaller than Minnesota)

Capital: Georgetown

Population: (1991 estimate) 748,000

Languages spoken: English, Guyanese Creole, Amerindian dialects

In 1498 Columbus sighted an area of northeastern South America, which he named Guiana. The area consisted of modern Guyana, Suriname, French Guiana, and parts of Brazil and Venezuela. The Dutch settled in Guyana in the late sixteenth century, but Dutch control was replaced by British in 1796. In 1815 the colonies of Essequibo, Demerara, and Berbice were officially ceded to the British by the Congress of Vienna and in 1831 were consolidated as British Guiana.

Slave revolts, such as the one in 1763 led by Guyanan hero Cuffy, stressed the desire to obtain basic rights and were underscored by a willingness to compromise. Following the abolition of slavery in 1834, indentured workers were brought primarily from India but also from Portugal and China. A scheme in 1862 to bring black workers from the United States was unsuccessful.

Independence was achieved in 1966, and Guyana became a republic on February 23, 1970, the anniversary of the Cuffy slave rebellion.

Suriname

Independence: November 25, 1975

Area: 63,037 sq. mi. (about twice the size of South Carolina)

Capital: Paramaribo

Population: (1991 estimate) 402,000

Official language: Dutch

Columbus first sighted the Suriname coast in 1498. Although the Spanish claimed the area in 1593, the Dutch took over the colony in 1667, naming it Dutch Guiana. Because of frequent uprisings by the slave population, Dutch Guiana did not thrive. Many of the slaves fled to the interior, where they resumed a West African culture and established the five major Bush Negro tribes in existence today: the Djuka, Saramaccaner, Matuwari, Paramaccaner, and Quinti.

Beginning in 1951 Suriname began to acquire an increasing measure of autonomy from the Netherlands. On December 15, 1954, Suriname became an autonomous part of the Kingdom of the Netherlands and gained independence on November 25, 1975.

Venezuela

Independence: July 5, 1821

Area: 352,143 sq. mi. (about the size of Texas and Utah combined)

Capital: Caracas

Population: (1991 estimate) 20.1 million.

Official language: Spanish

About 900,000 of Venezuela's 17,000,000 people are black and another 500,000 are Zambos. In the sixteenth and seventeenth centuries, Caracas was a major center for the import of slaves. In the early nineteenth century, blacks and mulattoes comprised more than one-half the population of the Captaincy General of Caracas, as Venezuela was known then. Blacks remain a significant part of the country; Caracas is close to the Caribbean and this oil-rich nation has been a source of employment opportunities.

North America

Canada

Independence: July 1, 1867

Area: 3,849,672 sq. mi. (slightly larger than the United States)

Capital: Ottawa

Population: 25.3 million

Official languages: English, French

Fewer than 25,000 blacks live in Canada, a sprawling nation with a population of more than 25,000,000. However, blacks played important roles in the early exploration and development of Canada. The first black slave of Canada is believed to have been a native of Madagascar and to have been sold to a French resident of Quebec in

1628. As French Canada expanded, slaves were purchased in the United States.

In 1749 the British brought slaves to Halifax, Nova Scotia, and slavery was legalized in British Canada in 1762. Slavery increased shortly thereafter, when the British took all of Canada in the French and Indian War. Many British fleeing from the revolutionary colonies to the south after 1775 brought slaves with them.

British slave codes were more severe than the French, under which slaves could marry, own property, and maintain parental rights. Slavery was formally abolished in Canada in 1833. However, as early as 1826 Canada defied the United States and formally refused to return **fugitive** slaves. In 1829 the legislature of Lower Canada announced that every slave that entered the Province would be freed immediately. This declaration gave rise to the Underground Railroad and inspired black Americans to resettle in Canada.

By 1861, at the outbreak of the Civil War in the United States, there were 50,000 blacks in Canada. However, after the Civil War, fear among white Canadians led to employment and educational discrimination against blacks. Many black Americans returned to the United States in the hope that a bright future awaited them. By 1871 the black population of Canada dipped to about 20,000.

Mexico

Independence: September 16, 1821

Area: 761,604 sq. mi. (about three times the size of Texas)

Capital: Mexico City

Population: (1991 estimate) 66.8 million

Official language: Spanish

Blacks accompanied Spanish conquerors of Mexico in the sixteenth century and later were brought in large numbers as slaves. It is estimated that there were 150,000 black slaves in Mexico in the sixteenth century. One of the earlier slaves, Estevanico, is credited with opening up the northern interior lands of what is now New Mexico and Arizona to Spanish conquest.

The use of slavery dropped sharply in the eighteenth and early nineteenth centuries. In 1829 Mexico abolished slavery in all its states except Texas (which did not join the union until 1845), allowing it to remain there to **pacify** the United States. As slavery in the United States moved westward into Texas, Mexico became a haven for escaped slaves.

Since the sixteenth century, most of Mexico's blacks have intermarried with Indians and whites so that their African heritage is no longer clearly identifiable.

4

Words

Letters, Laws, Speeches, Songs, and Other Chronicles of African American History, 1661-1993

"I find, in being black, a thing of beauty: a joy; a strength; a secret cup of gladness."—Ossie Davis, from Purlie Victorious

History lives especially through words. In this chapter, words are the focus. No matter what form they take (a letter to a schoolgirl from W. E. B. Du Bois, a famous court ruling, a little-known news story, a classic speech by Martin Luther King, Jr., or a poem by Maya Angelou), words convey a sense of time, a sense of place, and a sense of action.

Fortunately for the student of African American history, there is a rich assortment of "word chronicles." Included below are just some of the thousands of common and not-so-common pieces of living history. These pieces can be viewed as parts of a vast jigsaw puzzle. Individually, they provide a meaningful glimpse of life at a given moment; together, they offer a complex and amazing picture of the passage of time and the gradual advancement of an entire race, from slavery to freedom and beyond.

New Netherlands Petition (1661)

Below is one of the earliest African American documents. Addressed to the leaders of New Netherlands (a Dutch colony that later became New York), this 1661 petition asked that Anthony van Angola, an orphan who had grown to young adulthood, be declared a free person. The leaders of New Netherlands agreed to this request.

To the Noble Right Honorable Director-General and Lords Councillors of New Netherlands

Herewith very respectfully declare Emanuel Pieterson, a free Negro, and Reytory, otherwise Dorothy, Angola, free Negro woman, together husband and wife, the very humble petitioners of your noble honors, that she, Reytory, in the year 1643, on the third of August, stood as godparent or witness at the Christian baptism of a little son of one Anthony van Angola, begotten with his own wife named Louise, the which aforementioned Anthony and Louise were both free

Negroes; and about four weeks thereafter the aforementioned Louise came to depart this world, leaving behind the aforementioned little son named Anthony, the which child your petitioner out of Christian affection took to herself, and with the fruits of her hands' bitter toil she reared him as her own child, and up to the present supported him, taking all motherly solicitude and care for him, without aid of anyone in the world, not even his father (who likewise died about five years thereafter), to solicit his nourishment; and also your petitioner [i.e., Emanuel] since he was married to Reytory, has done his duty and his very best for the rearing ... to assist ... your petitioners ... very respectfully address themselves to you, noble and right honorable lords, humbly begging that your noble honors consent to grant a stamp in this margin of this [document], or otherwise a document containing the consent and approval of the above-mentioned adoption and nurturing, on the part of your petitioner, in behalf of the aforementioned Anthony with the intent [of declaring] that he himself, being of free parents, reared and brought up without burden or expense of the [West Indian] Company, or of anyone else than your petitioner, in accordance therewith he may be declared by your noble honors to be a free person: this being done, [the document] was signed with the mark of Anthony Pieterson.

The Omitted Antislavery Clause to the Declaration of Independence (1776)

Thomas Jefferson's attitudes regarding African slaves changed during the course of his life. In his early years, Jefferson thought Africans were inferior—that they represented a lower form of humanity—and that enslaving them was therefore not really wrong. Later, he decided that slavery had a harmful, lasting affect upon Africans and should be stopped.

When Jefferson was given the job of writing the Declaration of Independence, he included a short, fiery attack on King George III's approval of slave trafficking. However, delegates from South Carolina and Georgia and northern delegates whose ports sheltered and profited from slave ships succeeded in removing Jefferson's clause from the final version.

[King George III] has waged cruel war against human nature itself, violating its most sacred rights of life and liberty in the person of a distant people who never offended him, captivating and carrying them into slavery in another hemisphere, or to incur miserable death in their transportation thither....

Benjamin Banneker, in a Letter to Thomas Jefferson (1791)

Benjamin Banneker (1731-1806) was a free black man of many talents and accomplishments. As an inventor, he built the first clock made in America. As a mathematician and astronomer, he predicted the solar eclipse of 1789. He also began publishing a regular almanac a few years later; this was the first scientific book by an African American. As a surveyor and mapmaker, he completed his most important work. Using his skills in this area, he served as part of a team that designed the original city of Washington, D.C.

In the letter below, Banneker begins by saying that he is proud of his African her-

Benjamin Banneker

WORDS TO KNOW

apprehension: an understanding of an issue; fear that something bad will occur; capture or arrest

compromise: something blending qualities of two different things

compulsory: necessary or required

dissenting: in legal matters, a *dissenting* opinion is one that differs from the majority, or ruling, opinion; dissenting opinions are offered by justices who think their fellow members on the bench have made an error in their ruling

emancipation: the act of freeing

enact: to pass into law

execution: the act of legally putting to death; carrying out of a task

genocide: the destruction or killing of an entire race

inauguration: the formal ceremony by which a person is placed in office

indemnity: protection

intimidation: to scare or make timid by means of threats or violence

jurisdiction: legal territory

liable: responsible by law

lynching: murder without trial, frequently by hanging

manumitted: to be freed from slavery

mulatto: a person who has one black and one white parent; any person of black-white ancestry

itage and thankful for his many blessings. He then points out that many of his fellow African Americans, his brethren, have not been so favored as he has. They have lived as slaves and he has lived as a free man.

In the second and third paragraphs, Banneker recalls the reasons for the Revolutionary War and the drafting of the Declaration of Independence.

In the last two paragraphs, the scientist and inventor points out how slavery goes against the principles behind America's fight for independence. He then closes with a hopeful view of what will happen when prejudice disappears.

Sir, I freely and cheerfully acknowledge, that I am of the African race, and in that color which is natural to them of the deepest dye; and it is under a sense of the most profound gratitude to the Supreme Ruler of the Universe, that I now confess to you, that I am not under that state of tyrannical thraldom, and inhuman captivity, to which too many of my brethren are doomed, but that I have abundantly tasted of the fruition of those blessings, which proceed from that free and unequalled liberty with which you are favored; and which, I hope, you will willing allow you have mercifully received, from the immediate hand of that Being, from whom proceedeth every good and perfect Gift.

Sir, suffer me to recall to your mind that time, in which the arms and tyranny of the British crown were exerted, with every powerful effort, in order to reduce you to a state of **servitude:** look back, I entreat you, on the variety of dangers to which you were exposed; reflect on that time, in which every human aid appeared unavailable, and in which even hope and fortitude wore the aspect of inability to the conflict, and you cannot but be led to a serious and grateful sense of your miraculous and providential preservation; you cannot but acknowledge, that the present freedom and tranquility which you enjoy you have mercifully received, and that it is the peculiar blessing of heaven.

This, Sir, was a time when you clearly saw into the injustice of a state of slavery, and in which you had just **apprehensions** of the horror of its condition. It was now that your abhorrence thereof was so excited, that you publicly held forth this true and invaluable doctrine [The Declaration of Independence], which is worthy to be recorded and remembered in all succeeding ages: "We hold these truths to be self-evident, that all men are created equal; that they are endowed by their Creator with certain unalienable rights, and that among these are, life, liberty, and the pursuit of happiness."

Here was a time, in which your tender feelings for yourselves had engaged you thus to declare, you were then impressed with proper ideas of the great violation of liberty, and the free possession of those blessings, to which you were entitled by nature; but, Sir, how pitiable is it to reflect, that although you were so fully convinced of the benevolence of the Father of Mankind, and of his equal and impartial distribution of these rights and privileges, which he hath conferred upon them, that you should at the same time counteract his mercies, in detaining by fraud and violence so numerous a part of my brethren, under groaning captivity, and cruel oppression, that you should at the same time be found guilty of that most criminal act, which you professedly detested in others, with respect to yourselves.

I suppose that your knowledge of the situation of my brethren, is too extensive to need a recital here; neither shall I presume to prescribe methods by which they may be relieved, otherwise than by recommending to you and all others, to wean yourselves from those narrow prejudices which you have imbibed with respect to them, and as Job proposed to his friends, "put your soul in their souls' stead"; thus shall your hearts be enlarged with kindness and benevolence towards them; and thus shall you need neither the direction of myself or others, in what manner to proceed herein....

A Letter between Two Anonymous Slave Rebels from Virginia (1793)

Below is a rare letter—rare because few slaves of the time could read or write, and rarer still because this is a secret letter written between slave rebels. There is no record of the rebels' later actions.

Dear Friend—The great secret that has been so long in being with our own color has come nearly to a head tho some in our Town has told of it but in such a slight manner it is not believed, we have got about five hundred Guns aplenty of lead but not much powder, I hope you have made a good collection of powder and ball and will hold yourself in readiness to strike whenever called for and never be out of the way it will not be long before it will take place, and I am fully satisfied we shall be in full possession of the whole country in a few weeks, since I wrote you last I got a letter from our friend in Charleston he tells me he has listed near six thousand men, there is a gentleman that says he will give us as much powder as we want, and when we begin he will help us all he can, the damn'd brutes patroles is going all night in Richmond but will soon [kill] them all, there an't many, we will appoint a night to begin with fire clubs and shot, we will kill all before us, it will begin in every town in one nite Keep ready to receive orders, when I hear from Charleston again I shall no and will rite to you, he that give you this is a good friend and don't let any body see it, rite me by the same hand he will give it to me out his hand he will be up next week don't be feared have a good heart fight brave and we will get free.... [Signed] Secret Keeper Richmond to secret keeper Norfolk.

> **WORDS TO KNOW**
>
> **petition:** a formal, signed request
>
> **plaintiffs:** those filing a lawsuit (*defendants* are those being accused or sued by the plaintiffs)
>
> **plebiscite:** an expression of the people's will, by ballot, on a political issue
>
> **proclamation:** an official announcement
>
> **propaganda:** ideas and information used to further or to hinder a movement or cause
>
> **prohibit:** to forbid or make illegal
>
> **provision:** something set aside for the future; a section in a legal document that outlines a special condition or requirement
>
> **ratified:** approved or passed
>
> **servitude:** slavery
>
> **suppression:** keeping from happening or being known

George Washington's Last Will and Testament (1799)

By the eighteenth century, slavery was a fact of life in America, particularly in the South. Yet Washington, at the writing of his will in 1799, decided to free all slaves whom he held in his "own right."

In the Name of God Amen

I, George Washington of Mount Vernon—a citizen of the United States,—and lately President of the same, do make, ordain and declare this Instrument; which is written with my own hand and every page thereof subscribed with my name, to be my last Will & Testament, revoking all other.... Upon the deceased of my wife, it is my Will & desire that all the Slaves which I hold in my *own right,* shall receive their freedom.... And whereas among those who will receive freedom according to this devise, there may be some, who from old age or bodily infirmities, and others who on account of their infancy, that will be unable to support themselves; it is my Will and desire that all who come under the first & second description shall be comfortably clothed & fed by my heirs while they live;—and that such of the latter description as have no parents living, or if living are unable, or unwilling to provide for them, shall be bound by the Court until they shall arrive at the age of twenty-five year;—and in cases where no record can be produced, whereby their ages can be ascertained, the judgment of the Court upon its own view of the subject, shall be adequate and final.—The Negros thus bound, are (by their Masters of Mistresses) to be taught to read & write; and to be brought up to some useful occupation, agreeably to the Laws of the Commonwealth of Virginia, providing for the support of Orphan and other poor Children.—And I do hereby expressly forbid the Sale, or transportation out of the said Commonwealth of any Slave I may die possessed of, under any pretence whatsoever.—And I do moreover most pointedly, and most solemnly enjoin it upon my Executors hereafter named, or the Survivors of them, to see that this clause respecting Slaves, and every part thereof be religiously fulfilled at the Epoch at which it is directed to take place; without evasion, neglect or delay, after the Crops which may then be on the ground are harvested, particularly as it respects the aged and infirm;—Seeing that a regular and permanent fund be established for their Support so long as there are subjects requiring it; not trusting to the uncertain **provision** to be made by individuals.—And to my **Mulatto** man William (calling himself William Lee) I give immediate freedom; or if he should prefer it (on account of the accidents which have befallen him, and which have rendered him incapable of walking or of any active employment) to remain in the situation he now is, it shall be optional in him to do so: In either case however, I allow him an annuity of thirty dollars during his natural life, which shall be independent of the victuals and cloaths he has been accustomed to receive, if he chooses last alternative; but in full, with his freedom, if he prefers the first;—& this I give him as a testimony of my sense of his attachment to me, and for his faithful services during the Revolutionary War.

The Earliest African American Petition to Congress (1797)

Below is a letter from four black men from North Carolina who moved to Philadelphia, Pennsylvania. They moved only after they were set free by their owners. Yet, because a North Carolina law forbade owners to free slaves, these men were forced to return to slavery. Their letter, asking for mercy and justice, was not accepted.

I, Jupiter Nicholson, of Perquimans county, N.C., after being set free by my master, Thomas Nicholson, and having been about two years employed as a seaman in the service of Zachary Nickson, on coming on shore, was pursued by men with dogs and arms; but was favored to escape by night to Virginia, with my wife, who was **manumitted** by Gabriel Cosand, where I resided about four years in the town of Portsmouth, chiefly employed in sawing boards and scantling; from thence I removed with my wife to Philadelphia, where I have been employed, at times, by water, working along shore, or sawing wood. I left behind me a father and mother, who were manumitted by Thomas Nicholson and Zachary Dickson; they have since been taken up, with a beloved brother, and sold into cruel bondage.

I, Jacob Nicholson, also of North Carolina, being set free by my master, Joseph Nicholson, but continuing to live with him till, being pursued night and day, I was obliged to leave my abode, sleep in the woods, and stacks in the fields, &c, to escape the hands of violent men who, induced by the profit afforded them by law, followed this course as a business; at length, by night, I made my escape, leaving a mother, one child, and two brothers, to see whom I dare not return.

I, Joe Albert, manumitted by Benjamin Albertson, who was my careful guardian to protect me from being afterwards taken and sold, providing me with a house to accommodate me and my wife, who was liberated by William Robertson; but we were night and day hunted by men armed with guns, swords, and pistols, accompanied with mastiff dogs....

I, Thomas Pritchet, was set free by my master Thomas Pritchet, who furnished me with land to raise provisions for my use, where I built myself a house, cleared a sufficient spot of woodland to produce ten bushels of corn; the second year about fifteen, and the third, had as much planted as I suppose would have produced thirty bushels; this I was obliged to leave about one month before it was fit for gathering, being threatened by Holland Lockwood, who married my said master's widow, that if I would not come and serve him, he would apprehend me, and send me to the West Indies....

We beseech your impartial attention to our hard condition, not only with respect to our personal sufferings, as freemen, but as a class of that people who, distinguished by color, are therefore with a degrading partiality, considered by many, even of those in eminent stations, as unentitled to that public justice and protection which is the great object of Government....

Submitting our cause to God, and humbly craving your best aid and influence, as you may be favored and directed by that wisdom which is from above, wherewith that you may be eminently dignified and rendered conspicuously, in the view of nations, a blessing to the people you represent, is the sincere prayer of your petitioners.

Act to Prohibit the Importance of Slaves (1807)

Signed by President Thomas Jefferson, this act was supposed to end the slave trade, though not slavery itself. However, the act was not very well enforced. Proof of this can be found in the fact that, between 1808 and 1860, some 250,000 slaves were illegally imported or brought into the United States.

An Act to **prohibit** the importation of Slaves into any port or place within the **jurisdiction** of the United States, from and after the first day of January, in the year of our Lord one thousand eight hundred and eight.

*Be it **enacted**,* that from and after the first day of January, one thousand eight hundred and eight, it shall not be lawful to import or bring into the United States or the territories thereof from any foreign kingdom, place, or country, any negro, mulatto, or person of colour, as a slave, or to be held to service or labour.

Section 2. That no citizen of the United States, or any other person, shall, from and after the first day of January, in the year of our Lord one thousand eight hundred and eight, for himself, or themselves, or any other person whatsoever, either as master, factor, or owner, build, fit, equip, load or to otherwise prepare any ship or vessel, in any port or place within the jurisdiction of the United States, nor shall cause any ship or vessel to sail from any port or place within the same, for the purpose of procuring any negro, mulatto, or person of colour, from any foreign kingdom, place, or country, to be transported to any port or place whatsoever within the jurisdiction of the United States, to be held, sold, or disposed of as slaves, or to be held to service or labour....

A Statement by Nat Turner before His Execution (1831)

*Nat Turner (1800-1831) was the leader of the most famous slave revolt in American history. All his life, it seemed, he was moving toward this defining moment. The uprising he led in Southampton County, Virginia, was prompted by his repeated religious visions as well as by his belief that slavery was wrong. In all, about sixty whites and more than one hundred blacks died during the uprising and its aftermath. More than two months passed before Turner was captured. On November 11, 1831, the leader calmly met his death, an **execution** by hanging. Below is Turner's own account, from prison, of how he came to lead the revolt.*

Nat Turner planning his revolt

My grandmother, who was very religious, and to whom I was much attached—my master, who belonged to the church, and other religious persons who visited the house, and whom I often saw at prayers, noticing the singularity of my manners, I suppose, and my uncommon intelligence for a child, remarked I had too much sense to be raised, and, If I was, I would never be of any service to any one as a slave. To a mind like mine, restless, inquisitive, and observant of everything that was passing, it is easy to suppose that religion was the subject to which it would be directed; and, although this subject principally occupied my thoughts, there was nothing that I saw or heard of to which my attention was not directed. The manner in which I learned to read and write, not only had great influence on my own mind, as I acquired it with the most perfect ease,—so much so, that I have no recollection whatever of learning the alphabet; but, to the astonishment of the family, one day, when a book was shown me, to keep me from crying, I began spelling the names of different objects. This was a source of wonder to all in the neighborhood, particularly the blacks—and this learning was constantly improved at all opportunities.... All my time, not devoted to my master's service, was spent either in prayer, or in making experiments in casting different things in moulds made of earth, in attempting to make paper, gunpowder, and many other experiments, that, although I could not perfect, yet convinced me of its practicability if I had the means....

By this time, having arrived to man's estate, and hearing the Scriptures commented on at meetings, I was struck with that particular passage which says, "Seek ye the kingdom of heaven, and all things shall be added unto you"....

About this time I was placed under an overseer, from whom I ran away, and after remaining in the woods thirty days, I returned, to the astonishment of the Negroes on the plantation, who thought I had made my escape to some other part of the country, as my father had done before. But the reason of my return was, that the Spirit appeared to me and said I had my wishes directed to the things of this world, and not to the kingdom of heaven, and that I should return to the service of my earthly master—"For he who knoweth his Master's will, and doeth it not, shall be beaten with many stripes, and thus have I chastened you." And the Negroes found fault, and murmured against me, saying that if they had my sense they would not serve any master in the world. And about this time I had a vision—and I saw white spirits and black spirits engaged in battle, and the sun was darkened—the thunder rolled in the heavens, and blood flowed in streams—and I heard a voice saying, "Such is your luck, such you are called to see; and let it come rough or smooth, you must surely bear it"....

And on the 12th of May, 1828, I heard a loud noise in the heavens, and the Spirit instantly appeared to me and said the Serpent was loosened, and Christ had laid down the yoke he had borne for the sins of men, and that I should take it on and fight against the Serpent, for the time was fast approaching when the first should be last and the last should be first. [Here Turner's witness interrupted with this question: "Do you not find yourself mistaken now?" Turner replied: "Was not Christ crucified?"] And by signs in the heavens that it would make known to me when I should commence the great work, and until the first sign appeared I should conceal it from the knowledge of men; and on the appearance of the sign (the eclipse of the sun, last February), I should arise and prepare myself, and slay my enemies with their own weapons....

Since the commence of 1830 I had been living with Mr. Joseph Travis, who was to me a kind master, and placed the greatest confidence in me; in fact, I had no cause to complain of his treatment to me. On Saturday evening, the 20th of August, it was agreed between Henry, Hark, and myself, to prepare a dinner the next day for the men we expected, and then to concert a plan, as we had not yet determined on any....

It was quickly agreed we should commence at home (Mr. J. Travis') on that night; and until we had armed and equipped ourselves, and gathered sufficient force, neither age nor sex was to be spared—which was invariably adhered to....

I sometimes got in sight in time to see the work of death completed; viewed the mangled bodies as they lay, in silent satisfaction, and immediately started in quest of other victims. Having murdered Mrs. Waller and ten children, we started for Mr. Wm. Williams',—having killed him and two little boys that were there; while engaged in this, Mrs. Williams fled and got some distance from the house, but she was pursued, overtaken, and compelled to get up behind one of the company, who brought her back, and, after showing her the mangled body of her lifeless husband, she was told to get down and lay by his side, where she was shot dead.

The white men pursued and fired on us several times. Hark had his horse shot under him, and I caught another for him as it was running by me; five or six of my men were wounded, but none left on the field. Finding myself defeated here, I instantly determined to go through a private way, and cross the Nottoway River at the Cypress Bridge, three miles below Jerusalem, and attack that place in the rear, as I expected they would look for me on the other road, and I had a great desire to get there to procure arms and ammunition. After going a short distance in this private way, accompanied by about twenty men, I overtook two or three, who told me the others were dispersed in every direction.

On this, I gave up all hope for the present; and on Thursday night, after having supplied myself with provisions from Mr. Travis', I scratched a hole under a pile of fence-rails in a field, where I concealed myself for six weeks, never leaving my hiding-place but for a few minutes in the dead of the night to get water, which was very near....

During the time I was pursued, I had many hair-breadth escapes, which your time will not permit you to relate. I am here loaded with chains, and willing to suffer the fate that awaits me.

Essays by African American Students in Cincinnati (1834)

In Cincinnati, the first school for black Americans was not opened until March 1834. Near the end of that year, students were asked to write on the topic: "What do you think most about?" Below are responses from five pupils.

Written by a seven-year-old: Dear schoolmates, we are going next summer to buy a farm and to work part of the day and to study the other part if we live to see it and come home part of the day to see our mothers and sisters and cousins if we are got any and see our kind folks and to be good boys and when we get a man to get the poor slaves from bondage. And I am sorrow to hear that the boat of Tiskilwa went down with two hundred poor slaves from up the river. Oh how sorrow I am to hear that, it grieves my heart so that I could faint in one minute.

Written by a twelve-year-old: Dear school-master, I now inform you in these few lines, that what we are studying for is to try to get the yoke of slavery broke and the chains parted asunder and slave holding cease for ever. O that God would change the hearts of our fellow men.

Written by an eleven-year-old: In my youthful days dear Lord, let me remember my creator, Lord. Teach me to do his will.

Bless the cause of abolition—bless the heralds of the truth that we trust God has sent out to declare the rights of man. We trust that it may be the means of moving mountains of sin off all the families. My mother and stepfather, my sister and myself were all born in slavery. The Lord did let the oppressed go free. Roll on the happy period that all nations shall know the Lord. We thank him for his many blessings.

Written by a ten-year-old: Dear Sir.—This is to inform you that I have two cousins in slavery who are entitled to their freedom. They have done everything that the will requires and now they wont let them go. They talk of selling them down the river. If this was your case what would you do? Please give me your advice.

Written by a sixteen-year-old: Let us look back and see the state in which the Britons and Saxons and Germans lived. They had no learning and had not knowledge of letters. But now look, some of them are our first men. Look at king Alfred and see what a great man he was. He at one time did not know his a, b, c, but before his death he commanded armies and nations. He was never discouraged but always looked forward and studied the harder. I think if the colored people study like king Alfred they will soon do away the evil of slavery. I cant see how the Americans can call this a land of freedom where so much slavery is.

Act to Suppress the Slave Trade in the District of Columbia (1850)

*Part of the **Compromise** of 1850, this act outlawed the slave trade in Washington, D.C., but kept it everywhere else throughout the South. Consequently, the breeding and trading of slaves remained a big business in such states as Maryland and Virginia, which served as headquarters for some of the nation's largest traders.*

Be it enacted, ... That from and after January 1, 1851, it shall not be lawful to bring into the District of Columbia any slave whatsoever, for the purpose of being sold, or for the purpose of being placed in depot, to be subsequently transferred to any other State or place to be sold as merchandise. And if any slave shall be brought into the said District by its owner, or by the authority or consent of its owner, contrary to the **provisions** of this act, such slave shall thereupon become liberated and free.

Frederick Douglass's Independence Day Address (1852)

An escaped slave, Frederick Douglass (1817-1895) was probably the greatest voice in the abolitionist movement of the nineteenth century. In 1852 more than three million blacks were being held as slaves in the United States. Douglass was among those who saw the incompatibility of slavery with the values of a country where independence was so eagerly celebrated every Fourth of July. The following is Douglass's powerful lecture on the topic, addressed to the citizens of Rochester, New York.

Fellow Citizens

Pardon me, and allow me to ask, why am I called upon to speak here today? What have I or those I represent to do with your national independence? Are the great principles of political freedom and of natural jus-

Frederick Douglass

tice, embodied in that Declaration of Independence, extended to us? And am I, therefore, called upon to bring our humble offering to the national altar, and to confess the benefits, and express devout gratitude for the blessings resulting from your independence to us?

Would to God, both for your sakes and ours, that an affirmative answer could be truthfully returned to these questions. Then would my task be light, and my burden easy and delightful. For who is there so cold that a nation's sympathy could not warm him? Who so obdurate and dead to the claims of gratitude, that would not thankfully acknowledge such priceless benefits? Who so stolid and selfish that would not give his voice to swell the hallelujahs of a nation's jubilee, when the chains of servitude had been torn from his limbs? I am not that man....

I am not included within the pale of this glorious anniversary! Your high independence only reveals the immeasurable distance between us. The blessings in which you this day rejoice are not enjoyed in common. The rich inheritance of justice, liberty, prosperity, and independence bequeathed by your fathers is shared by you, not by me. The sunlight that brought life and healing to you has brought stripes and death to me. This Fourth of July is *yours*, not *mine*. You may rejoice, I must mourn. To drag a man in fetters into the grand illuminated temple of liberty, and call upon him to join you in joyous anthems, were inhuman mockery and sacrilegious irony. Do you mean, citizens, to mock me, by asking me to speak today?...

Fellow citizens, above your national, tumuituous joy, I hear the mournful wail of millions, whose chains, heavy and grievous yesterday, are today rendered more intolerable by the jubilant shouts that reach them. If I do forget, if I do not remember those bleeding children of sorrow this day, "may my right hand forget her cunning, and may my tongue cleave to the roof of my mouth!" To forget them, to pass lightly over their wrongs, and to chime in with the popular theme, would be treason most scandalous and shocking, and would make me a reproach before God and the world. My subject, then, fellow citizens, is "American Slavery." I shall see this day and its popular characteristics from the slave's point of view. Standing here, identified with the American bondman, making his wrongs mine, I do not hesitate to declare, with all my soul, that the character and conduct of this nation never looked blacker to me than on this Fourth of July. Whether we turn to the declarations of the past, or to the professions of the present, the conduct of the nation seems equally hideous and revolting. America is false to the past, false to the present, and solemnly binds herself to be false to the future. Standing with God and the crushed and bleeding slave on this occasion, I will, in the name of humanity, which is outraged, in the name of Liberty, which is fettered, in the name of the Constitution and the Bible, which are disregarded and trampled upon, dare to call in question and to denounce, with all the emphasis I can command, everything that serves to perpetuate slavery—the great sin and shame of America! "I will not equivocate; I will not excuse"; I will use the severest language I can command, and yet not one word shall escape me that any man, whose judgment is not blinded by prejudice, or who is not at heart a slave-holder, shall not confess to be right and just.

But I fancy I hear some of my audience say it is just in this circumstance that you and your brother Abolitionists fail to make a favorable impression on the public mind. Would your argue more and denounce less, would you persuade more and rebuke less, your cause would be much more likely to succeed. But, I submit, where all is plain there is nothing to be argued. What point in the anti-slavery creed would you have me argue? On what branch of the subject do the people of this country need light? Must I undertake to prove that the slave is a man? That point is conceded already. Nobody doubts it. The slave-holders themselves acknowledge it in the enactment of laws for their government....

For the present it is enough to affirm the equal manhood of the Negro race. Is it not astonishing that, while we are plowing, planting, and reaping, using all kinds of mechanical tools, erecting houses, constructing bridges, building ships, working in metals of brass, iron, copper, silver, and gold; that while we are reading, writing, and ciphering, acting as clerks, merchants, and secretaries, having among us lawyers, doctors, ministers, poets, authors, editors, orators, and teachers; that while we are engaged in all the enterprises common to other men—digging gold in California, capturing the whale in the Pacific, feeding sheep and cattle on the hillside, living, moving, acting, thinking, planning, living in families as husbands, wives, and children, and above all, confessing and worshipping the Christian God, and looking hopefully for life and immortality beyond the grave—we are called upon to prove that we are men?...

At a time like this, scorching irony, not convincing argument, is needed. Oh! had I the ability, and could I reach the nation's ear, I would today pour out a fiery stream of biting ridicule, blasting reproach, withering sarcasm, and stern rebuke. For it is not light that is needed, but fire; it is not the gentle shower, but thunder. We need the storm, the whirlwind, and the earthquake. The feeling of the nation must be quickened; the conscience of the nation must be startled; the hypocrisy of the nation must be exposed; and its crimes against God and man must be denounced.

What to the American slave is your Fourth of July? I answer, a day that reveals to him more than all other days of the year, the gross injustice and cruelty to which he is the constant victim. To him your celebration is a sham; your boasted liberty an unholy license; your national greatness, swelling vanity; your sounds of rejoicing are empty and heartless; your denunciation of tyrants, brass-fronted impudence; your shouts of liberty and equality, hollow mockery; your prayers and hymns, your sermons and thanksgivings, with all your religious parade and solemnity, are to him mere bombast, fraud, deception, impiety, and hypocrisy—a thin veil to cover up crimes which would disgrace a nation of savages. There is not a nation of the earth guilty of practices more shocking and bloody than are the people of these United States at this very hour.

Go where you may, search where you will, roam through all the monarchies and despotisms of the Old World, travel through South America, search out every abuse and when you have found the last, lay your facts by the side of the every-day practices of this nation, and you will say with me that, for revolting barbarity and shameless hypocrisy, America reigns without a rival.

A Description of a Slave Auction by Solomon Northrup, from His *Twelve Years a Slave* (1853)

Solomon Northrup was kidnapped and kept as a slave for twelve years. Below is his account of a slave auction held in New Orleans in 1841.

In the first place we were required to wash thoroughly, and those with beards to shave. We were then furnished with a new suit each, cheap, but clean. The men had hat, coat, shirt, pants and shoes; the women frocks of calico, and handkerchief to bind about their heads. We were now conducted into a large room in the front part of the building to which the yard was attached, in order to be properly trained, before the admission of customers. The men were arranged on one side of the room, the women at the other. The tallest was placed at the head of the row, then the next tallest, and so on in the order of their respective heights. Emily was at the foot of the line of women. Freeman [Theophilus Freeman was the owner of the slave-pen] charged us to remember our places; exhorted us to appear smart and lively,—sometimes threatening, and again, holding out various inducements. During the day he exercised us in the art of "looking smart," and of moving to our places with exact precision....

Next day many customers called to examine Freeman's "new lot." The latter gentleman was very loquacious, dwelling at much length upon our several good points and qualities. He would make us hold up our heads, walk briskly back and forth, while customers would feel of our hands and arms and bodies, turn us about, ask us what we could do, make us open our mouths and show our teeth, precisely as a jockey examines a horse which he is about to barter for or purchase. Sometimes a man or woman was taken back to the small house in the yard, stripped, and inspected more minutely. Scars upon a slave's back were considered evidence of a rebellious or unruly spirit, and hurt his sale....

[Randall] was made to jump, and run across the floor, and perform many other feats, exhibiting his activity and condition. All the time the trade was going on, Eliza was crying aloud, and wringing her hands.

Engraving showing a slave auction

She besought the man not to buy him, unless he also bought herself and Emily. She promised, in that case, to be the most faithful slave that ever lived. The man answered that he could not afford it, and then Eliza burst into a paroxysm of grief, weeping plaintively. Freeman turned round to her, savagely, with his whip in his uplifted hand, ordering her to stop her noise, or he would flog her. He would not have such work—such snivelling; and unless she ceased that minute, he would take her to the yard and give her a hundred lashes. Yes, he would take the nonsense out of her pretty quick—if he didn't, might he be d——d. Eliza shrunk before him, and tried to wipe away her tears, but it was all in vain. She wanted to be with her children, she said, the little time she had to live. All the frowns and threats of Freeman, could not wholly silence the afflicted mother. She kept on begging and beseeching them, most piteously, not to separate the three. Over and over again she told them how she loved her boy. A great many times she repeated her former promises—how very faithful and obedient she would be; how hard she would labor day and night, to the last moment of her life, if he would only buy them all together. But it was of no avail; the man could not afford it. The bargain was agreed upon, and Randall must go alone. Then Eliza ran to him; embraced him passionately; kissed him again and again; told him to remember her—all the while her tears falling in the boy's face like rain.

Freeman damned her, calling her a blubbering, bawling wench, and ordered her to go to her place, and behave herself, and be somebody. He swore he wouldn't stand such stuff but a little longer. He would soon give her something to cry about, if she was not mighty careful and *that* she might depend upon.

The planter from Baton Rouge, with his new purchase, was ready to depart.

"Don't cry, mama. I will be a good boy. Don't cry," said Randall, looking back, as they passed out of the door.

What has become of the lad, God knows. It was a mournful scene indeed. I would have cried myself if I had dared.

Emancipation Proclamation (1863)

Hoping to bring an end to the Civil War, President Abraham Lincoln issued a warning in September 1862 that slavery would be abolished in any state that continued to rebel. He followed this warning on January 1, 1863, with the **Emancipation Proclamation.** *This document freed slaves in Confederate states but it did not free slaves in Union or Union-occupied states. As a result, some 800,000 northern blacks still lacked their freedom and most southern blacks experienced little change in conditions until the war was over and the Thirteenth Amendment was ratified [see below].*

By the President of the United States of America: A Proclamation

Whereas on the 22d day of September, A.D. 1862, a proclamation was issued by the President of the United States, containing, among other things, the following, to wit:

"That on the 1st day of January, A.D. 1863, all persons held as slaves within any State or designated part of a State the people whereof shall then be in rebellion against the United States shall be then, henceforward, and forever free; and the executive government of the United States, including the military and naval authority thereof, will recognize and maintain the freedom of such persons and will do no act or acts to repress such persons, or any of them, in any efforts they may make for their actual freedom"....

And I hereby enjoin upon the people so declared to be free to abstain from all violence, unless in necessary self-defense; and I recommend to them that, in all cases when allowed, they labor faithfully for reasonable wages.

And I further declare and make known that such persons of suitable condition will be received into the armed service of the United States to garrison forts, positions, stations, and other places, and to man vessels of all sorts in said service.

And upon this act, sincerely believed to be an act of justice, warranted by the Constitution upon military necessity, I invoke the considerate judgment of mankind and the gracious favor of Almighty God.

Amendment Thirteen to the United States Constitution (1865)

Approved on December 18, 1865, the

WORDS

President Abraham Lincoln's Emancipation Proclamation

Thirteenth Amendment abolished slavery throughout the United States.

Section 1. Neither slavery nor involuntary servitude, except as a punishment for crime whereof the party shall have been duly convicted, shall exist within the United States, or any place subject to their jurisdiction.

Section 2. Congress shall have power to enforce this article by appropriate legislation.

Black Codes of Mississippi (1865)

Following emancipation many states forced unfair rules and laws upon African Americans. These restrictions served to turn back history to pre-Civil War times. Black codes imposed heavy penalties for vagrancy (wandering without money or work), insulting gestures, curfew violations, and seditious speeches (speeches intended to stir up rebellion). In November 1865, Mississippi became the first state to enact such laws.

Note below that in the first paragraph, the master and apprentice relationship in special cases perpetuated a form of servitude.

An act to regulate the relation of master and apprentice, as relates to freedmen, free Negroes, and mulattoes.

Section 1. It shall be the duty of all sheriffs, justices of the peace, and other civil officers of the several counties in this State, to report to the probate courts of their respective counties semiannually, at the January and July terms of said courts, all freedmen, free negroes, and mulattoes, under the age of eighteen, in their respective counties, beats, or districts, who are orphans, or whose parent or parents have not the means or who refuse to provide for and support said minors; and thereupon it shall be the duty of said probate court to order the clerk of said court to apprentice said minors to some competent and suitable person on such terms as the court may direct, having a particular care to the interest of said minor: Provided, that the former owner of said minors shall have the preference when, in the opinion of the court, he or she shall be a suitable person for that purpose....

An act to amend the vagrant laws of the State.

Section 1. All rogues and vagabonds, idle and dissipated persons, beggars, jugglers, or persons practicing unlawful games or plays, runaways, common drunkards, common night-walkers, pilferers, lewd, wanton, or lascivious persons, in speech or behavior, common railers and brawlers, persons who neglect their calling or employment, misspend what they earn, or do not provide for the support of themselves or their families, or dependents, and all other idle and disorderly persons, including all who neglect all lawful business, habitually misspend their time by frequenting houses of ill-fame, gaming-house, or tippling shops, shall be deemed and considered vagrants, under the provisions of this act, and upon conviction thereof shall be fined not exceeding one hundred dollars, with all accruing costs, and be imprisoned, at the discretion of the court, not exceeding ten days....

An act to confer civil rights on freedmen, and for other purposes.

Section 3. All freedmen, free negroes or mulattoes who do now and have hereberfore lived and cohabited together as husband and wife shall be taken and held in law as legally married, and the issue shall be taken and held as legitimate for all purposes; and it shall not be lawful for any freedman, free negro or mulatto to intermarry with any white person; nor for any person to intermarry with any freedman, free negro or mulatto; and any person who shall so intermarry shall be deemed guilty of felony, and on conviction thereof shall be confined in the State penitentiary for life; and those shall be deemed freedmen, free negroes and mulattoes who are of pure negro blood, and those descended from a negro to the third generation, inclusive, though one ancestor in each generation may have been a white person.

Civil Rights Act (1866)

The Civil Rights Act of 1866 was designed to protect recently freed African Americans from black codes and other unjust laws.

An Act to protect all Persons in the United States in their Civil Rights, and furnish the Means of their Vindication

Be it enacted... That all persons born in the United States and not subject to any foreign power, excluding Indians not taxed, are hereby declared to be citizens of the United States; and such citizens, of every race and color, without regard to any previous condition of slavery or involuntary servitude, except as a punishment for crime whereof the party shall have been duly convicted, shall have the same right in every State and Territory in the United States, to make and enforce contracts, to sue, be parties, and give evidence, to inherit, purchase, lease, sell, hold, and convey real and personal property, and to full and equal benefit of all laws and proceedings for the security of person and property, as is enjoyed by white citizens, and shall be subject to like punishment, pains, and penalties, and to none other, any law, statute, ordinance, regulation, or custom, to the contrary notwithstanding.

Section 10. *And be it further enacted,* That upon all questions of law arising in any cause under the provisions of this act a final appeal may be taken to the Supreme Court of the United States.

Amendment Fourteen to the United States Constitution (1868)

Ratified on July 23, 1868, the Fourteenth Amendment provided a definition of both national and state citizenship. When the Supreme Court heard the case Dred Scott v. Sandford *in 1857, it ruled that African slaves and their descendants could not become citizens of the United States. The Fourteenth Amendment reversed this.*

The amendment also reversed the traditional federal-state relationship in the area of citizen's rights. The federal government now had power over individual states. For example, the Black Codes of Mississippi could now be ruled unfair to African Americans. The battle for comprehensive civil rights, though, was far from over.

Section 1. All persons born or naturalized in the United States, and subject to the jurisdiction thereof, are citizens of the United States and of the State wherein they reside. No state shall make or enforce any law which shall abridge the privileges or immunities of citizens of the United States; nor shall any State deprive any person of life, liberty, or property, without due process of law; nor deny to any person within its jurisdiction the equal protection of the laws.

Amendment Fifteen to the United States Constitution (1870)

The Fifteenth Amendment, ratified March 30, 1870, was meant to protect the right of all citizens to vote. However, the amendment failed to completely end such unjust voting requirements as literacy tests (which less educated blacks could not pass) and poll taxes (which poor blacks could not afford).

Section 1. The right of citizens of the United States to vote shall not be denied or abridged by the United States or by any State on account of race, color, or previous conditions of servitude.

Section 2. The Congress shall have power to enforce this article by appropriate legislation.

Ku Klux Klan Act (1871)

*Following the Civil War, white terrorist groups began to spring up throughout the South. The members of these organizations were mainly Confederate veterans. They met regularly and terrorized both blacks and the whites who aided them. Known as the Knights of the White Camelia, the Jayhawkers, or the Ku Klux Klan, these groups had become quite popular by 1871. The Ku Klux Klan Act of 1871 was an attempt by Congress to end **intimidation** and violence by such organizations. However, the law failed to erase the Klan, which survives to this day.*

A Ku Klux Klan cross burning near Edinburg, Mississippi

Be it enacted, ... that any person who, under color of any law, statute, ordinance, regulation, custom, or usage of any State, shall subject, or cause to be subjected, any person within the jurisdiction of the United States to the deprivation of any rights, privileges, or immunities secured by the Constitution of the United States, shall, any such law, statute, ordinance, regulation, custom, or usage of the State to the contrary notwithstanding, be **liable** to the party injured in any action at law, suit in equity, or other proper proceeding for redress; such proceeding to be prosecuted in the several district or circuit courts of the United States, with and subject to the same rights of appeal, review upon error, and other reme-

Booker T. Washington

dies provided in like cases in such courts, under the provisions of the [Civil Rights Act of April 9, 1866] ... and the other remedial laws of the United States which are in their nature applicable in such cases.

Booker T. Washington's "Atlanta Compromise" Speech (1895)

An educator and author, Booker T. Washington (1856-1915) was a major force in the movement for the betterment of African Americans. He was criticized by many, though, for being too willing to compromise with whites. In the following address to the 1895 Atlanta Exposition, Washington outlines his guiding beliefs.

Mr. President and Gentlemen of the Board of Directors and Citizens:

One-third of the population of the South is of the Negro race. No enterprise seeking the material, civil, or moral welfare of this section can disregard this element of our population and reach the highest success. I but convey to you, Mr. President and Directors, the sentiment of the masses of my race when I say that in no way have the value and manhood of the American Negro been more fittingly and generously recognized than by the managers of this magnificent Exposition at every stage of its progress. It is a recognition that will do more to cement the friendship of the two races than any occurrence since the dawn of our freedom.

Not only this, but the opportunity here afforded will awaken among us a new era of industrial progress. Ignorant and inexperienced, it is not strange that in the first years of our new life we began at the top instead of at the bottom; that a seat in Congress or the State Legislature was more sought than real estate or industrial skill; that the political convention or stump speaking had more attractions than starting a dairy farm or truck garden.

A ship lost at sea for many days suddenly sighted a friendly vessel. From the mast of the unfortunate vessel was seen a signal: "Water, water; we die of thirst!" The answer from the friendly vessel at once came back: "Cast down your bucket where you are." A second time the signal, "Water, water; send us water!" ran up from the distressed vessel, and was answered: "Cast down your bucket where you are." And a third and fourth signal for water was answered: "Cast down your bucket where you are." The captain of the distressed vessel, at last heeding the injunction, cast down his bucket, and it came up full of fresh, sparkling water from the mouth of the Amazon River. To those of my race who depend on bettering their condition in a foreign land, or who underestimate the importance of cultivating friendly relations with the Southern white man, who is their next door neighbor, I would say: "Cast down your bucket where you are"—cast it down in making friends in every manly way of the people of all races by whom we are surrounded.

Cast it down in agriculture, mechanics, in commerce, in domestic service, and in the professions. And in this connection it is well to bear in mind that whatever other sins the South may be called to bear, when it comes to business, pure and simple, it is in the South that the Negro is given a man's chance in the commercial world, and in nothing is this Exposition more eloquent than in emphasizing this chance. Our greatest danger is, that in the great leap from slavery to freedom we may overlook the fact that the masses of us are to live by the productions of our hands, and fail to keep in mind that we shall prosper in proportion as we learn to dignify and glorify common labor, and put brains and skill into the common occupations of life; shall prosper in proportion as we learn to draw the line between the superficial and the substantial, the ornamental gewgaws of life and the useful. No race can prosper till it learns that there is as much dignity in tilling a field as in writing a poem. It is at the bottom of life we must begin, and not at the top. Nor should we permit our grievances to overshadow our opportunities....

In conclusion, may I repeat that nothing in thirty years has given us more hope and encouragement, and drawn us so near to you of the white race, as this opportunity offered by the Exposition; and here bending, as it were, over the altar that represents the results of the struggle of your race and mine, both starting practically empty-handed three decades ago, I pledge that, in your effort to work out the great and intricate problem which God has laid at the doors of the South, you shall have at all time the patient, sympathetic help of my race; only let this be constantly in mind that, while from representations in these buildings of the product of field, of forest, of mine, of factory, letters, and art, much good will come, yet far above and beyond material benefits will be that higher good, that let us pray God will come, in a blotting out of sectional differences and racial animosities and suspicions, in a determination to administer absolute justice, in a willing obedience among all classes to the mandates of law. This, coupled with our material prosperity, will bring into our beloved South a new heaven and a new earth.

Plessy v. Ferguson (1896)

On February 23, 1869, the Louisiana legislature passed a law prohibiting segregation on public transportation. In 1878 the U.S. Supreme Court overturned this law and set back the progress of civil rights. Later still, the Supreme Court case of Plessy v. Ferguson *upheld a "separate but equal" doctrine. This doctrine paved the way for segregation of blacks in all walks of life.*

The "separate but equal" doctrine paved the way for segregation of blacks in all walks of life

The Plessy case came about after Homer Adolph Plessy, a black traveling by train from New Orleans to Covington, Louisiana, was arrested when he refused to ride in the "colored" railway coach. Such types of separation continued until the Brown v. Board of Education *decision of 1954. Note especially Justice John Marshall Harlan's **dissenting** opinion, which follows the opinion of Justice Brown and the rest of the court.*

Justice Brown delivered the opinion of the Court.

2. By the Fourteenth Amendment, all persons born or naturalized in the United States, and subject to the jurisdiction thereof, are made citizens of the United States and of the state wherein they reside; and the states are forbidden from making or enforcing any law which shall abridge the privileges or immunities of citizens of the United States, or shall deprive any person of life, liberty, or property without due process of law, or deny to any person within their jurisdiction the equal protection of the laws....

The object of the amendment was undoubtedly to enforce the absolute equality of the two races before the law, but in the nature of things it could not have been intended to abolish distinctions based upon color, or to enforce social, as distinguished from political, equality, or a commingling of the two races upon terms unsatisfactory to

97

either. Laws permitting, and even requiring, their separation in places where they are liable to be brought into contact do not necessarily imply the inferiority of either race to the other, and have been generally, if not universally, recognized as within the competency of the state legislatures in the exercise of their police power. The most common instance of this is connected with the establishment of separate schools for white and colored children, which has been held to be a valid exercise of the legislative power even by courts of states where the political rights of the colored race have been longest and most earnestly enforced....

So far, then, as a conflict with the Fourteenth Amendment is concerned, the case reduces itself to the question whether the statute of Louisiana is a reasonable regulation, and with respect to this there must necessarily be a large discretion on the part of the legislature. In determining the question of reasonableness it is at liberty to act with reference to the established usages, customs, and traditions of the people, and with a view to the promotion of their comfort, and the preservation of the public peace and good order. Gauged by this standard, we cannot say that a law which authorizes or even requires the separation of the two races in public conveyances is unreasonable or more obnoxious to the Fourteenth Amendment than the acts of Congress requiring separate schools for colored children in the District of Columbia, the constitutionality of which does not seem to have been questioned, or the corresponding acts of state legislatures....

The judgment of the court below is therefore, *Affirmed*.

Justice Harlan Dissenting

In respect of civil rights, common to all citizens, the Constitution of the United States does not, I think, permit any public authority to know the race of those entitled to be protected in the enjoyment of such rights. Every true man has pride of race, and under appropriate circumstances with the rights of others, his equals before the law, are not to be affected, it is his privilege to express such pride and to take such action based upon it as to him seems proper. But I deny that any legislative body or judicial tribunal may have regard to the race of citizens when the civil rights of those citizens are involved. Indeed, such legislation, as that here in question, is inconsistent not only with that equality of rights which pertains to citizenship, national and state, but with the personal liberty enjoyed by everyone within the United States....

I am of opinion that the statute of Louisiana is inconsistent with the personal liberty of citizens, white and black, in that state, and hostile to both the spirit and letter of the Constitution of the United States. If laws of like character should be enacted in the several states of the Union, the effect would be in the highest degree mischievous. Slavery, as an institution tolerated by law, would, it is true, have disappeared from our country, but there would remain a power in the states, by sinister legislation, to interfere with the full enjoyment of the blessings of freedom; to regulate civil rights, common to all citizens, upon the basis of race, and to place in a condition of legal inferiority a large body of American citizens, now constituting a part of the political community called the People of the United States, for whom, and by whom through representatives, our government is administered. Such a system is inconsistent with the guarantee given by the Constitution to each state of a republican form of government, and may be stricken down by congressional action, or by the courts in the discharge of their solemn duty to maintain the supreme law of the land, anything in the constitution or laws of any state to the contrary notwithstanding.

For the reasons stated, I am constrained to withhold my assent from the opinion and judgment of the majority....

A Newspaper Account of the Lynching of Postmaster Baker (1898)

The following account, dated February 26, 1898, is taken from the Cleveland Gazette, *a black-owned newspaper. The reporter ends this tragic story of the murders of an innocent man and his newborn child with a note of bitter irony.*

Lake City, S.C.—George Washington's birthday was ushered in in this section on Tuesday morning a 1 o'clock with the most revolting crime ever perpetrated.... Postmaster Baker, an Afro-American of this little town, and his family at the time stated above were burned out of their home, the postmaster and a babe in arms killed, his wife and three daughters shot and maimed for life, and his son wounded.

Mr. Baker was appointed postmaster three months ago. Lake City is a town of 500 inhabitants, and the Afro-American population in the vicinity is large. There was the usual prejudiced protest at his appointment. Three months ago as the postmaster was leaving the office at night in company with several men of our class, he was fired on from ambush. Since then he moved his family into a house in which he also established the post office.

Last week Tuesday night a body of scoundrels (white) who were concealed behind buildings and fences in the neighborhood, riddled the building with shot and rifle bullets. They shot high and no one was hurt. It was simply an effort to intimidate him. A short time before Senators Tillman and McLauren and Congressman Horton had asked the postmaster general to remove Mr. Baker because of his color and the request had been refused. The refusal was wired here. Mr. Baker did not remove his family and gave no evidence of being frightened. Being a government official he felt confident of protection from Washington.

At 1 o'clock Tuesday morning a torch was applied to the post office and house. Back, just within the line of light, were over a hundred white brutes—murderers—armed with pistols and shotguns. By the time the fire aroused the sleeping family, consisting of the postmaster, his wife, four daughters, a son and an infant at the breast, the crowd began firing into the building. A hundred bullet holes were made through the thin boarding and many found lodgment in members of the family within.

The postmaster was the first to reach the door and he fell dead just within the threshold, being shot in several places. The mother had the baby in her arms and reached the door over her husband's body, when a bullet crashed through its skull, and it fell to the floor. She was shot in several places. Two of the girls had their arms broken close to the shoulders and will probably lose them. Another of the girls is fatally wounded. The boy was also shot.

Only two of the seven occupants of the house escaped with slight injuries. The bodies of Mr. Baker and the infant were cremated in the building. All mail matter was destroyed. A coroner's jury was impanelled Tuesday evening. It visited the charred remains and adjourned until today. Nothing will be done to apprehend the infernal brutes and murderers. The whelps that shot almost to death some time ago Isaac H. Loftin, the Afro-American postmaster of Hogansville, Ga., are still at liberty—walking the streets of that town, with more freedom than the man they all but murdered. No effort to arrest and punish them has ever been or ever will be made by local, state or federal authorities. The same will be true in this case. This is a great country, a great government! Not even Spain respects it.

A Speech by Ida B. Wells-Barnett, Addressed to President McKinley (1898)

*Ida B. Wells-Barnett (1864-1931) devoted her life to speaking out against **lynching** and for upholding the civil rights of African Americans. As the chosen representative of a large antilynching group that had recently met in Chicago, Barnett pleaded the case of Postmaster Baker before President William McKinley, seeking justice in the courts. McKinley pledged his support but nothing was done to punish the lynchers from Cleveland.*

Mr. President, the colored citizens of this country in general, and Chicago in particular, desire to respectfully urge that some action be taken by you as chief magistrate of this great nation, first, for the **apprehension** and punishment of the lynchers of Postmaster Baker, of Lake City, S.C.; second, we ask **indemnity** for the widow and children, both for the murder of the husband and father, and for injuries sustained by themselves; third, we most earnestly desire that national legislation be enacted for the **suppression** of the national crime of lynching.

For nearly twenty years lynching crimes, which stand side by side with Armenian and Cuban outrages, have been committed and permitted by this Christian nation. Nowhere in the civilized world save the United States of America do men, possessing all civil and political power, go out in bands of 50 to 5,000 to hunt down, shoot, hang or burn to death a single individual, unarmed and absolutely powerless. Statistics show that nearly 10,000 American citizens have been lynched in the past 20 years. To our appeals for justice the stereotyped reply has been that the government could not interfere in a state matter. Postmaster Baker's case was a federal matter, pure and simple. He died at his post of duty in defense of his country's honor, as truly as did ever a soldier on the field of battle. We refuse to believe this country, so powerful to defend its citizens abroad, is unable to protect its citizens at home. Italy and China have been indemnified by this government for the lynching of their citizens. We ask that the government do as much for its own.

"Lift Every Voice and Sing" (1901)

Originally used in a Jacksonville, Florida school program to celebrate Lincoln's birthday, "Lift Every Voice and Sing" has become known as the black "national anthem." The song's words, written by poet and civil rights leader James Weldon Johnson, serve as a tribute to African American heritage. The song's music was composed by Johnson's brother and songwriting partner, J. Rosamond Johnson.

> Lift every voice and sing
> Till earth and heaven ring,
> Ring with the harmonies of Liberty;
> Let our rejoicing rise
> High as the listening skies,
> Let it resound loud as the rolling sea.
> Sing a song full of the faith that the dark past has taught us,
> Sing a song full of the hope that the present has brought us,
> Facing the rising sun of our new day begun
> Let us march on till victory is won.
>
> Stony the road we trod,
> Bitter the chastening rod,
> Felt in the days when hope unborn had died;
> Yet with a steady beat,
> Have not our weary feet
> Come to the place for which our fathers sighed?
> We have come over a way that with tears have been watered,
> We have come, treading our path through the blood of the slaughtered,
> Out from the gloomy past,
> Till now we stand at last
> Where the white gleam of our bright star is cast.
>
> God of our weary years,
> God of our silent tears,
> Thou who has brought us thus far on the way;
> Thou who has by Thy might
> Led us into the light,
> Keep us forever in the path, we pray.
> Lest our feet stray from the places, Our God, where
> We met Thee,
> Lest, our heart's drunk with the wine of the world,
> We forget Thee;
> Shadowed beneath Thy hand,
> May we forever stand.
> True to our God,
> True to our native land.

A Letter from W. E. B. Du Bois to Vernealia Fareira, a Pennsylvania Student (1905)

W. E. B. Du Bois (1868-1963) ranks among the most important blacks of the twentieth century. The first of his race to earn a Ph.D. from Harvard University, Du Bois was also one of the founders of the National Association for the Advancement of Colored People (NAACP). A historian, educator, civil rights leader, and author, Du Bois believed that African Americans should not set limits to the goals they set for themselves. In the following letter he conveys this view to a young student from Pennsylvania.

I wonder if you will let a stranger say a word to you about yourself? I have heard that you are a young woman of some ability but that you are neglecting your school work because you have become hopeless of trying to do anything in the world. I am very sorry for this. How any human being whose wonderful fortune it is to live in the 20th century should under ordinarily fair advantages despair of life is almost unbelievable. And if in addition to this that person is, as I am, of Negro lineage with all the hopes and yearnings of hundreds of millions of human souls dependent in some degree on her striving, then her bitterness amounts to crime.

There are in the U.S. today tens of thousands of colored girls who would be happy beyond measure to have the chance of educating themselves that you are neglecting. If you train yourself as you easily can, there are wonderful chances of usefulness before you: you can join the ranks of 15,000 Negro women teachers, of hundreds of nurses and physicians, of the growing number of clerks and stenographers, and above all of the host of homemakers. Ignorance is a cure for nothing. Get the very best training possible & the doors of opportunity will fly open before you as they are flying before thousands of your fellows. On the other hand every time a colored person neglects an opportunity, it makes it more difficult for others of the race to get such an opportunity. Do you want to cut off the chances of the boys and girls of tomorrow?

Marcus Garvey's Speech at Liberty Hall, New York City (1922)

Marcus Garvey, black nationalist and founder of the Universal Negro Improvement Association, dedicated his life to uplifting Africans throughout the world. In this 1922 address, Garvey outlined the goals of the Universal Negro Improvement Association.

Marcus Garvey

Over five years ago the Universal Negro Improvement Association placed itself before the world as the movement through which the new and rising Negro would give expression of his feelings. This Association adopts an attitude not of hostility to other races and peoples of the world, but an attitude of self-respect....

The Universal Negro Improvement Association stands for the Bigger Brotherhood; the Universal Negro Improvement Association stands for human rights, not only for Negroes, but for all races. The Universal Negro Improvement Association believes in the rights of not only the black race, the white race, the yellow race and the brown race. The Universal Negro Improvement Association believes that the white man has as much right to be considered, the yellow man has as much right to be considered, the brown man has as much right to be considered as the black man of Africa. In view of the fact that the black man of Africa has contributed as much to the world as the white man of Europe, and the brown man and yellow man of Asia, we of the Universal Negro Improvement Association demand that the white, yellow and brown races give to the black man his place in the civilization of the world. We ask for nothing more than the rights of 400,000,000 Negroes. We are not seeking ... to destroy or disrupt the society of the government of other races, but we are determined that 400,000,000 of us shall unite ourselves to free our motherland from the grasp of the invader....

We are not preaching a **propaganda** of hate against anybody. We love the white man; we love all humanity.... The white man is as necessary to the existence of the Negro as the Negro is necessary to his existence. There is a common relationship that we cannot escape. Africa has certain things that Europe wants, and Europe has certain things that Africa wants, ... it is impossible for us to escape it. Africa has oil, diamonds, copper, gold and rubber and all the minerals that Europe wants, and there must be some kind of relationship between Africa and Europe for a fair exchange, so we cannot afford to hate anybody.

The question often asked is what does it require to redeem a race and free a country? If it takes man power, if it takes scientific intelligence, if it takes education of any kind, or if it takes blood, then the 400,000,000 Negroes of the world have it.

It took the combined power of the Allies to put down the mad determination of the Kaiser to impose German will upon humanity. Among those who suppressed his mad ambition were two million Negroes who have not yet forgotten how to drive men across the firing line ... when so many white men refused to answer to the call and dodged behind all kinds of excuses, 400,000 black men were ready without a question. It was because we were told it was a war of democracy; it was a war for the liberation of the weaker peoples of the world. We heard the cry of Woodrow Wilson, not because we liked him so, but because the things he said were of such a nature that they appealed to us as men. Wheresoever the cause of humanity stands in need of assistance, there you will find the Negro ever ready to serve.

He has done it from the time of Christ up to now. When the whole world turned its back upon the Christ, the man who was said to be the Son of God, when the world cried out "Crucify Him," when the world spurned Him and spat upon Him, it was a black man, Simon, the Cyrenian, who took up the cross. Why? Because the cause of humanity appealed to him. When the black man saw the suffering Jew, struggling under the heavy cross, he was willing to go to His assistance, and he bore that cross up to the heights of Calvary. In the spirit of Simon, the Cyrenian, 1900 years ago, we answered the call of Woodrow Wilson, the call to a larger humanity, and it was for that we willingly rushed into the war....

We shall march out, yes, as black American citizens, as black British subjects, as black French citizens, as black Italians or as black Spaniards, but we shall march out with a greater loyalty, the loyalty of race. We shall march out in answer to the cry of our fathers, who cry out to us for the redemption of our own country, our motherland, Africa.

We shall march out, not forgetting the blessings of America. We shall march out, not forgetting the blessings of civilization. We shall march out with a history of peace before and behind us, and surety that history shall be our breast-plate, for how can man fight better than knowing that the cause for which he fights is righteous?... Glorious shall be the battle when the time comes to fight for our people and our race.

We should say to the millions who are in Africa to hold the fort, for we are coming 400,000,000 strong.

"How It Feels to Be Colored Me," by Zora Neale Hurston (1928)

An important—and for a long time underappreciated—writer of the Harlem Renaissance, Zora Neale Hurston (1891-1960) was born and raised in Eatonville, Florida, the first incorporated all-black town in America. Hurston was known particularly for her upbeat view of life as an African American woman. Below, in one of her first published articles, she memorably explains this view.

I am not tragically colored. There is no great sorrow dammed up in my soul, nor lurking behind my eyes. I do not mind at all. I do not belong to the sobbing school of Negrohood who hold that nature somehow has given them a lowdown dirty deal and whose feelings are all hurt about it. Even in the helter-skelter skirmish that is my life, I have seen that the world is to the strong regardless of a little pigmentation more or less. No, I do not weep at the world—I am too busy sharpening my oyster knife.

Someone is always at my elbow reminding me that I am the granddaughter of slaves. It fails to register depression with me. Slavery is sixty years in the past. The operation was successful and the patient is doing well, thank you. The terrible struggle that made me an American out of a potential slave said "On the line!" The Reconstruction said "Get set!"; and the generation before said "Go!" I am off to a flying start and I must not halt in the stretch to look behind and weep. Slavery is the price I paid for civilization, and the choice was not with me. It is a bully adventure and worth all that I have paid through my ancestors for it....

I have no separate feeling about being an American citizen and colored. I am merely a fragment of the Great Soul that surges within the boundaries. My country, right or wrong.

Sometimes, I feel discriminated against, but it does not make me angry. It merely astonishes me. How *can* any deny themselves the pleasure of my company? It's beyond me.

An Appeal from the Scottsboro Boys (1932)

On April 6, 1931, nine black youths accused of raping two white women went on trial for their lives in Scottsboro, Alabama. The case attracted international attention, with African American organizations (such as the NAACP), liberal whites, and the

Eight of the nine Scottsboro boys

American Communist Party (represented by the International Labor Defense) all competing to defend "the Scottsboro Boys."

Although there was little evidence against them, the defendants were quickly convicted. Their innocence was later proven by medical testimony and by the withdrawal of charges by one of the women. However, it was not until 1950 that all of the nine who were accused finally gained their freedom, either by parole, appeal, or escape.

On April 1, 1932, eight of the Scottsboro Boys sent the following appeal to workers everywhere. The appeal appeared in the May 1932 issue of The Negro Worker.

From the death cell here in Kilby Prison, eight of us Scottsboro boys is writing this to you.

We have been sentenced to die for something we ain't never done. Us poor boys been sentenced to burn up on the electric chair for the reason that we is workers—and the color of our skin is black. We like any one of you workers is none of us older than 20. Two of us is 14 and one is 13 years old.

What we guilty of? Nothing but being out of a job. Nothing but looking for work. Our kinfolk was starving for food. We wanted to help them out. So we hopped a freight—just like any one of you workers might a done—to go down to Mobile to hunt work. We was taken off the train by a mob and framed up on rape charges.

At the trial they give us in Scottsboro we could hear the crowds yelling, "Lynch the Niggers." We could see them toting those big shotguns. Call 'at a fair trial?

And while we lay here in jail, the bossman make us watch 'em burning up other Negroes on the electric chair. "This is what you'll get," they say to us.

What for? We ain't done nothing to be in here at all. All we done was to look for a job. Anyone of you might have done the same thing—and got framed up on the same charge just like we did.

Only ones helped us down here been the International Labor Defense and the League of Struggle for Negro Rights. We don't put no faith in the National Association for the Advancement of Colored People [N.A.A.C.P.]. They give some of us boys eats to go against the other boys who talked for the I.L.D. But we wouldn't split. Nohow. We know our friends and our enemies.

Working class boys, we asks you to save us from being burnt on the electric chair. We's only poor working class boys whose skin is black. We shouldn't die for that.

We hear about working people holding meetings for us all over the world. We asks for more big meetings. It'll take a lot of big meetings to help the I.L.D. and the L.S.N.R. to save us from the boss-man down here. Help us boys. We ain't done nothing wrong. We are only workers like you are. Only our skin is black. [Signed] Andy Wright, Olen Montgomery, Ozie Powell, Charlie Weems, Clarence Norris, Haywood Patterson, Eugene Williams, Willie Robertson.

Executive Order No. 8802 (1941)

Issued by President Franklin D. Roosevelt on June 25, 1941, Executive Order 8802 was intended to rid the defense industries of discrimination during World War II.

I do hereby reaffirm the policy of the United States that there shall be no discrimination in the employment of workers in defense industries or Government because of race, creed, color, or national origin, and I do hereby declare that it is the duty of employers and of labor organizations, in furtherance of said policy and of this order, to provide for the full and equitable participation of all workers in defense industries, without discrimination because of race, creed, color, or national origin....

Executive Order No. 9981 (1948)

Signed by President Harry S Truman on July 26, 1948, Executive Order 9981 was designed to end segregation in the Armed Forces of the United States.

1. It is hereby declared to be the policy of the President that there shall be equality of treatment and opportunity for all persons in the armed services without regard to race,

Before the *Brown* decision, black children often attended poorly funded schools

color, religion or national origin. This policy shall be put into effect as rapidly as possible, having due regard to the time required to effectuate-any necessary changes without impairing efficiency or morals.

Brown v. Board of Education of Topeka, Kansas (1954)

Beginning in the late 1930s the Supreme Court began to review many cases dealing with segregation in public education. By the 1950s it had become obvious that segregated educational facilities were not equal.

In the landmark case of Brown v. Board of Education, *the Supreme Court ruled unanimously, or in total agreement, that racial segregation in public schools was not constitutional. Attorney Thurgood Marshall, who later became a Supreme Court justice, argued for the NAACP legal team that won the case on behalf of Linda Brown, a Topeka public school student.*

Chief Justice Warren delivered the opinion of the Court.

In each of these cases, minors of the Negro race, through their legal representatives, seek the aid of the courts in obtaining admission to the public schools of their community on a nonsegregated basis. In each instance, they had been denied admission to schools attended by white children under laws requiring or permitting segregation according to race. This segregation was alleged to deprive the **plaintiffs** of the equal protection of the laws under the Fourteenth Amendment. In each of the cases other than the Delaware case, a three-judge federal district court denied relief to the plaintiffs on the so-called "separate but equal" doctrine announced by this Court in *Plessy* v. *Ferguson*.... Under that doctrine, equality of treatment is accorded when the races are provided substantially equal facilities, even though these facilities be separate. In the Delaware case, the Supreme Court of Delaware adhered to that doctrine, but ordered that the plaintiffs be admitted to the white schools because of their superiority to the Negro schools.

Today, education is perhaps the most important function of state and local governments. **Compulsory** school attendance laws and the great expenditures for education both demonstrate our recognition of the importance of education to our democratic society. It is required in the performance of our most basic public responsibilities, even service in the armed forces. It is the very foundation of good citizenship. Today it is a principal instrument in awakening the child to cultural values, in preparing him for later professional training, and in helping him to adjust normally to his environment. In these days, it is doubtful that any child may reasonably be expected to succeed in life if he is denied the opportunity of an education.

WORDS

Federal troops escorting black students to class at Little Rock's Central High School

Such an opportunity, where the state has undertaken to provide it, is a right which must be made available to all on equal terms.

We come then to the question presented: Does segregation of children in public schools solely on the basis of race, even though the physical facilities and other "tangible" factors may be equal, deprive the children of the minority group of equal educational opportunities? We believe that it does....

Executive Order No. 10730 (1957)

In September 1957, Arkansas Governor Orval Faubus called on the Arkansas National Guard in an effort to prevent black students from entering Little Rock's Central High School. As a result, on September 24, President Dwight D. Eisenhower issued an executive order authorizing the use of the National Guard and the Air National Guard of the United States to assist in desegregation in Little Rock.

The Little Rock incident was the most serious clash between a state government and the federal government in modern times. Faubus and a mob of whites backed down in the face of military power and finally allowed nine black children to begin attending a desegregated high school on September 25.

Section 1. I hereby authorize and direct the Secretary of Defense to order into the active military service of the United States as he may deem appropriate to carry out the purposes of this Order, any or all of the units of the National Guard of the United States and of the Air National Guard of the United States within the State of Arkansas to serve in the active military service of the United States for an indefinite period and until relieved by appropriate orders.

Section 2. The Secretary of Defense is authorized and directed to take all appropriate steps to enforce any orders of the United States District Court for the Eastern District of Arkansas for the removal of obstruction of justice in the State of Arkansas with respect to matters relating to enrollment and attendance at public schools in the Little Rock School District, Little Rock, Arkansas. In carrying out the provisions of this section, the Secretary of Defense is authorized to use the units, and members thereof, ordered into the active military service of the United States pursuant to Section 1 of this Order.

Section 3. In furtherance of the enforcement of the aforementioned orders of the United States District Court for the Eastern District of Arkansas, the Secretary of Defense is authorized to use such of the armed forces of the United States as he may deem necessary.

Section 4. The Secretary of Defense is authorized to delegate to the Secretary of the Army or the Secretary of the Air Force, or both, any of the authority conferred upon him by this Order.

Excerpt from Martin Luther King, Jr.'s "I Have a Dream" Speech, Delivered at the Lincoln Memorial, Washington, D.C. (1963)

On August 28, 1963, some 250,000 people gathered at the Lincoln Memorial in Washington, D.C. Together they formed the largest single protest demonstration in U.S. history. The day was immortalized when Martin Luther King, Jr., the nation's foremost civil rights leader, delivered his "I Have a Dream" speech.

I say to you today, my friends, that even though we must face the difficulties of today and tomorrow, I still have a dream. It is a dream deeply rooted in the American dream that one day this nation will rise up and live out the true meaning of its creed—we hold these truths to be self-evident, that all men are created equal.

I have a dream that one day on the red hills of Georgia, sons of former slaves and sons of former slave-owners will be able to sit down together at the table of brotherhood.

I have a dream that one day, even the state of Mississippi, a state sweltering with the heat of injustice, sweltering with the heat of oppression, will be transformed into an oasis of freedom and justice.

I have a dream my four little children will one day live in a nation where they will not be judged by the color of their skin but by the content of their character. I have a dream today!

I have a dream that one day, down in Alabama, with its vicious racists, with its governor having his lips dripping with the words of interposition and nullification, that one day, right there in Alabama, little black boys and black girls will be able to join hands with white boys and white girls as sisters and brothers. I have a dream today.

I have a dream that one day every valley shall be exalted, every hill and mountain shall be made low, the rough places shall be made plain, and the crooked places shall be

A crowd of 250,000 gather in Washington, D.C., August 1963

made straight, and the glory of the Lord will be revealed, and all flesh shall see it together.

This is our hope. This is the faith that I go back to the South with.

With this faith we will be able to hew out of the mountain of despair a stone of hope. With this faith we will be able to transform the jangling discords of our nation into a beautiful symphony of brotherhood.

With this faith we will be able to work together, to pray together, to struggle together, to go to jail together, to stand up for freedom together, knowing that we will be free one day. This will be the day when all of God's children will be able to sing the new meaning—"my country 'tis of thee; sweet land of liberty; of thee I sing; land where my fathers died; land of the pilgrim's pride; from every mountain side, let freedom ring"—and if America is to be a great nation this must become true.

> So let freedom ring from the prodigious hilltops of New Hampshire.
> Let freedom ring from the mighty mountains of New York.
> Let freedom ring from the heightening Alleghenies of Pennsylvania.
> Let freedom ring from the snowcapped Rockies of Colorado.
> Let freedom ring from the curvaceous peaks of California.
> But not only that.
> Let freedom ring from Stone Mountain of Georgia.
> Let freedom ring from Lookout Mountain of Tennessee.
> Let freedom ring from every hill and mole hill of Mississippi, from every mountainside, let freedom ring.

And when we allow freedom to ring, when we let it ring from every village and hamlet, from every state and city, we will be able to speed up that day when all God's children—black men and white men, Jews and Gentiles, Catholics and Protestants—will be able to join hands and sing in the words of the old Negro spiritual, "Free at last, free at last; thank God Almighty, we are free at last."

Civil Rights Act of 1964 (1964)

This civil rights act was signed by President Lyndon B. Johnson on July 2, 1964, though it had been initiated by President John F. Kennedy in June 1963 (Kennedy was assassinated in November 1963).

More detailed than previous acts, the 1964 act contained eleven "titles" covering the areas of voting rights, access to public facilities, federal aid to schools engaged in the process of desegregation, discrimination in federally funded programs, and discrimination in employment. The act also strengthened earlier voter registration protection; made racial discrimination in restaurants, hotels, and motels illegal; provided for equal access to public parks, pools, and other facilities; outlined unlawful employment practices, and; ordered the creation of a federal Equal Employment Opportunity Commission.

Following is one of the most important sections, a direct result of the civil rights movement sparked by Rosa Parks.

Sec. 201. (a) All persons shall be entitled to the full and equal enjoyment of the goods, services, facilities, privileges, advantages,

WORDS

President Lyndon B. Johnson signs the Civil Rights Act of 1964. Looking on are Edward Brooke (left), Walter Mondale (right), and Thurgood Marshall

and accommodations of any place of public accommodation ... without discrimination or segregation on the ground of race, color, religion, or national origin.

The Black Panther Manifesto (1966)

The Black Panther Party relied on strict rules to mold its members into a unified force. Like the Muslims, the Black Panthers denounced all intoxicants, drugs, and artificial stimulants "while doing party work." Below is the ten-point program of the party, which every member was expected to know, understand, and even memorize.

1. We want FREEDOM. We want power to determine the destiny of our Black Community.

We believe that black people will not be free until we are able to determine our destiny.

2. We want full employment for our people.

WORDS

Black Panther Party founders Bobby Seale (left) and Huey Newton

We believe that the federal government is responsible and obligated to give every man employment or a guaranteed income. We believe that if the white American businessman will not give full employment, then the means of production should be taken from the businessmen and placed in the community so that the people of the community can organize and employ all of its people and give a high standard of living.

3. We want an end to the robbery by the CAPITALIST of our Black Community.

We believe that this racist government has robbed us and now we are demanding the overdue debt of forty acres and two mules. Forty acres and two mules was promised 100 years ago as restitution for slave labor and mass murder of black people. We will accept the payment in currency which will be distributed to our many communities. The Germans are now aiding the Jews in Israel for the **genocide** of the Jewish people. The Germans murdered six million Jews. The American racist has taken part in the slaughter of over fifty million black people, therefore, we feel that this is a modest demand that we make.

4. We want decent housing, fit for shelter of human beings.

We believe that if the white landlords will not give decent housing to our black community, then the housing and the land should be made into cooperatives so that our community, with government aid, can build and make decent housing for its people.

5. We want education for our people that exposes the true nature of this decadent American society. We want education that teaches us our true history and our role in the present-day society.

We believe in an educational system that will give to our people a knowledge of self. If a man does not have knowledge of himself and his position in society and the world, then he has little chance to relate to anything else.

6. We want all black men to be exempt from military service.

We believe that Black people should not be forced to fight in the military service to defend a racist government that does not protect us. We will not fight and kill other people of color in the world who, like black people, are being victimized by the white racist government of America. We will protect ourselves from the force and violence of the racist police and the racist military, by whatever means necessary,

7. We want an immediate end to POLICE BRUTALITY and MURDER of black people.

We believe we can end police brutality in our black community by organizing black self-defense groups that are dedicated to defending our black community from racist police oppression and brutality. The Second Amendment to the Constitution of the United States gives a right to bear arms. We therefore believe that all black people should arm themselves for self-defense.

8. We want freedom for all black men held in federal, state, county, and city prisons and jails.

We believe that all black people should be released from the many jails and prisons because they have not received a fair and impartial trial.

9. We want all black people when brought to trial to be tried in court by a jury of their peer group or people from their black communities, as defined by the constitution of the United States.

We believe that the courts should follow the United States Constitution so that black people will receive fair trials. The 14th Amendment of the U.S. Constitution gives a man a right to be tried by his peer group. A peer is a person from a similar economic, social, religious, geographical, environmental, historical, and racial background. To do this the court will be forced to select a jury from the black community from which the black defendant came. We have been, and are being tried by all-white juries that have no understanding of the "average reasoning man" of the black community.

10. We want land, bread, housing, education, clothing, justice, and peace. And as our major political objective, a United Nations-supervised **plebiscite** to be held throughout the black colony in which only black colonial subjects will be allowed to participate, for the purpose of determining the will of black people as to their national destiny.

When, in the course of human events, it becomes necessary for one people to dissolve the political bands which have connected them with another, and to assume, among the powers of the earth, the separate and equal station to which the laws of nature and nature's God entitle them, a decent respect to the opinions of mankind requires that they should declare the causes which impel them to the separation.

We hold these truths to be self-evident, that all men are created equal; that they are endowed by their Creator with certain inalienable rights; that among these are life, liberty, and the pursuit of happiness.

That, to secure these rights, governments are instituted among men, deriving their just powers from the consent of the governed; that, whenever any form of government becomes destructive of these ends, it is the right of the people to alter or to abolish it, and to institute a new government, laying its foundation on such principles, and organizing its powers in such form, as to them shall seem most likely to effect their safety and happiness.

Prudence, indeed, will dictate that governments long established should not be changed for light and transient causes; and, accordingly, all experience hath shown, that mankind are more disposed to suffer, while evils are sufferable, than to right themselves by abolishing the forms to which they are accustomed. But, when a long train of abuses and usurpations, pursuing invariably the same object, evinces a design to reduce them under absolute despotism, it is their right, it is their duty, to throw off such government, and to provide new guards for their future security.

Martin Luther King, Jr.'s Last Speech, "I See the Promised Land," Delivered at Mason Temple, Memphis, Tennessee (1968)

King's reputation as a civil rights leader was suffering near the end of his life. On the one side, there were many blacks who disagreed with his nonviolent tactics. On the other side, there were many within the white establishment, including the Federal Bureau of Investigation (FBI), who distrusted him and wanted him removed from power.

Shrugging off the depression that grew out of this state of affairs and the continual threats on his life, King agreed to travel to Memphis to deliver an important speech. The purpose for the speech was to cheer on sanitation workers in the city, who were striking against unfair labor practices.

What resulted was a rousing, highly personal sermon, King's last—and one of his greatest.

Let us rise up tonight with a greater readiness. Let us stand with a greater determination. And let us move on in these powerful days, these days of challenge to make America what it ought to be. We have an opportunity to make America a better nation. And I want to thank God, once more, for allowing me to be here with you.

You know, several years ago, I was in New York City autographing the first book that I had written. And while sitting there autographing books, a demented black woman came up. The only question I heard from her was, "Are you Martin Luther King?"

And I was looking down writing, and I said yes. And the next minute I felt something beating on my chest. Before I knew it I had been stabbed by this demented woman. I was rushed to Harlem Hospital. It was a dark Saturday afternoon. And that blade had gone through, and the X-rays revealed that the tip of the blade was on the edge of my aorta, the main artery. And once that's punctured, you drown in your blood—that's the end of you.

It came out in the *New York Times* the next morning, that if I had sneezed, I would have died. Well, about four days later, they allowed me, after the operation, after my chest had opened, and the blade had been taken out, to move around in the wheel chair in the hospital. They allowed me to read some of the mail that came in, and from all over the states, and the world, kind letters came in. I read a few, but one of them I will never forget. I had received one from the President and Vice-President. I've forgotten what those telegrams said. I'd received a visit and a letter from the Governor of New York, but I've forgotten what the letter said. But there was another letter that came from a little girl, a young girl who was a student at the White Plains High School. And I looked at that letter, and I'll never forget it. It said simply, "Dear Dr. King: I am a ninth-grade student at the White Plains High School." She said, "While it should not matter, I would like to mention that I am a white girl. I read in the paper of your misfortune, and of your suffering. And I read that if you had sneezed, you would have died. And I'm simply writing you to say that I'm so happy that you didn't sneeze."

And I want to say tonight, I want to say that I am happy that I didn't sneeze. Because if I had sneezed, I wouldn't have been around here in 1960, when students all over the South started sitting-in at lunch counters. And I knew that as they were sitting in, they were really standing up for the best in the American dream. And taking the whole nation back to those great wells of democracy which were dug deep by the Founding Fathers in the Declaration of Independence and the Constitution. If I had sneezed, I wouldn't have been around in 1962, when Negroes in Albany, Georgia, decided to straighten their backs up. And whenever men and women straighten their backs up, they are going somewhere, because a man can't ride your back unless it is bent. If I had sneezed, I wouldn't have been here in 1963, when the black people of Birmingham, Alabama, aroused the conscience of this nation, and brought into being the Civil Rights Bill. If I had sneezed, I wouldn't have had a chance later that year, in August, to try to tell America about a dream that I had had. If I had sneezed, I wouldn't have been down in Selma, Alabama, to see the great movement there. If I had sneezed, I wouldn't have been in Memphis to see the community rally around those brothers and sisters who are suffering. I'm so happy that I didn't sneeze.

And they were telling me, now it doesn't matter now. It really doesn't matter what happens now. I left Atlanta this morning, and as we got started on the plane, there were six of us, the pilot said over the public address system, "We are sorry for the delay, but we have Dr. Martin Luther King on the plane. And to be sure that all of the bags were checked, and to be sure that nothing would be wrong with the plane, we had to check out everything carefully. And we've had the plane protected and guarded all night."

And then I got into Memphis. And some began to say the threats, or talk about the threats that were out. What would happen to me from some of our sick white brothers?

Well, I don't know what will happen now. We've got some difficult days ahead. But it doesn't matter with me now. Because I've been to the mountaintop. And I don't mind. Like anybody, I would like to live a long life. Longevity has its place. But I'm not concerned about that now. I just want to do God's will. And He's allowed me to go up to the mountain. And I've looked over. And I've seen the promised land. I may not get there with you. But I want you to know tonight, that we, as a people, will get to the promised land. And I'm happy tonight. I'm not worried about anything. I'm not fearing any man. Mine eyes have seen the glory of the coming of the Lord.

Jesse L. Jackson's Address to the Democratic National Convention (1988)

In 1984 Jesse L. Jackson made his first run as a Democratic candidate for president. In 1988 Jackson ran again and most thought he would not fare much better than he had in his previous attempt. Yet, with the support of most black leaders, most African Americans, and many liberal whites, Jackson made the primaries of 1988 exciting and memorable.

In a field of seven candidates, Jackson was one of the two who remained in the running until the time of the convention, coming in second behind the Democratic nominee, Michael Dukakis.

The following are excerpts from Jackson's inspiring speech to the Democratic National Convention on July 19, 1988.

Tonight, we pause and give praise and honor to God for being good enough to allow us to be at this place at this time. When I look out at this convention, I see the face of America, red, yellow, brown, black and white. We are all precious in God's sight—the real rainbow coalition. All of us—all of us who are here think that we are seated. But we're really standing on someone's shoulders. Ladies and gentlemen, Mrs. Rosa Parks. The mother of the civil rights movement....

My right and my privilege to stand here before you has been won—won in my lifetime—by the blood and the sweat of the innocent.... Dr. Martin Luther King Jr. lies only a few miles from us tonight. Tonight he must feel good as he looks down upon us. We sit here together, a rainbow coalition—the sons and daughters of slavemasters and the sons and daughters of slaves sitting together around a common table, to decide the direction of our party and our country. His heart would be full tonight.

As a testament to the struggles of those who have gone before; as a legacy for those who will come after; as a tribute to the endurance, the patience, the courage of our forefathers and mothers; as an assurance that their prayers are being answered, their work has not been in vain, and hope is eternal, tomorrow night my name will go into nomination for the presidency of the United States of America.

We meet tonight at the crossroads, a point of decision. Shall we expand, be inclusive, find unity and power; or suffer division and impotence.

We've come to Atlanta, the cradle of the old South, the crucible of the new South.

Tonight there is a sense of celebration because we are moved, fundamentally moved from racial battlegrounds by law, to economic common ground, with the moral challenge to move to higher ground; common ground!... Common ground! That's the challenge of our party tonight....

Left wing. Right wing. Progress will not come through boundless liberalism nor static conservatism, but at the critical mass of mutual survival....

[Don't] despair. Be as wise as my grandma. Pull the patches and the pieces together, bound by a common thread. When we form a great quilt of unity and common ground, we'll have the power to bring about health care and housing and jobs and education and hope.... We the people can win....

We can win. We must not lose to the drugs and violence, premature pregnancy, suicide, cynicism, pessimism and despair. We can win. Wherever you are tonight, now I challenge you to hope and to dream. Don't submerge your dreams. Exercise above all else—even on drugs, dream of the day you are drug-free. Even in the gutter, dream of the day that you will be up on your feet again. You must never stop dreaming....

Dream of peace. Peace is rational and reasonable. War is irrational ... and unwinnable.

And I was not supposed to make it. You see, I was born of a teenage mother, who was born of a teenage mother. I understand. I know abandonment, and people being mean to you, and saying you're nothing and nobody and can never be anything. I understand....

Wherever you are tonight, you can make it. Hold your head high. Stick your chest out. You can make it. It gets dark sometimes, but the morning comes. Don't you surrender. Suffering breeds character, character breeds faith, in the end faith will not disappoint.

You must not surrender. You may or may not get there but just know that you're qualified and you hold on and hold out. We must never surrender.

America will get better and better. Keep hope alive. Keep hope alive. Keep hope alive for tomorrow night and beyond. Keep hope alive....

President George Bush's Message to the Senate upon Returning without Approval the Civil Rights Act of 1990 (Oct. 22, 1990)

In June 1989, the United States Supreme Court delivered opinions in several cases dealing with racial discrimination in employment. The Court's rulings, which appeared harmful to the progress of blacks in the workplace, were protested by civil rights organizations.

On October 16 and 17, 1990, both houses of Congress approved a bill designed to reverse the Court's rulings. On October 22, President Bush vetoed the bill, claiming that the bill's provisions would encourage employers to establish hiring quotas.

To the Senate of the United States.

I am today returning without my approval [Separate Bill] 2104, the "Civil Rights Act of 1990." I deeply regret having to take this action with respect to a bill bearing such a title, especially since it contains certain provisions that I strongly endorse.

Discrimination, whether on the basis of race, national origin, sex, religion, or disability, is worse than wrong. It is a fundamental evil that tears at the fabric of our society, and one that all Americans should and must oppose. That requires rigorous enforcement of existing antidiscrimination laws....

Despite the use of the term "civil rights" in the title of S. 2104, the bill actually employs a maze of highly legalistic language to introduce the destructive force of quotas into our Nation's employment system....

Our goal and our promise has been equal opportunity and equal protection under the law. That is a bedrock principle from which we cannot retreat. The temptation to support a bill—any bill—simply because its title includes the words "civil rights" is very strong. This impulse is not entirely bad. Presumptions have too often run the other way, and our Nation's history on racial questions cautions against complacency. But when our efforts, however well intentioned, result in quotas, equal opportunity is not advanced but thwarted. The very commitment to justice and equality that is offered as the reason why this bill should be signed requires me to veto it.

Civil Rights Act of 1991 (1991)

After vetoing Congress's 1990 civil rights legislation, the Bush administration joined both houses of Congress in working on alternative bills. Following months of talks, the Senate passed Senate Bill 1745 on October 30; the House passed the bill on November 7. On November 21, President George Bush signed the Civil Rights Act of 1991.

Included below are findings from the "Glass Ceiling" section of the act. Glass ceiling is a term used to describe the invisible barrier that women and minorities sometimes encounter when they try to advance to the highest rungs of the "corporate ladder."

Title II—Glass Ceiling

Sec. 202 Findings and Purpose.

(a) Findings—Congress finds that—

WORDS

President George Bush meets with civil rights leaders, 1990; Dorothy Heights and Benjamin Hooks are pictured

(1) despite a dramatically growing presence in the workplace, women and minorities remain underrepresented in management and decision-making positions in business;

(2) artificial barriers exist to the advancement of women and minorities in the workplace;

(3) United States corporations are increasingly relying on women and minorities to meet employment requirements and are increasingly aware of the advantages derived from a diverse work force;

(4) the "Glass Ceiling Initiative" undertaken by the Department of Labor, including the release of the report entitled "Report on the Glass Ceiling Initiative," has been instrumental in raising public awareness of—

(A) the underrepresentation of women and minorities at the management and decision-making levels in the United States work force;

(B) the underrepresentation of women and minorities in line functions in the United States work force;

(C) the lack of access for qualified women and minorities to credential-building developmental opportunities; and

(D) the desirability of eliminating artificial barriers to the advancement of women and minorities to such levels;

(f) the establishment of a commission to examine issues raised by the Glass Ceiling Initiative would help—

(A) focus greater attention on the importance of eliminating artificial barriers to the advancement of women and minorities to management and decision-making positions in business; and

(B) promote work force diversity....

On the Pulse of Morning, by Maya Angelou, Read at President Bill Clinton's Inauguration (January 20, 1993)

A widely respected poet, Maya Angelou (1928-) is nevertheless best known for her I Know Why the Caged Bird Sings *(1970), the first of her series of five autobiographical novels. In addition to writing, Angelou has enjoyed success as a singer and actress and even received an Emmy nomination in 1977 for her performance in the television miniseries* Roots.

On January 20, 1993, Angelou became the first poet in 32 years to deliver a reading at a presidential **inauguration** *(the last had been Robert Frost, at the inauguration of John F. Kennedy). The full text of the poem she wrote for the occasion, with words full of hope for the human species, is included below.*

A Rock, A River, A Tree
Hosts to species long since departed,
Marked the mastodon,
The dinosaur, who left dried tokens
Of their sojourn here
On our planet floor,
Any broad alarm of their hastening doom
Is lost in the gloom of dust and ages.

But today, the Rock cries out to us, clearly, forcefully,
Come, you may stand upon my
Back and face your distant destiny,
But seek no haven in my shadow,
I will give you no hiding place down here.

You, created only a little lower than
The angels, have crouched too long in
The bruising darkness
Have lain too long
Facedown in ignorance.
Your mouths spilling words

Armed for slaughter.
The Rock cries out to us today,
You may stand upon me;
But do not hide your face.

Across the wall of the world,
A River sings a beautiful song. It says,
Come, rest here by my side.

Each of you, a bordered country,
Delicate and strangely made proud,
Yet thrusting perpetually under siege.

WORDS

Your armed struggles for profit
Have left collars of waste upon
My shore, currents of debris upon my breast.
Yet today I call you to my riverside,
If you will study war no more.

Come, clad in peace,
And I will sing the songs
The Creator gave to me when I and the
Tree and the Rock were one.
Before cynicism was a bloody sear across your brow
And when you yet knew you still knew nothing.
The River sang and sings on.

There is a true yearning to respond to
The singing River and the wise Rock.
So say the Asian, the Hispanic, the Jew
The African, the Native American, the Sioux,
The Catholic, the Muslim, the French, the Greek,
The Irish, the Rabbi, the Priest, the Sheik,
The Gay, the Straight, the Preacher,
The privileged, the homeless, the Teacher.
They hear. They all hear
The speaking of the Tree.

They hear the first and last of every Tree
Speak to humankind today.
Come to me,
Here beside the River.
Plant yourself beside the River.

Each of you, descendant of some passed
On traveler, has been paid for.
You, who gave me my first name, you
Pawnee, Apache, Seneca, you
Cherokee Nation, who rested with me, then
Forced on bloody feet,
Left me to the employment of
Other seekers—desperate for gain,
Starving for gold.
You, the Turk, the Arab, the Swede,
The German, the Eskimo, the Scot,
The Italian, the Hungarian, the Pole,
You the Ashanti, the Yoruba, the Kru, bought,
Sold, stolen, arriving on a nightmare
Praying for a dream.

Maya Angelou

Here, root yourselves beside me.
I am that Tree planted by the River,
Which will not be moved.
I, the Rock, I, the River, I, the Tree
I am yours—your passages have been paid.
Lift up your faces, you have a piercing need
For this bright morning dawning for you.
History, despite its wrenching pain,
Cannot be unlived, but if faced
With courage, need not be lived again.

Lift up your eyes
Upon this day breaking for you.
Give birth again
To the dream.

Women, children, men,
Take it into the palms of your hands,
Mold it into the shape of your most
Private need. Sculpt it into
The image of your most public self.
Lift up your hearts
Each new hour holds new chances
For a new beginning.

Do not be wedded forever
To fear, yoked eternally
To brutishness.

The horizon leans forward,
Offering you space
To place new steps of change
Here, on the pulse of this fine day
You may have the courage
To look up and out and upon me,
The Rock, the River, the Tree, your country.
No less to Midas than the mendicant.
No less to you now than the mastodon then.

Here, on the pulse of this new day
You may have the grace to look up and out
And into your sister's eyes,
And into Your brother's face,
Your country,
And say simply
Very simply
With hope—
Good morning.

5

Places

African American Landmarks around the United States

The United States

"This colored people going to be a people."—Sojourner Truth

African Americans have made a deep and lasting imprint on the history and landscape of the United States. Virtually every state contains notable sites honoring the African American experience. Many of these landmarks commemorate black participation in the settlement and defense of this nation. Many others recognize African Americans' quest for knowledge. Still others trace the black race's long history from slavery to freedom to modern-day struggles for civil rights. And yet others recognize the historical achievements of blacks in sports, science, and the arts.

Just as the documents from the previous chapter represent living history so, too, do landmarks. From Beckwourth, California, to Eatonville, Florida, from Motown to Montgomery, the struggles and accomplishments of black people have been preserved. Because of this, all Americans may relive a past that, in many cases, would otherwise be all but forgotten.

THE MIDWEST

Illinois

Chicago

Daniel Hale Williams House

445 East 42nd Street

This house was the home of one of America's first black surgeons, whose accomplishments include establishing black-run Provident Hospital [see below] in 1891 and performing a pioneering open-heart operation in 1893.

Daniel Hale Williams was born in Hollidaysburg, Pennsylvania. He managed a barber shop prior to studying under Henry Palmer, who was surgeon-general of Wisconsin. Williams received his medical degree from Chicago Medical College in 1883 and later opened an office in Chicago. In 1913 he became the first black to win a fellowship from the American College of Surgeons. The Williams house was designated a National Historic Landmark on May 15, 1975.

The Midwest
Illinois • Indiana • Iowa • Michigan • Minnesota • Ohio • Wisconsin

The Northeast
Connecticut • Delaware • Maine • Maryland • Massachusetts • New Hampshire • New Jersey • New York • Pennsylvania • Rhode Island • Vermont

South Central States
Alabama • Arkansas • Kentucky • Louisiana • Mississippi • Missouri • Tennessee

The Southeast
Florida • Georgia • North Carolina • South Carolina • Virginia •·Washington, D.C. • West Virginia

The West
Alaska • Arizona • California • Colorado • Hawaii • Idaho • Kansas • Montana • Nebraska • Nevada • New Mexico • North Dakota • Oklahoma • Oregon • South Dakota • Texas • Utah • Washington •·Wyoming

---

Du Sable Museum of African-American History and Art

740 East 56th Place

Established in 1961 and named for pioneer fur trader Jean Baptiste Pointe Du Sable, the Du Sable Museum includes sev-

PLACES

Jean Baptiste Pointe Du Sable and the fur-trading settlement that became the city of Chicago

eral galleries of African art and American works. Special collections include those focusing on the history of blacks in Chicago and the events of the 1960s across the nation.

Ida B. Wells-Barnett House
3624 South Dr. Martin Luther King, Jr., Drive

This house was the home of civil rights crusader and early feminist Ida B. Wells-Barnett. The Wells house was designated a National Historic Landmark on May 30, 1974.

Jean Baptiste Pointe Du Sable Homesite
401 North Michigan Avenue

Born in Haiti to a French father and a black mother, Jean Baptiste Pointe Du Sable immigrated to French Louisiana and became a fur trapper. He established trading posts on the sites of the present cities of Michigan City, Indiana; Peoria, Illinois; and Port Huron, Michigan. But the most important post was at the mouth of the Chicago River. This site, where he constructed a log home for his wife and family, is recognized as the first settlement of what became Chicago. In 1796 Du Sable sold his Chicago home and went to live with his son in St. Charles, Missouri, where he died in 1814.

The homesite was designated a National Historic Landmark on May 11, 1976. The site of Du Sable's home is marked by a plaque on the northeast approach to the

Michigan Avenue Bridge. Two other plaques recognizing Du Sable exist—one in the Chicago Historical Society Museum, at North Avenue and Clark Street, the other in the lobby of Du Sable High School, at 49th and State Streets.

Milton L. Olive Park
Lake Shore Drive

Milton L. Olive Park was dedicated by Chicago mayor Richard Daley in honor of the first black soldier to be awarded a Congressional Medal of Honor during the Vietnam War. Olive died in action after displaying extraordinary heroism that saved the lives of several other soldiers exposed to a live grenade.

Oscar Staton DePriest House
4538 Dr. Martin Luther King, Jr., Drive

This house served as the residence of the first black American elected to the U.S. House of Representatives from a northern state. Born in Florence, Alabama, Oscar DePriest moved with his family to Kansas and later to Chicago. While in Chicago, he worked as a real estate broker. In 1928 he was elected to the House of Representatives, where he served three terms.

DePriest then returned to the real estate business but remained politically active in Chicago, including serving as vice-chairman of the Cook County Republican Committee. The DePriest house was designated a National Historic Landmark on May 15, 1975.

Provident Hospital and Training School
500 East 51st Street and Vincennes Avenue

This facility was the first training school for black nurses in the United States. It was founded by Daniel Hale Williams [see above], a famous black surgeon who performed one of the first successful open-heart operations in 1893. The current hospital was opened in 1933.

WORDS TO KNOW

alma mater: (Latin for *fostering mother*) the particular school or college a person attended

alumni: persons who have attended or graduated from a particular college or school

archives: a place where important papers, documents, and other memorabilia are kept; the papers, documents, and memorabilia that are kept in such a place

attaché: a person with special duties, particularly in connection with international relations

bequest: money or other personal property that is awarded by means of a will; the act of giving money or personal property

bourgeoisie: a social class between the wealthy and the working class; the middle class

catafalque: a wooden framework used to hold a coffin during elaborate funerals

collateral: a form of security that is offered to a lender until a loan is repaid

diaspora: a scattering or dispersion of people who share a common background

endowment: a gift, generally money, to an institution or person; a natural talent or ability

PLACES

Robert S. Abbott House
4742 Martin Luther King Drive

This house was occupied by Robert Sengstacke Abbott from 1926 until his death in 1940. Abbott's newspaper, the *Chicago Defender,* targeted black readers.

Probably more than any other publication, the *Defender* was responsible for the large northward migration of blacks during the first half of the twentieth century. The Abbott house was named a National Historic Landmark on December 8, 1976.

Victory Monument
35th Street and South Parkway

Victory Monument honors the black soldiers of Illinois who served in World War I. The monument and tomb of Stephen A. Douglas, once the owner of much of the land in the area, is also located near 35th Street.

Quincy

Father Augustine Tolton Grave Site
St. Peter's Cemetery
Broadway and 32nd Street

Augustine Tolton was the first black American to become a Roman Catholic priest. Ordained in 1886, Tolton opened a school for black children, was pastor at St. Joseph's Church in Quincy, and later served as pastor at St. Monica's Church in Chicago. He died in 1897.

INDIANA

Bloomingdale

Underground Railroad Marker
U.S. Route 41

This marks one of several points used to assist fugitive slaves seeking freedom and safety in Canada. One such slave, William Trail, liked Indiana so much he decided to stay to farm. He was successful and became one of many prosperous farmers in Union County, Indiana.

Fountain City

Levi Coffin House
North Main Street

Born in North Carolina in 1798, Levi Coffin was a Quaker abolitionist who also became known as "The President of the Underground Railroad." He used his own Fountain City home as a way station for runaway slaves on their way to Illinois, Michigan, or Canada. Between 1827 and 1847, Coffin hid more than 300 slaves.

Coffin then left Fountain City for Ohio, where he continued his activities, eventually helping over 3,000 slaves escape from the South. He was still engaged in the resettlement of former slaves long after the Civil War had ended. Coffin died in Avondale, Ohio, in 1877.

IOWA

Des Moines

Fort Des Moines Provisional Army Officer Training School
Southwest Ninth Street

Once a cavalry post, Fort Des Moines was reopened in 1917 as a base for training black officers to lead segregated troops in World War I. Between June and December of that year, hundreds of junior officers were trained at the facility. Black units led by men trained at the school were assembled in

Sojourner Truth's grave site

France as the 92nd Division. The camp was abandoned at the end of the war, and the site was designated a National Historic Landmark on May 30, 1974.

Sioux City

Pearl Street

Sioux City was a refuge for many slaves escaping from Missouri. Pearl Street, once the city's main thoroughfare, was named for a black pioneer who had arrived in the town by boat more than a century earlier and achieved widespread popularity as a cook.

MICHIGAN

Battle Creek

Sojourner Truth Grave Site
Oak Hill Drive, Oak Hill Cemetery

This site in the Oak Hill Cemetery marks the resting place of one of the most powerful abolitionists and lecturers of the nineteenth century, Sojourner Truth. Truth settled in Battle Creek after the Civil War, but continued to travel and lecture until a few years before her death on November 26, 1883.

According to popular accounts, Truth was once delivering an antislavery speech and was heckled from someone in the crowd. "Old woman," someone in the audience asked, "do you think your talk about slavery does any good? I don't care any more about it than I do for the bite of a flea."

"Maybe not," she answered. "But the Lord willing, I'll keep you scratching."

Truth was invited to the White House, where she met with Abraham Lincoln in 1864. A portrait of her reading the Bible with the president hung in Battle Creek until it was destroyed by fire in 1898.

Detroit

Afro-American Museum of Detroit
1553 West Grand Boulevard

This museum houses a collection of African and American items and includes memorabilia of actor-singer Paul Robeson.

Elijah McCoy Home Site
5730 Lincoln

PLACES

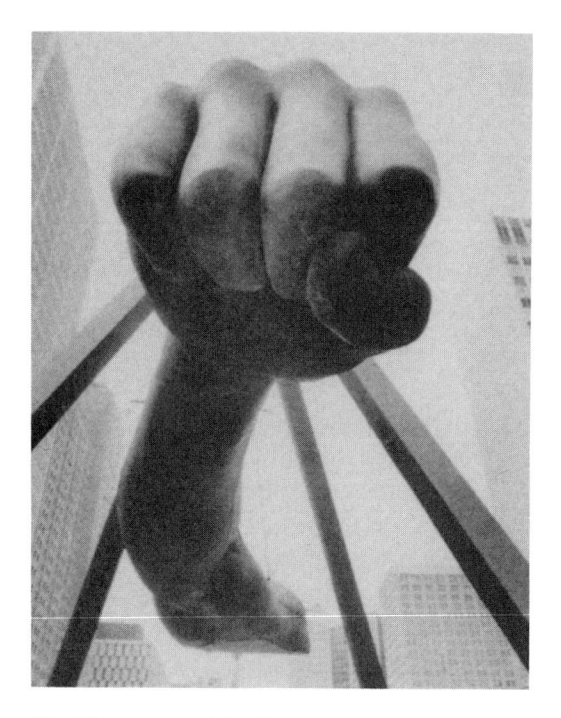

The Fist, a memorial to boxing champ Joe Louis

Born in Ontario, Canada, inventor Elijah McCoy settled in the Detroit area and opened his own manufacturing company in 1870. McCoy is best known for his work connected with the automatic lubrication of moving machinery. Over a 40-year period, McCoy received 57 patents for his inventions. A plaque marks his homesite.

Joe Louis Memorials
Cobo Convention Center
Corner of Woodward and Jefferson Avenues

Born in Lafayette, Alabama, Joe Louis grew up in Detroit and became the city's biggest hero, one of the most popular black fighters in the history of boxing. In 1934 Louis turned professional. His quickness and power took him swiftly to the highest level in heavyweight boxing and on June 22, 1937, he knocked out Jim Braddock to become the new heavyweight champion of the world.

Exactly one year later he faced the only man who had ever beaten him during his pro career, Max Schmeling of Germany. When Louis destroyed Schmeling in one round the entire country celebrated and the fighter from Detroit became one of the earliest black national sports hero.

Long after the construction of the Joe Louis Arena, at 600 Civic Center Drive in downtown Detroit, two other memorials to Louis were added. The first was unveiled in 1986 and became the city's most controversial piece of art. Made by Robert Graham and titled *The Fist,* this Louis memorial is a 24-foot-long outdoor sculpture of a black arm and clenched fist.

A more traditional tribute to Louis was put in place the following year inside the Cobo Convention Center. Designed by Ed Hamilton, this memorial is a 12-foot high statue of Louis in a typical boxing stance.

Motown Museum (Hitsville U.S.A.)
2648 West Grand Boulevard

This location served as the early headquarters of Motown Records, founded in 1958 by songwriter and independent record producer Berry Gordy, Jr. Performers including the Four Tops, Marvin Gaye, the Jackson Five, Martha and the Vandellas, Smokey Robinson, the Supremes, the Temptations, Mary Wells, and Stevie Wonder all played an important part in the early success of Motown.

Although the company moved its headquarters from Detroit to Los Angeles, Cali-

Motown Museum

fornia, in 1972, this site maintains a museum containing restored sound studios and mementoes.

National Museum of the Tuskegee Airmen
Historic Fort Wayne

This museum houses memorabilia of the Tuskegee Airmen, an all-black unit of fighter pilots active during World War II. The airmen, who were trained at Tuskegee Institute, played an important role in the combat against racial discrimination in the armed forces.

Ralph Bunche Birthplace
5685 West Fort Street

Ralph Bunche served the United Nations in several capacities, including that of

---

Gothic: a style of architecture that stresses pointed arches and steep roofs; a style of fiction that suggests horror, mystery, and gloom; anything ornate

Jim Crow: a reference (taken from a minstrel song) to laws and practices supporting the segregation of blacks and whites

liberal arts: a course of study that provides a broad background in literature, philosophy, languages, history, and abstract sciences; the opposite of a vocational or technical course of study

patron: a person, usually wealthy, who finances and supports another person, cause, or institution

pueblo: a close-knit village of sun-dried bricks and stone built by Native Americans in the southwestern United States; Pueblo Indian cultures include the Hopi and Zuni

seminary: a school where one is trained to become a minister, priest, or rabbi

Victorian: a nineteenth-century style of architecture characterized by largeness and ornamentation; anything dating from the reign of Queen Victoria (1837-1901)

women's suffrage: a movement for the right of women to vote

---

undersecretary, from 1946 until 1971. In 1950 Bunche became the first African American to receive the Nobel Peace Prize, which was awarded for his work as a United Nations mediator following the Arab-Israeli

PLACES

war of 1948. A plaque marks the site of his birthplace.

Underground Railroad Marker
Second Baptist Church
441 Monroe

One of many stops along the Underground Railroad, the basement of the Second Baptist Church was used to hide runaway slaves. The church, founded in 1836, boasts one of the oldest African American congregations in the Midwest.

Marshall

Crosswhite Boulder
Michigan Avenue and Mansion Street

The southern part of Michigan was settled by New Englanders who brought with them a burning hatred of slavery. Slave families escaping from Kentucky often settled in these communities. One such family was that of Adam Crosswhite.

In 1846 a band of slave hunters arrived in the town and demanded that the Crosswhites be turned over as fugitives. When the band tried to seize the family, town officials arrested the Kentucky slavers and charged them with attempted kidnapping. The Crosswhites were then taken to safety in Canada before the Kentuckians were released. The lawsuit that followed the incident led to the passing of the Fugitive Slave Law of 1850, which gave slaveowners the right to retrieve escaped blacks anywhere in the United States. The Crosswhite Boulder marks the site where the slave hunters were arrested.

Minnesota

Minneapolis-St. Paul

Fort Snelling State Historical Park

Set high on a bluff overlooking the junction of the Mississippi and Minnesota Rivers, Fort Snelling was once the northwesternmost outpost of the federal government. The lands beyond were unknown and unmapped.

Named for Colonel Josiah Snelling, its first commander, the fort was completed in 1825. Eleven years later, the new post surgeon, John Emerson, arrived from St. Louis and brought with him a black slave named Dred Scott.

The two men lived here only two years. But it was due to his residence in antislavery territory that Scott would eventually sue for his freedom.

A handful of black slaves lived at Fort Snelling at this time. One of them, James Thompson, who owned a business near the fort, was given his freedom when residents of the Wisconsin Territory (Minnesota did not become a state until 1858) raised funds to help him. More importantly, in 1836 a slave girl named Rachel won her freedom in a St. Louis court because she had lived at Fort Snelling. Scott's lawyers cited this case as a **precedent.**

Harriet Robinson was another slave living at the fort. In the summer of 1837 she married Scott and was given her freedom. The following spring, as the Scotts were returning to St. Louis by boat, she gave birth to a daughter north of the Missouri Compromise line; the baby was thus legally free. These events also figured into the historic series of trials of Dred Scott.

Ohio

Akron

John Brown Monument

132

The John Brown Monument was built in honor of the abolitionist whose ill-fated Harpers Ferry revolt led to his conviction for treason and execution by hanging in 1859.

Cincinnati

Harriet Beecher Stowe House
2950 Gilbert Avenue

The Harriet Beecher Stowe House has been preserved as a memorial to the internationally known author of *Uncle Tom's Cabin*. The house served as the Beecher family residence from 1832 to 1836.

Dayton

Paul Laurence Dunbar House
219 North Summit Street

Dunbar, the first black poet after Phillis Wheatley to gain a wide reputation in the United States, was also the first to concentrate on dialect poetry and black themes. Thus he became known as the "Poet Laureate of the Negro Race." His first collection of poetry, *Oak and Ivy,* was published before he was twenty. In 1896 his second volume of poetry, *Majors and Minors,* had won critical favor in a *Harper's Weekly* review by editor William Dean Howells.

Dunbar contracted tuberculosis in 1899 and was in failing health until his death on February 9, 1906. The Dunbar House was purchased by the State of Ohio in 1935 and became the first memorial in the United States dedicated to a black author.

Oberlin

John Mercer Langston House
207 East College Street

Elected township clerk in 1855, John Mercer Langston is believed to have been the first black American elected to public office. Langston later served for the Freedmen's Bureau, became the first dean of the Howard University Law School, and served as a United States Minister Resident to Haiti. The Langston House was designated a National Historical Landmark on May 15, 1975.

Oberlin College

Before the Civil War, Oberlin was one of the centers of secret abolitionist planning. The college was one of the first institutions to graduate blacks and women. Three of John Brown's raiding party at Harpers Ferry were identified as blacks from Oberlin.

After the war, Oberlin was able to devote more time to its stated mission: providing quality education to all regardless of race. Among the distinguished **alumni** of Oberlin was Blanche K. Bruce, who served a full term in the United States Senate (1875–1881).

Ripley

John Rankin House and Museum

Situated above the Ohio River across from slaveholding Kentucky, the Rankin House was one of the most important entry points on the Underground Railroad. It is believed that between 1825 and the end of the Civil War, John Rankin and his family sheltered more than 2,000 escaping slaves, as many as a dozen at a time, and helped them head north to Canada.

Their proudest claim was that they never lost a passenger to slave hunters. One of the stories Rankin delighted in retelling was the daring winter escape of a young woman, who crossed the river on ice floes while clutching her children in her arms. The story

133

was later used by Rankin's friend, Harriet Beecher Stowe, for the episode involving the character of Eliza in *Uncle Tom's Cabin.*

Wilberforce

Colonel Charles Young House
Route 42 between Cliffton and Stevenson Roads

This address was the residence of the highest ranking black officer in World War I and the first black military **attaché.** Colonel Charles Young was the son of former slaves and was born in Mays Lick, Kentucky. Army doctors had declared Young physically unfit because of his high blood pressure. To prove that he was fit, Young rode 500 miles on horseback from Wilberforce to Washington, D.C., in sixteen days. The Army, however, stood by its ruling. The house was declared a National Historical Landmark on May 30, 1974.

National Afro-American Museum
Wilberforce University, Brush Row Road

The museum is located on the original campus of Wilberforce University, the oldest black-run institution of higher learning in the country. Originally part of a **seminary** established in 1856 by the African Methodist Episcopal church, it combined seven years later with another church-run school and was renamed Wilberforce, in honor of a British abolitionist. Wilberforce has moved to a new campus nearby and the historic campus is now part of the museum conference center.

Walk into this museum and you return to the America of 1955, a nation at the crossroads of civil rights history. Funded by a 1971 act of Congress, the museum takes a unique approach to the era it covers. It documents both the small details of daily life and the great issues and events of the times. The galleries deal with typical businesses, churches, and homes in the African American communities of the 1950s. The museum also examines how music influenced these communities, and how the northern migration and the consequences of World War II shaped the civil rights movement. Other attractions include an art gallery with a permanent collection and changing exhibits of contemporary African American painting and sculpture.

Wisconsin

Janesville

Tallman Restorations
440 North Jackson Street

Wisconsin was among the most liberal of northern states. Many settlers who arrived here in the 1840s were refugees from failed revolutionary movements in Europe. They reacted strongly against slavery and enthusiastically provided shelter to fugitive slaves. The Janesville area contains two of the most noteworthy structures employed in this fashion.

William M. Tallman was a wealthy attorney and outspoken abolitionist when he moved here from New York. The mansion he built in Janesville, completed in 1857, was regarded as a marvel of the northwestern frontier. It featured running water, central heating, plumbing, and other conveniences known only to the great cities of the East. It also contained space in its 26 rooms for hiding slaves. One of the most lavish stops on the Underground Railroad, the house also welcomed Abraham Lincoln as an overnight guest in 1859, the year before his election brought about the Civil War.

The Stone House, also on the property, was built in 1842 and is designed to show the life of those with lesser means.

Madison

Wisconsin Historical Society
816 State Street

One of the largest **archives** of material relating to the civil rights movement is being assembled here. It contains material that dates back to the founding of the National Association for the Advancement of Colored People (NAACP; 1909), and focuses on the 1950s through the 1970s. Included in this collection are the complete papers of the Congress on Racial Equality.

The Historical Society occasionally mounts exhibits drawn from the archive materials, but it is primarily a research facility.

Milton

Milton House and Museum
18 South Janesville Street

The Milton House, the first structure made of poured concrete in the United States, was once used as a hideaway for fugitive slaves escaping by means of the Underground Railroad. The house first served as a stagecoach inn. The inn's basement was connected by a tunnel to a nearby log cabin and it was here that innkeeper Joseph Goodrich hid slaves who passed through the area.

Portage

Ansel Clark Grave Site
Silver Lake Cemetery

Ansel Clark, "born a slave, died a respected citizen," settled in Wisconsin after the Civil War. During the war he was forced to serve as a laborer for the Confederate cause. After escaping, he became a nurse in a Union hospital. After the war he was brought to Portage by a Wisconsin man he had treated. Clark became the town's constable and deputy sheriff; for thirty years he stood up to the town's rough characters, keeping them in line with his "firmness and dignity."

THE NORTHEAST

Connecticut

Canterbury

Prince Goodin Homestead

This parcel of land in Canterbury was once the home of Prince Goodin, a free black man who fought on the British side in the French and Indian War. While serving at Fort William Henry, he was captured during a French attack upon the fort and taken to Montreal, where he was sold into slavery. After three years of captivity, Goodin was freed when the British claimed the city in 1760.

Enfield

Paul Robeson Residence
1221 Enfield Street

Purchased by Paul Robeson and his wife in 1940, this residence served as their home until 1953. Robeson, a singer, actor, and civil rights activist, is best known for his roles in the play and film versions of *The Emperor Jones* and the musical and film versions of *Show Boat.*

Farmington

First Church of Christ
75 Main Street

In the last week of August 1839, the U.S. Navy brig *Washington,* engaged in a coastal survey near Montauk Point, Long Island, came upon a mysterious ship. Manned by Africans who spoke no English, the slave ship *Amistad* would soon become the focus of the growing abolitionist movement and would pit two U.S. presidents against each other.

Two months earlier, the slave ship had left Havana on a routine delivery of slaves to plantations along the Cuban coast. But among its human cargo was a natural leader and orator named Joseph Cinqué. Brutally beaten and desperate, the recently kidnapped slaves mutinied under Cinqué's direction. Most of the crew was killed in the first rush on deck. Two Cuban planters who had purchased the blacks were kept alive on condition that they sail the ship back to Sierra Leone, on Africa's west coast.

While the Cubans sailed east by day under Cinqué's watchful eye, they doubled back at night to the northwest. After six weeks of this zig-zag journey they found themselves off Montauk Point. When the sailors from the *Washington* boarded the *Amistad,* the Cubans greeted them as rescuers. They demanded to be returned with their slaves to Cuba. However, the press soon picked up the story and abolitionists demanded protection for the slaves.

President Martin Van Buren's administration backed the Cubans. A legal battle followed. By February 1941 the case had advanced to the U.S. Supreme Court. At this stage the slaves were represented by one of the most celebrated men in New England, former president John Quincy Adams.

While awaiting the outcome of the legal fight (which they would eventually win), the *Amistad* revolutionaries were taken to Farmington, a town with strong abolitionist sympathies. They were given schooling and religious instruction, while funds were raised for their defense and return to Africa. The First Church of Christ was the center of their community life during their stay. The church was designated a National Historic Landmark on December 8, 1976. In nearby Farmington Cemetery is a memorial to a member of the *Amistad* group, Foone, who accidentally drowned while in Farmington.

Washington

Jeff Liberty Grave Site
Judea Cemetery

This cemetery contains the grave site of Jeff Liberty, a black soldier in the Continental Army during the Revolution. His grave marker, erected by the Sons of the American Revolution, states simply "in remembrance of Jeff Liberty and his colored patriots." Liberty, a slave at the time of the rebellion, asked his owner to be allowed to serve in the struggle for independence. His request granted, he fought throughout the Revolution with an all-black regiment and was granted freedman status at the end of the war.

PLACES

Delaware

Wilmington

Asbury Methodist Episcopal Church
Third and Walnut Streets

The Asbury Methodist Episcopal Church was dedicated in 1789 by the distinguished orator Bishop Francis Asbury. Tradition has it that on one occasion a number of the town's leading citizens, many of whom were eager to hear Asbury preach but considered Methodism socially beneath them, refused to enter the church but stayed outside within hearing distance of the sermon.

The listeners were impressed by the eloquence of the man they heard. As it turned out, the voice and inspiring testimony they heard was not that of the bishop but of his black servant Harry.

In its early years, the church welcomed black members. However, by 1805 blacks had left this church, driven out by the decision of white worshippers to confine black members to the gallery.

Maine

Brunswick

First Parish Church
Main Street

While listening to her husband, Calvin Stowe, preaching an antislavery sermon here, Harriet Beecher Stowe was inspired to write *Uncle Tom's Cabin.* Built in 1846, the First Parish Church has a long activist tradition; Martin Luther King, Jr., was among those who graced its pulpit.

Peary-McMillan Arctic Museum
Bowdoin College, First floor of Hubbard Hall

Bowdoin College graduated some of New England's most famous nineteenth-century writers, including Harriet Beecher Stowe. It was also a home base for Arctic exploration. Admiral Robert E. Peary was a Bowdoin man, and the college supported his repeated quests for the North Pole. Exhibits on Peary and co-explorer Matthew Henson are a major part of the displays in the Peary-McMillan Arctic Museum.

Stowe House
63 Federal Street

From 1832 to 1836, Harriet Beecher Stowe lived in Cincinnati, Ohio, and witnessed slavery firsthand. But here, in a picturesque college town far removed from that atmosphere, Stowe proceeded to write *Uncle Tom's Cabin,* the novel that would make her famous. The Stowe House is now a restaurant.

Maryland

Annapolis

Banneker-Douglass Museum
84 Franklin Street

This museum, located in the city's historic district, is dedicated to black surveyor and inventor Benjamin Banneker and abolitionist Frederick Douglass, both of whom were born in Maryland.

Matthew Henson Memorial
Maryland State House

The Matthew Henson Memorial, first unveiled in 1961, honors the memory of the codiscoverer of the North Pole. Henson claimed until his death in 1955 that he had reached the Pole before his fellow explorer Admiral Robert E. Peary.

PLACES

Matthew Henson

"I was in the lead that final morning," he said in a newspaper interview in 1934, "and when Peary took his sights we found out that we had overshot the mark a couple of miles. We went back then and I could see that my footprints were the first at the spot." It was also Henson who planted the American flag at the Pole, since Peary was too weak to get up from his sledge.

Henson spent the 30 years after his polar trip working quietly as a clerk in the federal customs house in New York. Only in the final years of his life was his role officially acknowledged. In 1945, years after Peary's death, Congress voted Henson a silver medal, identical to that awarded to Peary. He was buried in a shared grave in New York, however, because his estate could not afford a separate plot.

Harvard history professor S. Allen Counter petitioned for years to have Henson's remains moved to Arlington National Cemetery. This was finally accomplished in April 1988 as Counter delivered these words at the new burial site: "A tragic wrong has been righted. Welcome home, Matthew Henson, to a new day in America. May your presence here inspire generations of explorers."

Baltimore

Benjamin Banneker Marker
Westchester Avenue at Westchester School

This marker is a tribute to Benjamin Banneker, the black mathematician, astronomer, and inventor who, in 1792, produced one of the most reliable scientific almanacs of the time. His scientific knowledge led to his assignment as a member of the surveying and planning team that helped lay out the nation's capital city.

Beulah M. Davis Collection
Soper Library, Morgan State University

Morgan State University houses an interesting collection of artifacts on Benjamin Banneker, noted astronomer, compiler of almanacs, and—together with Pierre-Charles L'Enfant—surveyor of Washington, D.C. It also houses a number of artifacts on abolitionist writer and speaker Frederick Douglass and explorer Matthew Henson.

Frederick Douglass Monument
Morgan State University

On the campus of Morgan State University is the Frederick Douglass memorial statue, created by the noted black sculptor James Lewis. The work, completed in 1956, stands 12 feet high. Its simple inscription reads "Frederick Douglass 1817-1895 Humanitarian, Statesman."

Rockville

Uncle Tom's Cabin

This is the site of the log cabin believed to have been the birthplace of Josiah Henson, the escaped slave immortalized as Uncle Tom in Harriet Beecher Stowe's famous abolitionist novel.

Born in 1789, Henson was sold at auction at an early age and transferred among many masters until he managed to escape in 1830. After setting up a community for fugitive slaves in Dawn, Canada, Henson frequently returned to the South to liberate others. Meeting with Stowe, Henson outlined his slave experiences, which later formed the basis for her celebrated story. In the introduction to Henson's autobiography, published some years later, Stowe acknowledged his story as the source of her own tale.

Massachusetts

Boston

Abiel Smith School and Museum of Afro-American History
46 Joy Street

Boston's Beacon Hill district contains the nation's largest collection of historical sites associated with the pre-Civil War black community. Massachusetts outlawed slavery in 1783, and newly freed blacks flocked to Boston, choosing to settle in this area of the city. Many of the sites have been stitched together to form the African American National Historic Site [see below].

The focus of the area was the corner of Joy Street and Smith Court. This is where the city's first school for black children was built in 1834, a building which now houses the Museum of Afro-American History. The school was named for Abiel Smith, a white merchant whose **bequest** to the city went specifically for the education of black children.

African American National Historic Site

This Beacon Hill area contains the African Meeting House, the Abiel Smith School [see above], and a number of other sites. The Black Heritage Trail is a walking tour through the district that includes 14 locations related to black history.

African Meeting House
8 Smith Court

This is the site of the first black church in Boston and the oldest surviving black church building in the United States. Built in 1806 and constructed by blacks, it was a center of political activity in the years before the Civil War. It was known as the Black Faneuil Hall, because the meetings held here corresponded in importance to those in Boston that preceded the American Revolution. Most of the leaders of the abolitionist movement, black and white, spoke from its pulpit. The Meeting House was designated a National Historic Site on May 30, 1974.

Bunker Hill Monument

Standing in the Charlestown district of Boston, the Bunker Hill Monument commemorates the famous Revolutionary War

PLACES

Plaque honoring Colonel Robert Gould Shaw and the 54th Massachusetts

battle of June 17, 1775 (which, contrary to popular belief, was actually fought on Breed's Hill). A number of blacks fought alongside the colonists during the battle, including Peter Salem, Salem Poor, Titus Coburn, Cato Howe, Alexander Ames, Seymour Burr, Pomp Fiske, and Prince Hall, founder of the Negro Masonic order.

Colonel Robert Gould Shaw Monument
Beacon and Park Streets

Fashioned by the famed sculptor Augustus Saint-Gaudens, the Shaw monument depicts Colonel Robert Gould Shaw and the 54th Massachusetts Volunteers, a black regiment that served in the Union Army during the Civil War. The regiment particularly distinguished itself in the battle for Fort Wagner, during which Shaw was killed. Sergeant William H. Carney's brave exploits during this battle later earned him the Medal of Honor.

Crispus Attucks Monument

The Crispus Attucks Monument, located in the Boston Common, was dedicated in 1888 to the five victims of the Boston Massacre—Crispus Attucks, Samuel Maverick, James Caldwell, Samuel Gray, and Patrick Carr. The site of the Massacre is marked by a plaque on State Street, near the Old State House.

Attucks is believed by many historians to have been the same man who was posted in 1750 as a runaway black slave from Framingham, Massachusetts. Although a stranger to Boston, he led a group that converged on a British garrison quartered in King Street.

One of the soldiers of the garrison panicked and fired, and Attucks was the first to fall. Gray and Caldwell were also killed on the same spot. Maverick and Carr died later of wounds sustained during the clash. The British soldiers were later tried for murder

Crispus Attucks Monument

140

and acquitted. The five men are buried a few blocks away in Granary Burying Ground, together with such famous Revolutionary figures as John Adams and John Hancock, as well as Governor William Bradford of Plymouth Colony.

William C. Nell House
3 Smith Court

From the 1830s to the end of the Civil War, William C. Nell was one of the leading black abolitionists. Born in Boston, Nell aspired to a career in law but refused to take an oath to be admitted to the bar because he did not want to support the Constitution of the United States, which compromised his position on the issue of slavery. He then began organizing meetings and lecturing in support of the antislavery movement. The Nell house was designated a National Historic Landmark on May 11, 1976.

Cambridge

Maria Baldwin House
196 Prospect and H Street

This house was the permanent address of Maria Baldwin from 1892 until her death in 1922. Baldwin served as principal and later as "master" of the Agassiz School in Cambridge, as a leader in organizations such as the League for Community Service, as a gifted and popular speaker on the lecture circuit, and as a sponsor of such charitable activities as establishing the first kindergarten in Atlanta, Georgia.

Baldwin's accomplishments served as a shining example of what blacks could accomplish in a largely white society. The house was designated as a National Historic Landmark on May 11, 1976.

Phillis Wheatley Folio
Harvard University

During her celebrated trip to England in 1773, Phillis Wheatley was presented with a folio edition of poet John Milton's *Paradise Lost*. This valuable edition is now housed in the library of Harvard University.

Wheatley, who came to America from west Africa in 1761 as a child, made rapid strides in mastering the English language. By the time she was fourteen she had already completed her first poem. Always in delicate health, Wheatley died in Boston on December 5, 1784.

Central Village

Paul Cuffe Memorial

Paul Cuffe, son of a freedman, was born in 1759 and became a wealthy merchant seaman. Cuffe resolved to use his money and power to campaign for civil rights for blacks. On one occasion, he refused to pay his personal property tax on the grounds that he was being denied full citizenship rights. A court of law agreed with him and he was granted the same privileges and protections enjoyed by white citizens of the state.

In 1815 Cuffe transported 38 blacks to Sierra Leone, Africa. This was the first attempt in what Cuffe hoped would be a continuing effort to return African Americans to their homeland. However, with the growth of abolitionism, this effort never became successful.

Great Barrington

W. E. B. Du Bois Homesite
Route 23

This location served as the boyhood home of William Edward Burghardt Du

141

Bois from 1868 to 1873. Du Bois, the prominent black sociologist and writer, was a major figure in the civil rights movement during the first half of the twentieth century. Du Bois fought discrimination against blacks through his writing, as a college professor, and as a lecturer. The Du Bois homesite was designated on May 11, 1976, as a National Historic Landmark.

Lynn

Jan Ernst Matzeliger Statue

The Matzeliger Statue is one of few memorials to this black inventor, whose shoe-last machine revolutionized the shoemaking industry and helped establish mass-produced shoes in the United States.

A native of Dutch Guiana, Matzeliger came to the United States in 1876, learned the cobbler's (shoemaker's) trade, and set out to design a machine that would simplify shoe manufacturing. Always sickly, he died at an early age, unable to capitalize on his successful patent, which was purchased by the United Shoe Machinery Company of Boston. After his death, Matzeliger was awarded a gold medal at the 1901 Pan-American Exposition.

New Bedford

New Bedford Whaling Museum

The museum maintains a treasury of whaling artifacts and information, including the names and histories of blacks who participated in the whaling industry. The museum also houses versions of the toggle harpoon—invented by Lewis Temple, a black metalsmith—which revolutionized the whaling industry.

Suffolk County

William Monroe Trotter House

97 Sawyer Avenue

This house served as the home of William Monroe Trotter, a noted black journalist and civil rights activist. Trotter, the first black member of Phi Beta Kappa, worked as an insurance and mortgage broker in Boston from 1897 to 1906. In 1901 he became publisher and editor of *The Guardian,* a crusading newspaper, until his death in 1934. The Sawyer Avenue house was designated a National Historical Landmark on May 11, 1976.

Westport

Paul Cuffe Farm and Memorial

1504 Drift Road

Paul Cuffe was a self-educated black man who became a prosperous merchant. He was a pioneer in the struggle for minority rights in the eighteenth and early nineteenth centuries and was active in the movement for black resettlement in Africa. The Paul Cuffe Farm was designated a National Historic Landmark on May 30, 1974.

New Hampshire

Jaffrey

Amos Fortune Grave Site

This grave site marks the resting place of African slave Amos Fortune. In 1770, at the age of 60, Fortune purchased his freedom. Nine years later Fortune was able to buy freedom for his wife, Violet Baldwin, and his adopted daughter, Celyndia.

In 1781 he moved to Jaffrey and set himself up as a tanner (someone who tans hides), employing both black and white apprentices. He soon became one of the leading citizens of his newly adopted hometown. In 1795, six years before his death, Fortune founded the Jaffrey Social Library. In his will he directed that money be left to the church and to the local school district.

The school fund begun by Fortune is still in existence. Proceeds from the fund are used to provide annual prizes for high-school speech and debating contests.

The Fortune house and barn still stand intact, and both Fortune and his wife lie in the meeting house burial ground. Fortune's freedom papers and several receipt slips for the sale of his leather are on file at the Jaffrey Public Library, located at 111 Main Street.

New Jersey

Lawnside

Site of Free Haven

Located just east of the city of Camden, New Jersey, is the town of Lawnside, originally known as Free Haven. The town was established by Quakers, and black presence in the area has been traced back to 1792. What is now the Mount Pisgah African Methodist Episcopal Church served as a primary Underground Railroad stop. William G. Still, a black journalist whose carefully kept records offer an eyewitness account of the era, based himself here. After the Civil War the community was favored by former slaves. When the railroad arrived in the 1880s, the name was changed to Lawnside.

Red Bank

T. Thomas Fortune House
94 West Bergen Pl.

From 1901 to 1915, this location was the home of black journalist T. Thomas Fortune. Born a slave in Marianna, Florida, Fortune was freed by the Emancipation Proclamation. He received training as a printer and founded the *New York Age* newspaper. The Fortune House was designated a National Historic Landmark on December 8, 1976.

New York

Albany

Emancipation Proclamation
New York State Library

The New York State Library houses President Abraham Lincoln's original draft of the Emancipation Proclamation, which was issued in September 1862. The draft was purchased by Gerritt Smith, a wealthy abolitionist and **patron** of the famed revolutionary John Brown. The January 1, 1863, version of the proclamation resides in the National Archives at Washington, D.C.

Auburn

Harriet Tubman House
180 South Street

Born a slave in Maryland, Harriet Tubman escaped from slavery at the age of 25, only to return to the South at least 19 times to lead more than 300 others to freedom. Rewards of up to $40,000 were offered for her capture, but she was never arrested, nor did she ever lose one of her "passengers" in transit.

During the Civil War, Tubman served as a spy for Union forces. At the close of the war, she settled in this house—years after it had outlived its original function as a major

PLACES

Abyssinian Baptist Church

way station on the northbound freedom route of fugitive slaves. In 1953 the house was restored at a cost of $21,000.

Greenburgh

Villa Lewaro

Designed by the noted black architect Vertner Woodson Tandy for Madame C. J. Walker, a successful cosmetics manufacturer, Villa Lewaro illustrates the achievements of blacks in both architecture and business. The Villa Lewaro was declared a National Historic Landmark on May 11, 1976.

Lake Placid

John Brown House and Grave Site

Just six miles south of Lake Placid on Route 86A is the farm John Brown purchased after he had left Ohio. The farm was part of 100,000 acres set aside for both freedmen and slaves by Gerritt Smith, a wealthy abolitionist. Smith hoped to build an independent community of former slaves who had learned farming and other trades. Brown joined Smith in the venture, but the idea failed to take hold and was eventually abandoned.

New York City

HARLEM AND UPPER MANHATTAN

The most famous black community in the world, Harlem is in itself an attraction. It stretches across the upper portion of Manhattan Island, from 90th Street to 178th Street and from the Hudson to the East and Harlem Rivers. It has been the home of some of the greatest American artists, politicians, entertainers, clergymen, and writers of the twentieth century.

In the 1920s the creative energies of the Harlem Renaissance sent a thrill through America's black community. It became a beacon for talented young African Americans. As the poet Langston Hughes, who came here at that time, said: "I stood there, dropped my bags, took a deep breath, and felt happy again."

Once a flourishing black middle-class community, Harlem has never really recovered from an economic decline that began in the 1950s. However, during the civil rights era the community was again the center of black intellectual activity, with such notable African Americans as Malcolm X, James Baldwin, and Imamu Amiri Baraka congregating there.

Abyssinian Baptist Church
132 West 138th Street

The Abyssinian Baptist Church is one of the oldest and largest black Baptist congregations in the United States. The church building was completed in 1923 under the leadership of the Adam Clayton Powell, Sr. In 1937 Powell retired and was succeeded by his son Adam Clayton Powell, Jr., who was elected to the United States Congress in 1960.

Amsterdam News
2293 Seventh Avenue

The *Amsterdam News* was founded on December 4, 1909, in the home of James H. Anderson on 132 West 65th Street. Then one of only fifty black "news sheets" in the country, the *Amsterdam News* consisted of six printed pages and sold for two cents a copy. The paper was later printed at several Harlem addresses. This building was designated a National Historic landmark on May 11, 1976.

The *Amsterdam News* is currently located at 2340 Frederick Douglass Boulevard.

Apollo Theater
West 125th Street and Adam Clayton Powell, Jr., Boulevard

When the color line kept blacks out of most American theaters and hotels, Harlem established two landmarks of its own. The Apollo became the summit of the black show business circuit. From the 1920s to the 1960s, stars were not really stars until they had played the Apollo. Eventually, the changing economics of show business closed the historic theater. However, in 1989 the Apollo reopened after a multimillion-dollar renovation and is once again showcasing the biggest names in black show business.

Freedom National Bank
275 West 125th Street

Freedom National Bank, Harlem's first black-chartered and black-run commercial

Harlem's legendary Apollo Theater

bank, was founded in 1965. Baseball great Jackie Robinson was a former chairman of the board of Freedom National.

Hotel Theresa
2090 Seventh Avenue at 125th Street

Built in 1913, the Hotel Theresa was once a luxury hotel that served white guests from lower Manhattan and accommodated "white only" dinner patrons in its Skyline Room. In 1936 a corporation headed by Love B. Woods tried to take over the hotel to transform it into a black business establishment to complement the Apollo Theater next door. This move failed when Seidenberg Estates, the realtor, set a price beyond the group's reach. Woods, however, was eventually able to purchase the hotel. Renamed Theresa Towers, the building now serves as an office center.

Schomburg Center for Research in Black Culture
515 Malcolm X Boulevard

The most complete research facility in the world for studies of black life and culture, this branch of the New York Public Library system began as a private collection. Arthur A. Schomburg was a Puerto Rican of African descent. A historian and book lover, Schomburg began to assemble rare material on the African **diaspora** early in this century.

In 1926 the Carnegie Foundation purchased the collection and presented it to the library, which built a special branch for it in Harlem. The material furnished a spark for the Harlem Renaissance, with the new perspectives it cast on the black experience inspiring writers and scholars.

The original collection contained 5,000 volumes, 3,000 manuscripts, and 2,000 etchings. It has now grown to more than 5,000,000 items and contains information on every important grouping of blacks in the world.

Sugar Hill

Sugar Hill is a handsome residential section in uptown Harlem. It is bordered on the west by Amsterdam Avenue, on the north by 160th Street, on the east by Colonial Park, and on the South by 145th Street. An area of tall apartment buildings and private homes, it is peopled largely by middle-class African Americans, sometimes referred to as the black **bourgeoisie.** The only other comparable areas of central Harlem are Riverton and Lenox Terrace.

LOWER MANHATTAN, QUEENS, AND BROOKLYN

Claude McKay Residence
180 West 135th Street

From 1941 to 1946 this residence was the home of Jamaican-born black poet and writer Claude McKay, who has often been called the father of the Harlem Renaissance. His residence was named a National Historic Landmark on December 8, 1976.

Edward Kennedy "Duke" Ellington Residence
935 St. Nicholas Avenue, Apt. 4A

When Duke Ellington recorded "Take the A Train" (to Harlem), he meant just that: the A train express, which stopped on St. Nicholas Avenue, was the quickest and fastest way for Ellington to get home. This St. Nicholas Avenue address was the long-term residence of Ellington, who was one of the most creative black composers of the twentieth century. The residence was designated a National Historic Landmark on May 11, 1976.

Fraunces Tavern
Broad and Pearl Streets

One of the most famous landmarks in New York City, Fraunces Tavern was bought in 1762 from a wealthy Huguenot by Samuel Fraunces, a West Indian of black and French extraction. Known as the Queen's Head Tavern, it served as a meeting place for numerous patriots.

Fraunces Tavern

On April 24, 1774, the Sons of Liberty and the Vigilance Committee met at the tavern to map out much of the strategy later used during the war. George Washington himself frequented the tavern, as did many of his senior officers. Washington's association with Fraunces continued for a number of years, and the tavern owner eventually came to be known as Washington's "Steward of the Household" in New York City. It was at Fraunces Tavern, in fact, that Washington took leave of his trusted officers in 1783 before retiring to Mount Vernon.

Much of the tavern's original furnishings and decor are still intact. The third floor, now a museum, contains several Revolutionary War artifacts. A restaurant is maintained on the ground floor.

James Weldon Johnson Residence
187 West 135th Street

From 1925 to 1938 this residence was the home of James Weldon Johnson, a composer, poet, and writer who was also general secretary of the National Association for the Advancement of Colored People (NAACP) and a leading civil rights activist. Johnson is best known for the song "Lift Every Voice and Sing," which has been called the black national anthem. The residence was named a National Historic Landmark on May 11, 1976.

John Roosevelt "Jackie" Robinson House
5224 Tilden Street, Brooklyn

This house served as the home of Jackie Robinson, the baseball player who in 1947 became the first black to play in the major leagues. His baseball contract broke the color barrier that prevented blacks from participating in professional sports. While a Brooklyn Dodger, Robinson lived for many years in the New York City borough where he played baseball. The residence was designated a National Historic Landmark on May 11, 1976.

Louis Armstrong House
3456 107th Street, Corona, Queens

For years this was the home of Louis Armstrong, the famous jazz musician whose talents entertained millions throughout the world. Whenever Armstrong was at his Corona home on a break from his concert dates, he was a favorite with neighborhood youngsters. He often entertained them in his home and on the street. The house was designated a National Historical Landmark on May 11, 1976.

Maiden Lane and William Street

In 1712, on Maiden Lane and William Street, the first organized slave revolt in New York City occurred. Approximately 30 slaves joined and attempted to fight their way to freedom. Many people were injured in the revolt before the slaves escaped to the woods with the militia close behind. Surrounded in the woods, several slaves committed suicide. The rest were captured and consequently executed.

Malcolm X Residence
23-11 97th Street, East Elmhurst, Queens

Black Muslim leader Malcolm X lived at this location with his family from 1954 until his death in 1965. The house, which was owned by the Nation of Islam while he and his family lived there, was the scene of a fire-bombing on February 13, 1965. Fortunately, Malcolm and his family escaped without injury.

Matthew Henson Residence
Dunbar Apartments, 246 West 150th Street

This residence was the home of Matthew Henson, the black explorer who was an assistant to Robert E. Peary. Henson's best known achievement came in 1909, when he became the first man to reach the North Pole. The residence was designated a National Historic Landmark on May 15, 1975.

Paul Robeson Residence
555 Edgecomb Avenue

Paul Robeson was a famous black actor and singer. Unfortunately, in the 1940s and 1950s, while he was widely acclaimed for his artistic talents, Robeson suffered public disapproval for his socialist politic stance. His residence was named a National Historic Landmark on December 8, 1976.

PLACES

Ralph Bunche House
115125 Grosvenor Road, Kew Gardens, Queens

This house served as the home of Ralph Bunche, the distinguished black diplomat and undersecretary to the United Nations. In 1950 Bunche was awarded the Nobel Peace Prize for his contribution to peace in the Middle East. The house was designated a National Historic Landmark on May 11, 1976.

Roy Wilkins House
147-15 Village Road, Jamaica, Queens

This location served as the home of civil rights leader and former National Association for the Advancement of Colored People (NAACP) executive secretary Roy Wilkins from 1952 until his death in 1981. Wilkins had served as executive secretary of the NAACP for 22 years before retiring in 1977.

St. George's Episcopal Church
Third Avenue and First Street

This was the church home of Harry Thacker Burleigh, the featured baritone soloist at St. George's for 53 years. Burleigh, more than any other individual, is credited with popularizing the black spiritual and adapting the music to the concert stage. He also composed more than 300 songs, the most notable being "Deep River." The church was designated a National Historical Landmark on December 8, 1976.

Will Marion Cook Residence
221 West 138th Street

This residence served as the home of the early twentieth-century black composer Will Marion Cook, whom Duke Ellington called "the master of all masters of our people." Cook was born in Washington, D.C. He began learning violin at 13, and at 15 he won a scholarship to study with Joseph Joachim at the Berlin Conservatory. Cook's operetta *Clorinda* introduced syncopated ragtime music to theatergoers in New York City. The residence was designated a National Historic Landmark on May 11, 1976.

Rochester

Frederick Douglass Monument
Central Avenue and Paul Street

In 1899 then New York governor Theodore Roosevelt dedicated the Frederick Douglass Monument. While a resident of Rochester, Douglass edited his famous newspaper, *The North Star*. Douglass died in 1895 in Washington, D.C, where he had lived for the last 13 years of his life. However, he was buried in Rochester's Mount Hope Cemetery, not far from the memorial.

South Granville

Lemuel Haynes House
Route 149

This house, located in Washington County, was built in 1793. It served as the home of Lemuel Haynes, the first black ordained minister in the United States. Haynes was also the first black to minister to a white congregation. The South Granville home site was declared a National Historic Landmark on May 15, 1975.

Pennsylvania

Erie

Harry T. Burleigh Birthplace
Harry T. Burleigh was a friend of famed Czech composer Antonin Dvorak and a

149

composer/arranger in his own right. Born in 1866, Burleigh set to music many of the stirring poems of Walt Whitman and arranged such unforgettable spirituals as "Deep River." He died in 1949.

Lancaster

Thaddeus Stevens Grave Site
Schreiner's Cemetery
Chestnut and Mulberry Street

Senator Thaddeus Stevens of Pennsylvania, a white abolitionist and civil rights activist, was one of the chief drafters of the Fourteenth Amendment to the Constitution. Upon his death in 1868, his body was escorted by five black and three white pallbearers to Washington, D.C., to lay in state—guarded by black soldiers of the 54th Massachusetts Regiment—on the same **catafalque** that had borne the body of Abraham Lincoln.

Stevens's body was then returned to Lancaster, where more than 10,000 blacks attended the funeral. Stevens, whose will rejected burial in a white cemetery because of segregationist policy, was buried in Schreiner's Cemetery, a cemetery for blacks.

LOWER MERION TOWNSHIP (MONTGOMERY TOWNSHIP)

James A. Bland Grave Site
Merion Cemetery

James A. Bland was a black composer who wrote "Carry Me Back to Old Virginny," now the state song of Virginia. Bland was one of the most popular black minstrels of the nineteenth century.

Philadelphia

Afro-American Historical and Cultural Museum
Seventh and Arch Streets

This museum contains art, artifacts, and sculpture as well as materials covering the slave trade, the Civil War and Reconstruction, black churches, and the civil rights movement.

Frances Ellen Watkins Harper House
1006 Bainbridge Street

This was the home of the black writer and social activist Frances Ellen Watkins Harper, who participated in the nineteenth-century abolition, **women's suffrage,** and temperance movements. The house was named a National Historical Landmark on December 8, 1976.

Henry O. Tanner House
2903 West Diamond Street

Born in Pittsburgh in 1859, Henry Ossawa Tanner was the first black to be elected to the National Academy of Design. The Diamond Street residence was the artist's boyhood home. The house was designated a historical landmark on May 11, 1976.

Mother Bethel African Methodist Episcopal Church
419 South Sixth Street

The current building, built in 1859, is the fourth church to be erected on the site where Richard Allen and Absalom Jones founded the Free African Society in 1787. This organization later grew into the African Methodist Episcopal Church, one of the largest black religious denominations in the United States.

Allen, the first black bishop, was born a slave and became a minister after winning his freedom. In 1814 he and James Forten organized a force of 2,500 free blacks to defend Philadelphia against the British. Sixteen years later, Allen organized the first black convention in Philadelphia and was instrumental in getting the group to adopt a solid platform denouncing slavery and encouraging abolitionist activities. Allen died in 1831 and was buried in the church crypt.

Forten had been born free in 1766, and despite his youth, served aboard a Philadelphia privateer (an armed private ship) during the Revolutionary War. In 1800 he was one of the signers of a petition requesting Congress to alter the Fugitive Slave Act of 1793. Opposed to the idea of resettling slaves in Africa, Forten chaired an 1817 meeting held at Bethel to protest existing colonization schemes. In 1833 he put up the funds that William Lloyd Garrison needed to found *The Liberator*. After his death, Forten's successors continued his work, remaining active in the abolitionist cause throughout the Civil War and fighting for black rights during Reconstruction. The Forten home served as a meeting place for many of the leading figures in the movement. The church was named a National Historic Landmark on May 30, 1974.

Negro Soldiers Monument
West Fairmount Park, Lansdowne Drive

The state of Pennsylvania erected the Negro Soldiers Monument in 1934 to pay tribute to its fallen black soldiers.

Rhode Island

Portsmouth

Black Regiment Memorial of the Battle of Rhode Island
RI 114

Unlike many subsequent wars in which the United States engaged, in the American Revolution black soldiers were integrated into regular army units. One notable exception was the First Rhode Island Regiment, organized by General Nathanael Greene into a separate fighting force.

In Rhode Island, the General Assembly approved freeing any slave who enlisted in the Continental Army. There were 200 such freedmen in Greene's force, which ferried across the Sakonnet River to move upon British troops at Newport. But the colonials were not supported by the French fleet and found themselves trapped on the peninsula. Greene's black soldiers were called on to hold the line against the British assault, while the main force freed itself. Beating off three charges against their position, the unit enabled Greene to organize an orderly retreat and saved the regiment from destruction. Fought on August 29, 1778, this was the only Revolutionary War battle fought on Rhode Island soil.

Providence

Rhode Island Black Heritage Society
1 Hilton Street

A museum and cultural center, the society holds periodic displays on local history and also sponsors discovery tours of black roots in Rhode Island.

PLACES

Vermont

Bennington

Garrison Marker and Bennington Museum
West Main Street

William Lloyd Garrison had a talent for clear and pointed writing. For more than 30 years, his antislavery publication *The Liberator* poured forth an unending stream of criticism of the Constitution (which it labeled "a covenant with hell"), slaveowners, those who opposed abolition, and any other target Garrison got in his sights. "I will be as harsh as truth, and as uncompromising as justice. I will not equivocate—I will not excuse—I will not retreat a single inch—AND I WILL BE HEARD," he wrote in his first issue. Dragged through the streets by a mob, he saw his presses smashed and his allies desert him. Still, Garrison functioned as the steadfast conscience of the nation.

The *Liberator* was published in Boston, but Garrison's career began here when he published *The Journal of the Times* in an office near Bennington Common.

The museum features copies of Garrison's publications as well as a portrait of black minister Lemuel Haynes preaching in the nearby First Congregational Church.

Windsor

Constitution House
U.S. 5

In the summer of 1777, as British troops overran their borders on the way to crushing defeat at Saratoga, a group of flinty Vermonters gathered in this town on the Connecticut River to put together an extraordinary document. The constitution of the Republic of Vermont was the first in North America to ban slavery and to grant universal suffrage without requiring voters to own property.

SOUTH CENTRAL STATES

Alabama

Florence

William Christopher Handy Birthplace

W. C. Handy, composer of "St. Louis Blues," was born in 1873. The cabin in which he was born was moved from its original site to its current location. The restored cabin contains his piano, trumpet, and other mementoes.

Montgomery

Civil Rights Memorial
Washington Street

Inscribed with the names of 40 civil rights martyrs and these words of Martin Luther King, Jr., "Until justice rolls down like waters and righteousness like a mighty stream," this memorial was commissioned by the Southern Poverty Law Center and dedicated in 1989.

Dexter Avenue Baptist Church
454 Dexter Avenue

The Dexter Avenue Baptist Church was where Martin Luther King, Jr., organized the 1955 boycott of Montgomery's segregated bus system. It was this boycott that brought King into national prominence as a civil rights leader.

King pastored the church from 1954 to 1959. In the church is housed a mural depicting scenes of the civil rights movement as well as a library containing personal mementoes of King and his family. The church, which has been in existence since 1878, was declared a National Historic Landmark in 1974.

Selma

Edmund Pettis Bridge

On Sunday, March 7, 1965, civil rights leaders started out from Selma on what was to be a 55-mile march to Montgomery, protesting the denial of voting rights to blacks who had attempted to register in Selma. Reaching the Edmund Pettis Bridge, the marchers were met by state troopers. Governor George Wallace had issued the orders to deploy the troopers in order to enforce his executive order forbidding such demonstrations. Many of the unarmed marchers, who were turned back by tear gas and night sticks, were injured.

On March 21 a second march started out, organized by Martin Luther King, Jr.; this march concluded five days later on the steps of the state capitol building in Montgomery.

Talladega

Talladega College and Swayne Hall

The first college for blacks in Alabama, Talladega was founded by the American Missionary Association as a primary school in 1867. The school prompted a **liberal arts** program at a time when vocational education dominated black institutions. Its Slavery Library houses three fresco panels (the celebrated Amistad Murals) by Hale

The chapel at Tuskegee Institute

Woodruff, who studied in France under the renowned Henry Ossawa Tanner.

Swayne Hall, built in 1857, is the oldest building on the campus of Talladega College. The building was constructed by slave labor before the school was established. It was declared a National Historic Landmark on December 2, 1974.

Tuskegee

Tuskegee Institute

Tuskegee Institute first opened on July 4, 1881. At the time, it consisted of a single shanty, a student body of thirty, and one teacher, Booker T. Washington. Tuskegee's sole purpose at that time was to train black teachers. It was the first school of its kind established in the United States. Eventually it came to specialize in agricultural and general labor training, areas which were to make

PLACES

both the school and Washington famous around the world.

In 1882 Washington moved the school to a 100-acre plantation and began a self-help program that enabled students to finance their education. Most of the early buildings were built with the aid of student labor.

Next to Washington, the most famous person to be associated with the institute was George Washington Carver, who became its director of agricultural research in 1896. Carver convinced many Southern farmers to raise crops such as peanuts and sweet potatoes in place of cotton, which was rapidly draining the soil of valuable nutrients. Ultimately, Carver's research programs helped develop 300 products made from peanuts and 188 from sweet potatoes. At one point, he even succeeded in making artificial marble from wood pulp.

Today, Tuskegee covers nearly 5,000 acres and has more than 150 buildings. Places to visit include the Founder's Marker, the site of Washington's original shanty; The Oaks, Washington's stately home; the Booker T. Washington Monument; the George Washington Carver Museum, which houses the scientist's plant, mineral, and bird collections and exhibits of various products he developed; and the Daniel "Chappie" James Aerospace Center, dedicated to Tuskegee graduate James, a war hero and the first black four-star general in U.S. history, and to the Tuskegee Airmen, a highly successful group of World War II black fighter pilots. Tuskegee is also home to the George Washington Carver Foundation, a research center founded by Carver in 1940.

Arkansas
Little Rock

Central High School
14th and Park Streets

Here, in the fall of 1957, the first major confrontation over implementing the Supreme Court's 1954 ruling outlawing racial segregation in public school took place. When black students arrived for classes on September 23, 1957, they were turned away by the Arkansas National Guard—Arkansas governor Orville Faubus had called out the guard to turn away any black student attempting to enter the school. President Dwight D. Eisenhower, responding to the crisis, issued an executive order on September 24 calling for the use of federal troops to enforce the Court's order to desegregate.

Philander-Smith College
812 West 13th Street

In 1877 this institution was opened as Walder College, under the sponsorship of the African Methodist Episcopal Church. After receiving a large donation that enabled the school to construct a permanent brick edifice, the college was renamed.

Kentucky
Berea

Lincoln Hall
Berea College

Berea College, which opened its doors in 1855, was the first college established in the United States for the specific purpose of educating blacks and whites together. The school's Lincoln Hall, built in 1887, was

Central High School in Little Rock

designated as a National Historic Landmark on December 2, 1974.

Louisiana

New Orleans

James H. Dillard House
571 Audubon Street

This was the home of James Dillard from 1894 to 1913. Dillard played an important role in black education in the nineteenth century, strengthening vocational and teacher-training programs. Dillard's home was designated a National Historic Landmark on December 2, 1975. Dillard University, founded in 1869, was named for this educator.

Melrose

Yucca Plantation
Route 119

The Yucca Plantation was established in the eighteenth century by a former slave and wealthy business woman. The African House located on the plantation, a unique

PLACES

structure with an umbrella–like roof, is believed to be of direct African derivation. The site was declared a National Historic Landmark on May 30, 1974.

Mississippi

Alcorn

Oakland Memorial Chapel and Alcorn State University

Alcorn State University, founded in 1871, is the oldest black land grant college in the United States. The chapel on the Alcorn University campus was built in 1838. The chapel was designated a National Historic Landmark on May 11, 1976.

Mound Bayou

Isiah Thornton Montgomery House
West Main Street

This location served as the home of Isiah Thornton Montgomery, who, in 1887, in the town of Mound Bayou, founded a place where black Americans could obtain social, political, and economic rights in a white supremacist South. The house was declared a National Historic Landmark on May 11, 1976.

Natchez

Natchez National Cemetery

This cemetery is the final resting place of many black war casualties, including landsman Wilson Brown, who was awarded a Medal of Honor during the Civil War. Brown and seaman John Lawson received their medals for courage in action while serving aboard the U.S.S. *Hartford* in its Mobile Bay engagement of August 5, 1864.

Missouri

Diamond

George Washington Carver Birthplace and National Monument
U.S. Route 71

Located in a park, Carver National Monument commemorates the place where the black scientist George Washington Carver was born and spent his early childhood.

Kidnapped when he was just six weeks old, Carver was eventually ransomed for a horse valued at $300. Raised in Missouri by the family of his owner Moses Carver, he made his way through Minnesota, Kansas, and Iowa before being "discovered" by Booker T. Washington in 1896. That same year, Carver joined the faculty of Tuskegee Institute, where he conducted most of the research for which he is now famous.

The monument, one of the first created in honor of an African American, consists of a statue of Carver as a boy and encloses several trails leading to some of the scientist's favorite places. The park also houses a visitors' center and a museum displaying many of his discoveries and personal belongings.

Jefferson City

Lincoln University

The 62nd and 65th U.S. Colored infantries raised the more than $6,000 that made up the initial **endowment** for the Lincoln Institute. Just a 22-square-foot room in which classes were to be held in 1866, the school began receiving state aid to expand its teacher-training program in 1870. It became a state institution nine years later and introduced college-level courses in 1887. It has been known as Lincoln Univer-

Houston Hall, Lincoln University

sity since 1921, and has offered graduate programs since 1940.

St. Louis

Old Courthouse
Jefferson National Expansion Memorial
11 North Fourth Street

It was in the Old Courthouse in 1847 that Dred Scott first filed suit to gain his freedom. The lawsuit was actually a test case.

When Scott's owner, John Emerson, died, Mrs. Emerson became the rightful owner. Because she was against slavery, her lawyers devised the plan of having Scott sue her in 1847 on the basis that his past residence at Fort Snelling (in the antislavery territory that was to become Minnesota) had made him a free man.

For the next ten years, the Dred Scott case was a burning political and social issue throughout America. In 1857 the case reached the Supreme Court, where Chief Justice Roger Taney handed down the decision that slaves could neither become free by escaping or by being taken into free territory, nor could they be considered American citizens. Scott himself was freed immediately after the decision was handed down. He died a year later of tuberculosis and Mrs. Emerson paid his funeral expenses.

Scott Joplin House
2658 Delmar Boulevard

Born in Texarkana, Texas, Scott Joplin was known as the "King of Ragtime." He came to St. Louis as a teenager in 1885, when ragtime music was developing in the city's black community. He later moved to Sedalia, Missouri, and studied advanced harmony and music theory at George Smith College. Joplin made his living by playing piano at the Maple Leaf Club, and in 1897 he published a rag that paid tribute to the club.

Within six months, the "Maple Leaf Rag" had sold an astonishing 75,000 copies; clearly a new music craze was sweeping the country (eventually, it would sell over one million copies). Financially successful, Joplin returned to St. Louis with his wife and bought the house on Delmar Boulevard. He lived there for three years, writing many of his most enduring songs (including "The Cascades," a salute to the 1904 World's Fair), before moving into a larger house, which has since been demolished.

The Delmar house is the Joplin's last surviving residence. It was declared a National Historic Landmark on December 8, 1976.

Tennessee

Henning

Alex Haley House
Haley Avenue at South Church Street

PLACES

Alex Haley (right) and Samba Fye at Haley's boyhood home

Alex Haley is best known for the television adaptation of his Pulitzer Prize-winning novel *Roots*. In this work as well as his other writings, Haley awakened both black and white Americans to the richness of African American history and culture. The house, built in 1918 by Haley's grandfather, served as the author's home from 1921 to 1929 and was where he heard many of the stories that inspired him to write *Roots*. Today the house serves as a museum.

Jackson
Casey Jones Railroad Museum
I-40 and U.S. 45

Casey Jones was immortalized through the song about his legendary train ride. Popularized in vaudeville and music halls, the song was written by Wallace Saunders, a black fireman who served aboard Jones's locomotive. The Railroad Museum serves as a reminder of the unsung contributions of blacks to the railroad industry in the United States.

Memphis
Beale Street Historic District
Beale Street from Main to Fourth Streets

"Blues" music was born on Beale Street when it was rip-roaring with saloons, gambling halls, and theaters. The street was immortalized by W. C. Handy, who composed "Beale Street Blues." Beale Street was designated a National Historic Landmark on May 23, 1966.

Lorraine Hotel
406 Mulberry Street

It was on the balcony of the Lorraine Hotel that Martin Luther King, Jr., was assassinated while emerging from a second-floor room. In the presence of King were his trusted advisers Ralph Abernathy and Jesse Jackson. King died in the emergency room of St. Joseph's Hospital on April 4, 1968. The Lorraine closed for business in 1988 and is now operated as the National Civil Rights Museum.

Tom Lee Memorial
Beale Street

On May 8, 1925, Tom Lee became a hero by rescuing 32 passengers of the M. E. *Norman,* an excursion boat that had capsized some 20 miles below Memphis near Cow Island. Alerted to the disaster, Lee pulled the passengers from the water onto his skiff. The Memphis Engineers Club honored Lee by providing him with money for the duration of his life. A fund was also raised to purchase Lee a home. After his death a committee raised the money to erect the 30-foot granite memorial, which was completed in 1954.

William Christopher Handy Park

The city of Memphis pays tribute to famed blues composer William Christopher Handy in the form of a park and a heroic bronze statue overlooking the very same Beale Street that he immortalized in the tune "Beale Street Blues." The statue, showing Handy poised with his horn, was created by Leone Tomassi of Italy and was dedicated in 1960, at the close of a memorial celebration of Handy.

Nashville

Fisk University, Meharry Medical School, and Jubilee Hall
17th Avenue North

Fisk University was founded following the Civil War by the American Missionary Association to provide a liberal arts education for blacks. Fisk first began operation as the Fisk Free School.

Jubilee Hall, a **Victorian Gothic** structure, is the oldest building on the Fisk University campus. The hall was named a National Historic Landmark on December 2, 1974.

James Weldon Johnson House
911 18th Avenue

Writer and civil rights leader James Weldon Johnson resided at this location from about 1930 until his death in 1938, teaching literature and writing at Fisk University. Johnson was born in 1871 in Jacksonville, Florida. Collaborating with his brother J. Rosamond Johnson, he composed the song "Lift Every Voice and Sing."

THE SOUTHEAST

Florida

Daytona Beach

Bethune-Cookman College
640 Second Avenue

One of the leading schools for black teachers in the South, Bethune-Cookman

College was founded in 1904 by Mary McLeod Bethune on "faith and a dollar-and-a-half." One of the most powerful and influential black women in the United States, Bethune served as advisor to Presidents Franklin D. Roosevelt and Harry S Truman.

In 1920 a two-story frame house was built on the campus for its founder. The Mary McLeod Bethune House was proclaimed a National Historic Landmark on December 2, 1974.

Eatonville

Zora Neale Hurston Memorial

The town that gave rise to novelist, folklorist, and anthropologist Zora Neale Hurston is in itself famous. Founded on August 18, 1887, Eatonville was the first incorporated community in the United States established by African Americans.

In January 1990, three years after the town's centennial, the Association to Preserve the Eatonville Community (P.E.C.) dedicated the Zora Neale Hurston Memorial. The dedication ceremony formed part of the first annual Zora Neale Hurston Festival of the Arts. A number of celebrities attended the festival, including Pulitzer Prize-winning author Alice Walker, who back in 1973 rediscovered Hurston's unmarked grave in Fort Pierce and placed an inscribed headstone at the site [see below].

Fort George Island

Kingsley Plantation

Zephaniah Kingsley traded heavily in slaves, and his operation was headquartered on this plantation on Fort George Island. The oldest known plantation in Florida, the Kingsley Plantation was established in 1763. Restored as a museum, it displays exhibits and furnishings that depict the plantation and island life during the period from 1763 to 1783.

Fort Pierce

Zora Neale Hurston Grave Site
Garden of Heavenly Rest

Hurston died on January 28, 1960, and was buried in an unmarked grave in the Garden of Heavenly Rest. In August 1973 writer Alice Walker, after learning of Hurston's sad fate, set out to find and mark the grave. The site was obscured by an overgrown field of weeds, but Walker succeeded in locating it. She then ordered a small gray tombstone erected there.

The town of Eatonville has since launched a campaign to retrieve Hurston's remains from Fort Pierce.

Sumatra

Fort Gadsen
FL 65

The British built Fort Gadsen as a base for recruiting Seminole Indians and runaway slaves during the War of 1812. When the war ended the British abandoned the fort, but their allies continued to use it as a refuge for slaves escaping from Georgia.

In 1816 Andrew Jackson's federal forces attacked the fort—variously known as British Fort or Fort Negro—as part of the First Seminole War. The general's instructions to his commanders were: "Blow it up. Return the Negroes to their rightful owners." Of the 334 defenders of the fort, all but 60 were killed in the fight. On May 15,

Ebenezer Baptist Church

1975, British Fort was named a National Historic Landmark.

Georgia

Andersonville

Andersonville Prison

Andersonville, the infamous Confederate prison where thousands of Union soldiers died from brutal treatment, is now a national monument. Corporal Henry Gooding of the black 54th Massachusetts regiment was imprisoned here; he died on July 19, 1864.

It was Gooding who initiated a protest regarding the pay of black soldiers, going over the heads of military brass to write to Abraham Lincoln. At that time the pay of blacks was a flat $7 per month. For whites, it ranged from $9 to $30. Encouraged by Colonel Robert Gould Shaw (whose story, along with that of the whole 54th, inspired the 1989 film *Glory*), the black soldiers of the 54th refused to accept any wages unless they were equal to those of their white comrades. Although Gooding won the battle for equal pay for his fellow soldiers, he died at Andersonville having never received a salary himself.

Atlanta

Clark Atlanta University

Founded in 1865, Atlanta University held its first classes for freed slaves in abandoned railway cars. Clark College was founded four years later. The two schools were merged in 1988 and today the campus of the Clark Atlanta University System is one of the most beautiful anywhere, housing not only Clark Atlanta University, but also Morris Brown, Morehouse, and Spelman Colleges.

Stone Hall, built in 1882, is the oldest building in the complex. It was named a National Historic Landmark on December 2, 1974.

Ebenezer Baptist Church

407 Auburn Avenue

Built in 1922, Ebenezer Baptist Church had, from 1960 to 1968, Martin Luther King, Jr., as its associate pastor. King's call for nonviolent protest spread across the nation from this church through the Southern Christian Leadership Conference (SCLC), over which he presided.

PLACES

The birthplace of Martin Luther King, Jr.

When King was assassinated on April 4, 1968, funeral services were held in this church. As millions watched on television, mourners lined up for miles behind the mule-drawn wagon that carried King from Ebenezer to Morehouse College, his **alma mater.** There memorable eulogies were delivered and more than 150,000 paid their last respects.

Martin Luther King, Jr., National Historic Site
Auburn Avenue

This historic district, which consists of several blocks of Atlanta's Auburn Avenue and Boulevard, includes Martin Luther King, Jr.'s birthplace and grave site and the Ebenezer Baptist Church [see above], where King served as assistant pastor. His childhood neighborhood is still largely unchanged. Private efforts to create a living monument to King and his beliefs have been carried on primarily through the Martin Luther King, Jr., Center for Non-Violent Social Change, Inc. The district was designated a National Historic Landmark on May 5, 1977.

South View Cemetery

South View cemetery was founded in 1886 by blacks who rejected a policy requiring that they be buried in the rear of the municipal cemetery. King was laid to rest in South View Cemetery, where a marble crypt was inscribed with a personal version of the words he used to conclude his famous "I Have a Dream" speech: "Free at last, free at last, thank God Almighty I'm free at last."

Sweet Auburn Historic District
Auburn Avenue

Although only a small portion of its original one-mile expanse has survived, the Sweet Auburn district was once known as a thriving center of black business in the post-Civil War period. Restricted by the forces of segregation, many wealthy blacks settled in the area. Auburn Avenue was once known as the "richest Negro street in the world." The district was designated a National Historic Landmark on December 8, 1976.

Columbus

Bragg Smith Grave Site and Memorial
Columbus Colored Cemetery
Fourth Street and Seventh Avenue

This memorial, located in the Columbus Colored Cemetery, was built in memory of Bragg Smith, who was killed while attempting to rescue a city engineer trapped in a cave-in. The marble memorial is believed to be the first civic memorial in the country to have been dedicated to an African American.

Savannah

Reverend George Lisle Memorial
First Bryan Baptist Church
559 West Bryan Street

Inside the First Bryan Baptist Church is a memorial dedicated to the George Lisle, the first black Baptist missionary. Following Lisle's death, his work was continued by his assistant, Andrew Bryan, after whom the church is named.

North Carolina

Durham

North Carolina Mutual Life Insurance Company
114–116 West Parish Street

This Parish Street address is the home office of North Carolina Mutual Life Insurance Company, a black-managed business founded in 1898 that achieved financial success in an age of **Jim Crowism.** The site was declared a National Historical Landmark on May 15, 1975.

Milton

The Yellow Tavern

For more than 30 years, the Yellow Tavern (also known as Union Tavern) was the workshop of Tom Day, one of the great black artisans and furniture-makers of the Deep South prior to the Civil War.

Day began making mahogany furniture in 1818 and within five years accumulated enough money to convert the old Yellow Tavern into a miniature factory. He also became known as an expert teacher of his trade and took on both white and black apprentices.

The citizens of Milton so revered Day for his artistry that they went to great pains to secure a special pardon from a North Carolina law that prohibited free blacks and mulattoes from migrating to the state. The Yellow Tavern was declared a National Historic Landmark on May 15, 1975. Examples of Day's furniture can be seen in the North Carolina State Museum.

Raleigh

John Chavis Memorial Park
East Lenoir and Worth Streets

This park is named after John Chavis, a black educator and preacher who founded an interracial school in Raleigh that produced a number of important public figures. However, as a result of the failed Nat Turner slave rebellion of 1831, blacks were barred from preaching in North Carolina. Thus Chavis was forced to retire from the pulpit. He died in 1838.

South Carolina

Beaufort

Robert Smalls House
511 Prince Street

A former slave, Robert Smalls served in both the state legislature and the United States Congress. While in office, he worked especially to ensure the rights of black Americans. He had lived in Beaufort both as a slave and as a free man. The Smalls house was designated a National Historic Landmark on May 30, 1973.

Charleston

Dubose Hayward House
76 Church Street

Dubose Hayward, the author of *Porgy,* the book upon which George Gershwin's opera *Porgy and Bess* was based, lived here from 1919 to 1924. The house was designated a National Historic Landmark on November 11, 1971.

Denmark Vesey House
56 Bull Street

This was the residence of Denmark Vesey, the Charleston carpenter whose plans to organize a slave insurrection were discovered in 1822. The Denmark Vesey House was declared a National Historic Landmark on May 11, 1976.

Columbia

Chapelle Administration Building
1530 Harden Street

This building is one of the finest works of John Anderson Lankfor, a pioneer black architect. The building was named a National Historical Landmark on December 8, 1976.

Frogmore

Penn School Historic District
Lands End Road

When the South Carolina Sea Islands were taken by the Union in 1862, two Quakers from Philadelphia arrived in a matter of weeks to establish the first schools for blacks. Laura Towne and Ellen Murray would stay on to run the Penn Normal Institute on St. Helena Island for 40 years. The women pioneered efforts to provide health care and training in agriculture and home economics for the island inhabitants.

The school sponsored the first farming co-op in the state, and at its peak had workshops for tanning, basketry, carpentry, and shoe-repairing. On December 2, 1974, the district was named a National Historic Landmark.

Georgetown

Joseph H. Rainey House
909 Prince Street

A former slave, Joseph Hayne Rainey was the first black to serve in the United States House of Representatives. His election in 1870, along with that of Hiram R. Revels (the first black to be elected to the U.S. Senate), marked the beginning of black participation in the federal government. The house was designated a National Historic Landmark on April 20, 1984.

Rantowles

Stono River Slave Rebellion Historic Site

This was the site of a 1739 slave insurrection, during which some 100 slaves escaped. Stono River was named a National Historic Landmark on July 4, 1974.

Virginia

Alexandria

Franklin and Armfield Office
1315 Duke Street

From 1828 to 1836 Franklin and Armfield was the South's largest slave-trading firm (during the company's operation, Alexandria was part of the District of Columbia). The building was designated a National Historic Landmark on June 2, 1978.

Arlington

Benjamin Banneker Boundary Stone
18th and Van Buren Streets

Benjamin Banneker helped survey the city of Washington, D.C., and was perhaps the most well-known black man in colonial America. Banneker, a mathematician and scientist, was born in Ellicott Mills, Maryland. The boundary stone was declared a National Historic Landmark on May 11, 1976.

Charles Richard Drew House
2505 First Street South

This house was the home of Charles Richard Drew from 1920 to 1939. Drew, a noted black physician and teacher, is best remembered for his discovery of how to preserve blood plasma. The house was named a National Historic Landmark on May 11, 1976.

Capahosic

Holley Knoll (Robert R. Moton) House
From 1935 to 1959 this house served as the retirement home of Robert R. Moton. Moton, who succeeded Booker T. Washington as head of Tuskegee Institute [see Tuskegee, Alabama] in 1915, guided the school's growth until 1930. An influential educator, he was active in many African American causes.

Chatham

Pittsylvania County Courthouse
U.S. Business Route 29

Hampton University

The Pittsylvania County Courthouse was closely associated with the 1878 court case *Ex parte Virginia*. Dealing with black jury participation, the case stemmed from a state official's attempt to deny citizens the equal protection of the law guaranteed by the Fourteenth Amendment. The courthouse was designated a National Historic Landmark on May 4, 1987.

Hampton

Hampton University
Founded in 1868 as Hampton Institute, this was one of the first colleges for blacks in the United States. Booker T. Washington attended Hampton Institute before he went to Tuskegee Institute. Washington also taught for a time at Hampton.

PLACES

Jamestown

Jamestown Settlement
Colonial Parkway

The first English colonists to settle permanently in North America landed here in 1607. Twelve years later the first boatload of black servants followed. Two of these servants, Anthony and Isabella, were married and in 1625 became the parents of William, the first black child born in the colonies.

An exhibit that opened in 1990 in Jamestown Gallery stresses the role of blacks during the first century of Virginia's existence. Nearby Colonial National Historical Park shows the archaeological work done on the site and the outline of the original settlement.

Norfolk

Black Civil War Veterans' Memorial
Elmwood Cemetery
Princess Anne Road

Norfolk fell to Union forces in May 1862 and was never again part of the Confederacy. It became instead a center for black refugees from the countryside. By the end of the war there may have been as many as 70,000 former slaves living in Norfolk.

In Elmwood Cemetery stands what is believed to be the only memorial to black soldiers of the Civil War. Their gravestones stand behind a granite monument, topped by a black version of a Yankee soldier. Later, black veterans of the Spanish-American War were also buried in this area.

Richmond

Jackson Ward Historic District

The Maggie Walker House

Bounded by Fourth Street, Marshall Street, Smith Street, and I-95, this was the foremost black community of Richmond during the post-Civil War era and into the early twentieth century. The best-known native of the neighborhood was probably Bill "Bojangles" Robinson, the "King of Tap Dancers." Others include banker Maggie Lena Walker [see below] and Baptist preacher John Jasper. The Sixth Mt. Zion Baptist Church, where Jasper preached, is located at the corner of Duval Street and St. John's Street. The district was named a National Historic Landmark on June 2, 1978.

166

PLACES

Maggie Lena Walker House
110A East Leigh Street

In 1903 Maggie Lena Walker, a black woman, founded the successful St. Luke Penny Savings Bank—and became the first woman to establish and head a bank. In addition to being the first woman president of a bank, she was a concerned community leader and editor of a widely respected newspaper. The house, located in the Jackson Ward Historic District, was declared a National Historic Landmark on May 15, 1975.

Rocky Mount

Booker T. Washington National Monument

The Burroughs plantation, on which educator and scholar Booker T. Washington was born, can be found in a 200-acre park located 22 miles southeast of Roanoke, Virginia. Born a slave, Washington lived here until the end of the Civil War, when he and his mother moved to Malden, West Virginia.

Washington, D.C.

Bethune Museum and Archives
1318 Vermont Avenue Northwest

Named for Mary McLeod Bethune, the Bethune Museum and Archives opened in November 1979 and was granted National Historic Site status in April 1982. A nonprofit organization, the Museum and Archives documents the contributions made by black women to society and reaches out to schoolchildren through educational programs and other services.

Blanche K. Bruce House
909 M Street Northwest

Blanche K. Bruce was the first African American to serve a full term in the United States Senate. Born in Farmville, Virginia, Bruce learned the printer's trade in Missouri. In 1861, prior to the Civil War, he escaped to Hannibal, Missouri, and built a school for blacks. He studied at Oberlin College in Ohio and, after moving to Mississippi, became a wealthy planter. A Republican, Bruce was elected to the U.S. Senate in 1874. The Blanche K. Bruce House was designated a National Historic Landmark on May 15, 1975.

Carter G. Woodson House and the Association for the Study of Negro Life and History
1538 Ninth Street Northwest

The Association for the Study of Negro Life and History was founded in 1915 to study and preserve the historical record of African American culture. The pioneer behind the association was Carter G. Woodson, who operated the organization out of his home until his death in 1950.

A scholar and lecturer, Woodson began publication of the *Journal of Negro History* in 1916. Ten years later, he introduced the idea of "Negro History Week," during which African American leaders were to be appropriately honored. Negro History Week has grown into what is now Black History Month.

The Woodson house was designated a National Historic Landmark on May 11, 1976. Today, the organization is headquartered at 1401 14th Street Northwest and is known as the Association for the Study of Afro-American Life and History.

PLACES

Charlotte Forten Grimké House
1608 R Street Northwest

Charlotte Forten Grimké, born of wealthy free black parents in Philadelphia, was among the first wave of Northerners engaged in educating slaves in the occupied Union territories of the South. Her activities as an activist, writer, poet, and educator paved the way for other black women. The house was designated a National Historic Landmark on May 11, 1976.

Edward Kennedy "Duke" Ellington Birthplace
1212 T Street Northwest

Born April 29, 1899, Duke Ellington was one of the world's great jazz composers and bandleaders. He formed his first band in Washington, D.C., in 1918; a few years later he moved to New York City and soon became one of the brightest stars of the Jazz Age.

Emancipation Statue
Lincoln Park
East Capitol Street

Former slaves were responsible for financing and erecting the oldest memorial to Abraham Lincoln in the Washington, D.C., area. Following Lincoln's assassination in 1865, Charlotte Scott of Marietta, Ohio, donated the first $5 for the statue. Contributions were soon pouring in, and Congress finally set aside grounds for Thomas Bell's statue depicting Lincoln breaking slavery's chains. The memorial was dedicated on April 14, 1876—the eleventh anniversary of Lincoln's assassination.

The Frederick Douglass House

Frederick Douglass House
1411 West Street Southeast

Cedar Hill, the 20-room colonial mansion in which Frederick Douglass lived for the last 13 years of his life, has been preserved as a monument to the great nineteenth-century abolitionist. In 1964 it was declared a National Historic Landmark.

Credit for the restoration and preservation of the home belongs largely to the National Association of Colored Women's Clubs, which worked hand-in-hand with the Douglass Association.

General Oliver Otis Howard House
Howard University

Located on what is now the campus of Howard University, this was the residence of the Union Civil War general who became head of the Freedmen's Bureau. Howard University is named in honor of General Howard; of the four original buildings on campus, only his house is still standing.

PLACES

Howard University

Founded in 1867, Howard University is the largest institution of higher learning established for African Americans in the period immediately following the Civil War.

Covering more than 50 acres, the campus is situated on one of the highest elevations in the District of Columbia. Of special interest is the university's famed Founders Library, which contains more than 300,000 volumes and includes the Moorland-Spingarn Collection, one of the finest collections on African American life and history in the United States.

Lincoln Memorial

The Lincoln Memorial has been the site of several important events underscoring African Americans' quest for dignity and struggle for equal opportunity. In 1939, when singer Marian Anderson was refused permission to appear at Constitution Hall by the Daughters of the American Revolution, she performed an Easter Sunday concert on the steps of the Lincoln Memorial before a crowd of 75,000.

Another pivotal event, the 1963 march on Washington, was climaxed by Martin Luther King, Jr.'s "I Have A Dream" speech.

Mary Ann Shadd Cary House
1421 West Street Northwest

Between 1881 and 1886 this house was the residence of Mary Ann Shadd Cary, the first black newswoman in America. Cary, a lecturer, writer, educator, lawyer, and abolitionist, appeared before audiences throughout the country, usually speaking on the topics of slavery and women's suffrage. The house was designated a National Historic Landmark on December 8, 1976.

Mary Church Terrell House
326 T Street Northwest

This house served as the residence of the first president of the National Association of Colored Women, Mary Church Terrell.

Mary McLeod Bethune Memorial
Lincoln Park

The Mary McLeod Bethune Memorial, unveiled in 1974, is the first monument to be erected on public land in the nation's capitol in honor of either a black or a woman. An educator and activist, Bethune was concerned about the children of the laborers working on the Florida East Coast Railroad. In 1904 she established the Daytona Normal and Industrial Institute for black girls. In 1926 she merged the institute with the Cookman Institute of Jacksonville to form the Bethune-Cookman College.

The monument, located in Lincoln Park, is inscribed with the following words:

I leave you love, I leave you hope. I leave you the challenge of developing confidence in one another. I leave you a thirst for education. I leave you respect for the use of power. I leave you faith. I leave you racial dignity.

National Museum of African Art
950 Independence Avenue Southwest

A part of the Smithsonian Institution, the National Museum of African Art maintains exhibitions, research components, and public programs on the art and culture of Africa south of the Sahara. The museum was established in 1964 and incorporated as a bureau of the Smithsonian in 1979.

PLACES

St. Luke's Episcopal Church
15th and Church Streets Northwest

From 1879 until 1934 the pulpit of St. Luke's Episcopal Church was graced by Alexander Crummell, a black scholar who became a leading spokesman for African and African American liberation. He was the founder of the American Negro Academy, a group of black intellectuals and scholars. The church was designated a National Historic Landmark on May 11, 1976.

Tidal Basin Bridge

Designed and constructed by black engineer Archie Alphonso Alexander, the Tidal Basin Bridge is one of Washington's major tourist attractions. Alexander, born in Ottumwa, Iowa, in 1888, became the first Republican governor of the Virgin Islands of the United States in 1954.

West Virginia

Harpers Ferry

Harpers Ferry National Historic Park

One of the most famous landmarks in African American history, Harpers Ferry is the sight of the antislavery raid conducted by John Brown and a party of eighteen men, including five blacks, during October 1859. Brown hoped to set up a fortress and refuge for slaves that he could transform into an important way station for black fugitives en route to Pennsylvania.

Brown lost two of his sons in the battle and was himself seriously wounded. Later tried and convicted of treason, he was hanged at nearby Charles Town on December 2, 1859.

The entire town of Harpers Ferry is a museum of the pre-Civil War era. The National Park Service has constantly expanded its holdings and is slowly recreating the appearance of Harpers Ferry in 1859. Guides assume living history roles of the townsfolk of that period. There are also scenic lookouts over the junction of the Potomac and Shenandoah Rivers.

Malden

Booker T. Washington Monument
U.S. Route 60

Erected in 1963, this monument marks the site where Booker T. Washington labored for several years in the salt works. At the time Washington credited his employer, Mrs. Violla Ruffner, with having encouraged him to pursue a higher education at Hampton Institute.

THE WEST

Alaska

Fairbanks

Pioneers' Home

One of the few black pioneers of Alaska, Mattie Crosby first came to the territory in 1900 with the Maine family who adopted her. Some blacks came into the territory during the era of the Gold Rush, and others could occasionally be seen aboard ships that brought in supplies. Still, for nearly 17 years, Mattie Crosby lived in Fairbanks without meeting another black.

Arizona

Tombstone

John Swain Grave Site
Boot Hill Cemetery

PLACES

Harpers Ferry National Historic Park

Born a slave in 1845, John Swain traveled to Tombstone in 1879 as a cowhand of John Slaughter. Swain was an expert rider and only one of several blacks to work for Slaughter.

In 1884 Swain is said to have fought and lost a one-round boxing match with John L. Sullivan, then heavyweight champion of the world. He died just three months short of his one-hundredth birthday and was buried with honors by the citizens of Tombstone. A special tablet stands on the grave site, commemorating the close ties between Swain and Slaughter.

California

Allensworth

Allensworth Colony

The town of Allensworth was founded by Allen Allensworth in 1910 as an all-black community. Now a state park, this landmark serves as a memorial to its founder.

A slave prior to the Civil War, Allensworth was a well-known racing jockey in Louisville, Kentucky. With the beginning of the Civil War, Allensworth was allowed to enter the navy, where he advanced to the rank of chief petty officer. Following the

PLACES

Jim Beckwourth, the frontiersman for whom Beckwourth Pass is named

war Allensworth studied for the ministry and returned to the military service as chaplain of the famed 24th U.S. Infantry. Around 1900 he moved to California, where he dedicated himself to improving the status of African Americans.

Arcadia

Santa Anita Race Track

Santa Anita Race Track is located on the former site of the E. J. "Lucky" Baldwin Ranch, where John Fisher was a prominent breeder and trainer. Fisher, a native of St. Louis and a former slave, was at first reluctant to follow Baldwin to California out of fear of Indians. Overcoming his fear, Fisher later became a foreman on the ranch.

Beckwourth

Beckwourth Pass

Beckwourth Pass, which runs through the Sierra Nevadas (a mountain range in eastern California), was discovered by James Beckwourth, one of a number of black traders and trappers dubbed "Mountain Men" by American historians.

Hornitos

Gold Mining Camp

This was the home of Moses Rodgers, a wealthy black mine-owner who was one of the finest engineers and metalworkers in the state. Rodgers was only one of several black miners who struck it rich in gold and quartz.

Red Bluff

Oak Hill Cemetery

This is the burial place of Alvin Aaron Coffey, the only black member of the Society of California Pioneers. Coffey, a descendant of an officer who fought under Andrew Jackson at the Battle of New Orleans in the War of 1812, came to California as a slave in 1849. By day he worked for his master. By night, as a cobbler, he accumulated money toward his $1,000 emancipation fee.

Betrayed by his owner, he was forced to return to Missouri and was sold. Coffey pleaded successfully with his new master to allow him to return to California and earn the necessary money to free himself and his family, whom he had left behind as **collateral.** Upon earning his and his family's freedom, Coffey was able to live a contented life as a Red Bluff farmer.

Sacramento

St. Andrew's African Methodist Episcopal Church

2131 Eighth Street

PLACES

"Aunt Clara" Brown, a pioneering citizen of Colorado

St. Andrew's was the first African Methodist Episcopal congregation in California. Organized in a private residence in 1850, the congregation founded a school for African, Asian, and Native American children in the church's basement within four years.

San Francisco

Leidesdorff Street

This street is named for William Alexander Leidesdorff, a wealthy and influential California pioneer of black and Danish ancestry and a native of the Danish West Indies. Leidesdorff operated the first steamer to pass through the Golden Gate strait, was later appointed United States vice-consul, and ultimately became a civic and educational leader in San Francisco.

Colorado

Central City

"Aunt Clara" Brown's Chair
Central City Opera House
Eureka Street

"Aunt Clara" Brown, believed to have been the first black resident of the Colorado Territory, was born a slave in Virginia. Brown moved to Missouri, but her husband and children were sold before she gained freedom through her owner's will. From Missouri she headed for Kansas and then for the gold fields of Colorado, where she opened the territory's first laundry. She soon began putting aside money from her earnings for the purchase of her family.

Even when the Emancipation Proclamation set her immediate family free, she returned to Missouri and brought back to Central City a group of 38 relatives. She remained in the mining community for the rest of her life, nursing the sick and performing other charitable works.

Brown died in 1877 and was buried with honors by the Colorado Pioneers Association, of which she was a member. The Central City Opera House Association dedicated a chair to her in 1932.

Denver

Inter-Ocean Hotel
16th and Market Streets

Built by Barney Ford, the Inter-Ocean Hotel was once a showplace for millionaires

PLACES

Pueblo

El Pueblo Museum
905 South Prairie Avenue

The El Pueblo museum houses a replica of the Gantt-Blackwell Fort, which black explorer, scout, and trader Jim Beckwourth claimed to have founded in 1842. The truth of this claim has not been established, for Beckwourth was sometimes a teller of tall tales.

Hawaii

Pearl Harbor

U.S.S. *Arizona* Memorial

The Japanese attack on Pearl Harbor came as a complete surprise. The men stationed at the huge U.S. Navy base here had no warning of what was to come shortly after dawn on December 7, 1941. But as bombs started to rain down upon the slumbering naval force, a few men reacted instinctively and did whatever they could to fight off the assault. Among them was Dorie Miller, an African American mess attendant on the battleship *Arizona*.

Miller was collecting laundry when the sirens started to blare. Like the overwhelming majority of black sailors, he was in a noncombat post. The most segregated of all the military branches, the Navy directed its black recruits into support duties rather than train them for combat. Even so, Miller rushed on deck, pulled an injured officer to safety, and took up an anti-aircraft gun. Although never trained to use this weapon, he brought down four Japanese planes before being ordered to abandon ship.

Five months later Miller was awarded the Navy Cross for "extraordinary courage" and

Messman Dorie Miller wears the Navy Cross, awarded for his display of heroism aboard the U.S.S. *Arizona* during the Japanese attack on Pearl Harbor

and presidents. Ford, a black entrepreneur active during the gold rush days, joined the fight over the organization of the Colorado Territory and the question of statehood.

Originally allowed to vote, Ford saw this privilege taken away by the Territorial constitution. He therefore tried to delay statehood for the Territory until black voting rights were reinstated. Requesting the help of Massachusetts abolitionist senator Charles Sumner, Ford urged President Andrew Johnson to veto the bill for statehood.

After Ford retired he spent the remainder of his life in Denver, where he died in 1902. He is buried in Denver's Riverside Cemetery.

Indians doubted that the slave York, a member of the Lewis and Clark expedition, was black-skinned. Here they are shown trying to rub off his natural color

toured black areas of the country to raise support for war bonds. Returned to the battle zone as a mess attendant, he was killed in action in the South Pacific while aboard the aircraft carrier *Liscome Bay* in 1943. Legislation was introduced in the U.S. House of Representatives to award him the Congressional Medal of Honor in 1988.

Idaho

Spalding

Nez Percé National Historical Park
U.S. 95

Although mainly dedicated to the preservation of Nez Percé Indian culture and history, this park in north-central Idaho contains the Lolo Trail, over which explorers Meriwether Lewis and William Clark traveled in 1805 and 1806.

For 12 days the Lewis and Clark expedition rested at the Canoe Camp site on the trail. One of the members of the expedition was York, a black slave, servant, guide, and interpreter. With each new encounter with Indian tribes, York became the center of attention because of his dark skin. Many Indians, apparently unfamiliar with blacks, thought York's pigmentation was artificial, perhaps painted on. On a number of occasions the Indians rubbed York's face to see if the pigment would come off.

At this particular spot, York finally lost all patience and drew a knife on an Indian who wanted to try the skin-rubbing test again. According to Marcella Thum in *Black America* (1991): "The legend of York continues among the Nez Percé, who called him 'make big eyes much white in eyes and look fierce at chief.'"

York was in fact very valuable to Lewis and Clark because of his strength, marksmanship, and the generally friendly relations he had with the Indians. He accompanied the expedition all the way to the Pacific coast of Oregon, which they reached in December 1805. At the conclusion of the long voyage back to St. Louis, York was given his freedom.

Kansas

Beeler

George Washington Carver Homestead
Route K-96

Along Route K96 in Ness County lies the plot of land once homesteaded by George Washington Carver, the famed agricultural

PLACES

Sod houses were built by the first settlers of Nicodemus

scientist. He spent two years here before attending college in Iowa.

Nicodemus

Nicodemus Colony
U.S. Route 24

The Nicodemus Colony (located along U.S. Route 24, two miles west of the Rooks-Graham county line) is the last surviving colony founded by the Exodusters—a group of black homesteaders who migrated to Kansas during the 1870s. The name "Nicodemus" came from a slave who, according to legend, predicted the coming of the Civil War.

The first settlers arrived in 1877 and lived in dugouts and burrows during the cold weather. From the outset, these pioneers were plagued by crop failures. Although never more than 500 in number, they managed nonetheless to establish a community with teachers, ministers, and civil servants. The state of Kansas has commemorated this site with a historical marker located in a roadside park in Nicodemus.

Osawatomie

John Brown Memorial State Park
10th and Main Streets

This state park, named in honor of abolitionist fighter John Brown, contains the cabin in which he lived during his brief stay in Kansas. Osawatomie still celebrates his

John Brown on his way to the gallows

residence there with a John Brown Jamboree, four days of entertainment held annually in the last week of June.

Topeka

Sumner Elementary School
330 Western Avenue

In 1951 Linda Brown was not allowed to attend Sumner Elementary School because she was black. What followed was the landmark case *Brown v. Board of Education*. Upon hearing the case, the United States Supreme Court concluded that separate schools were unequal and that segregation in education should be declared illegal.

Montana

Big Horn Station

Fort Manuel Marker
Captain William Clark and his expedition, which included a slave named York, camped at this site on July 26, 1806, a year before Manuel Lisa established Montana's first trading post. Major Andrew Henry chose this site as the Rocky Mountain Fur Company's first trading post. The leader of that expedition was Edward Rose, another of the famed black mountain men and explorers active in the territory.

Nebraska

Nebraska City

Mayhew Cabin, John Brown's Caves
Nebraska 2, near 20th Street

This frontier town on the Missouri River was one of the westernmost stations of the Underground Railroad in the 1850s. Fugitive slaves making their way north from the Missouri and Kansas territories were hidden here until they could be taken across to Iowa after dark and outfitted for the trip to Canada.

Many believe abolitionist John Brown ran the station. Brown lived for a time in Osawatomie, Kansas. But in recent years, Allen B. Mayhew has been credited for this stop on the railroad. An underground passage connects the log cabin to caves along the river, and when danger was signalled to the hidden slaves they were instructed to make their way to the water. They are still known as John Brown's Caves.

Omaha

Great Plains Black Museum
2213 Lake Street

The northern plains have never been an area with a large black population. Yet the history of many of these plains communities is filled with such figures as Mary Fields,

PLACES

who ran a stagecoach stop in Cascade, Montana, and Aunt Sally Campbell, who mined for gold in Deadwood, South Dakota, and is credited with being the first non-Indian woman to enter the Black Hills.

The Great Plains Black Museum is intended to expand the historical record of this part of the country. Emphasizing especially the achievements of black women, the museum contains photographs, artifacts, and other historical material on these all but forgotten pioneers.

Nevada

Reno

Beckwourth Pass

In the early days of pioneer settlement, the barren stretch of trail between Reno and the California line was the last obstacle before passing through to the West Coast. The original trail was laid out by black explorer and legendary mountain man Jim Beckwourth.

New Mexico

Lincoln

Old Court House

During the Lincoln County Cattle War of 1877-78, outlaw Billy the Kid was held in custody at the Old Court House, now a frontier museum. Black cowhands were involved on both sides of this struggle and, on one occasion, a group of black cavalrymen is said to have surrounded Billy the Kid during a particularly bloody battle.

Zuni

Hawikuh Pueblo

The first non-Native American to enter the Southwest was a black man named Estevanico, or Esteban. Born in Morocco, a country in North Africa, Estevanico was a slave who accompanied Spanish explorers to Florida in 1528.

Much later, in the spring of 1539, Estevanico led an advance group of explorers into what is now Arizona and New Mexico in search of the legendary Seven Cities of Gold. When he arrived in Zuni, Estevanico demanded to speak to the Indian chief. The Zuni Indians refused Estevanico's order and told him to leave or face execution. Convinced that untold gold treasures were nearby, the explorer proceeded to the **pueblo,** where he was taken prisoner and killed. A year later, explorer Francisco Coronado entered the region, which had been claimed by Spain. The Cities of Gold, of course, were never found.

North Dakota

Buford

Fort Buford State Historic Site; Fort Union National Historic Site
ND 1804

Built in 1866, Fort Buford was the headquarters for the all-black 10th Cavalry and 25th Infantry. Although primarily a supply base for other western forts, Buford is probably best remembered as the site of Chief Sitting Bull's surrender in 1881.

A few miles from Fort Buford is Fort Union. From 1829 to 1867 Fort Union served as the chief fur-trading depot in the Upper Missouri River region. Trapper and explorer Jim Beckwourth was among the blacks who traded at the fort. During the

1830s the Fort Union commander selected Beckwourth to trade with the Crow Indians; some years earlier, Beckwourth had lived with the Crows and formed a lasting bond with them.

Oklahoma

Boley

Boley Historic District

This is the largest of the black towns in Oklahoma, which were built to provide African Americans with the opportunity for self-government during a time of widespread racism and segregation. The Boley Historic District was designated a National Historic Landmark on May 15, 1975.

Ponca City

101 Ranch

During the last half of the nineteenth century, the 101 Ranch was one of the largest and most famous in the West. Established in 1879, the ranch employed several black cowhands, of whom the most celebrated was Bill Pickett.

The inventor of bulldogging, or steer wrestling, Pickett also perfected a unique rodeo style unlike any used by his fellow wranglers. He died on April 21, 1932, after being kicked by a horse, and was buried on a knoll near the White Eagle Monument. Pickett had outlasted all the original ranch hands. The ranch was declared a National Historic Landmark on May 15, 1975.

Oregon

Astoria

Fort Clatsop National Memorial
U.S. 101

Named for the local Clatsop Indians, Fort Clatsop was built by the Lewis and Clark Expedition as quarters for the winter of 1805-06. The explorers had spent the previous winter in a Native American village along the Missouri River, in what is now North Dakota. But now there were no other dwellings available.

They voted on where to build a shelter. This site was selected for its good hunting, access to the ocean for salt, and protection from the winds. The party's black member, York, who had begun the trek as a slave of co-leader William Clark, was given a full vote in the proceedings. York's courage and strength during hard times had won the respect of everyone in the expedition, and by this time his position was equal to any held by his fellow explorers.

When the expedition returned home the following summer, York was granted his freedom. Ironically, Clark later became governor of the slave-holding state of Missouri.

South Dakota

Deadwood

Adams Memorial Museum

Only one of the many cowboys who claimed the title "Deadwood Dick" was black, but that man was as likely a candidate as any. Nat Love backed up his claim with a colorful autobiography that takes the reader through his childhood in slavery, his early bronco-busting efforts, and his fabled life as a range rider and Indian fighter in the old West.

Love said he won the title during a public competition held in Deadwood on the Fourth of July in 1876. The presence of other black

PLACES

Nat Love

cowboys, gambling house operators, and escort soldiers in the area during these years, as well as the convincing style of Love's narrative, lend a high degree of credibility to his adventurous tales. However, like Jim Beckwourth and other Wild West figures, Love was no stranger to telling tall tales.

Texas

Amarillo

First Black School

Matthew Bones Hooks was born in central Texas in 1867. The story goes that he rode wild horses at the age of eight, had his first paid job as a cowhand at the age of ten, and later herded cattle for Colonel Charles Goodnight, taking them from Texas to Dodge City, Kansas. Hooks homesteaded in New Mexico, rode broncos in Roma, Texas, and then moved to Amarillo, where he established the first school for blacks in that city.

He also founded the Dogie Club, an organization for underprivileged boys, in cooperation with the Boy Scouts. Hooks was the only black member of the old Settlers Association of Amarillo and the first black of Amarillo to serve on a grand jury.

Utah

Salt Lake City

Fort Douglas Military Museum
Wasatch Drive

Built during the Civil War, Fort Douglas was home to the all-black 24th Infantry Regiment as well as the 9th Cavalry Regiment. The 24th served in the trenches of San Juan Hill in Cuba during the Spanish-American War. They also helped combat a yellow fever epidemic on the island. When they returned to an enthusiastic welcome in New York, however, they were so weakened by their ordeal that they were barely able to get through the parade. More men died of yellow fever in Cuba than of wounds sustained in battle.

Washington

Centralia-Chehalis

George Washington Park; Chehalis County Museum

The park is named after a Virginia-born slave who escaped to Missouri, where he was adopted and raised by a white couple. Unable because of his color to attend school, Washington was tutored at home. By

Troop H of the Tenth Cavalry

the time he was in his thirties, he ran a sawmill in St. Joseph, Missouri. However, he grew tired of the restrictions of the slave-holding state and in 1850 joined a wagon train on the Oregon Trail.

Again entering the lumbering business, he established a homestead on the Chehalis River. But his farm lay in the path of the Northern Pacific Railroad, and with the cash settlement he received, Washington decided to plan a new town. He called it Centerville and set aside acreage for parks, a cemetery, and churches. Soon over 2,000 lots were in the hands of a thriving population. Washington remained there for the rest of his life as an honored citizen, though the name he selected for the town was changed.

Washington is buried in Centralia Cemetery. The museum, located four miles north in Chehalis, contains exhibits on Washington's life and displays of the history of logging and pioneer life in the area.

Wyoming
Lander

Fort Washakie Blockhouse
Windriver Indian Reservation, WY 287

The blockhouse served as headquarters from 1880 through 1890 for black troops of both the 9th and 10th Cavalry regiments. On one occasion, the 9th rescued a unit of infantry from Fort Steele—near Rawlins, Wyoming—which was being attacked by Ute Indians. The Fort Steele infantrymen, exhausted and low on supplies in their dugouts, were relieved to be reinforced by the black cavalrymen, who drove off the Indians. The 9th Cavalry later began construction of Fort Duchesne in northeastern Utah.

181

FURTHER READING

Aptheker, Herbert, ed., *A Documentary History of the Negro People in the United States,* New York: Carol Publishing Group, 1990.

Bennett, Lerone, *Before the Mayflower,* 6th ed., Chicago: Johnson Publishing Company, 1987.

Berry, Mary Frances, and John W. Blassingame, *Long Memory: The Black Experience in America,* New York and Oxford: Oxford University Press, 1982.

Billingsley, Andrew, *Climbing Jacob's Ladder: The Enduring Legacy of African-American Families,* New York: Simon & Schuster, 1992.

Bing, Léon, *Do or Die,* New York: HarperCollins Publishers, 1991.

Bogle, Donald, *Toms, Coons, Mulattoes, Mammies, and Bucks: An Interpretive History of Blacks in American Films,* New York: Continuum Publishing Company, 1989.

Clark, Joe, with Joe Picard, *Laying Down the Law: Joe Clark's Strategy for Saving Our Schools,* Washington, D.C.: Regnery Gateway, 1989.

Collins, Charles M., and David Cohen, eds., *The African Americans,* New York: Viking Studio Books, 1993.

Copage, Eric V., *Black Pearls: Daily Meditations, Affirmations, and Inspirations for African Americans,* New York: William Morrow, 1993.

Durham, Michael S., *Powerful Days: The Civil Rights Photography of Charles Moore,* New York: Stewart, Tabori & Chang, 1991.

Edwards, Audrey, and Craig K. Polite, *Children of the Dream: The Psychology of Black Success,* New York: Doubleday, 1992.

Franklin, John Hope, and Alfred A. Moss, Jr., *From Slavery to Freedom: A History of Negro Americans,* New York: McGraw Hill, 1988.

Haber, Louis, *Black Pioneers of Science and Invention,* San Diego: Harcourt Brace Jovanovich, 1987.

Hampton, Henry, and Steve Fayer, *Voices of Freedom: An Oral History of the Civil Rights Movement from the 1950s through the 1960s,* New York: Bantam, 1990.

Hardnett, Carolyn J., and Dawne A. Johnson, "Black Year in Review," *Emerge,* December/January 1994, pp. 55-60.

Harley, Sharon, et al., *The African American Experience: A History,* Englewood Cliffs, New Jersey: Simon & Schuster, 1992.

Haskins, James, *Black Music in America: A History through Its People,* New York: Crowell Junior Books, 1987.

Hughes, Langston, Milton Meltzer, and C. Eric Lincoln, *A Pictorial History of Blackamericans,* New York: Crown Publishers, 1983.

Johnson, John H., with Lerone Bennett, Jr., *Succeeding against the Odds,* New York: Warner Books, 1989.

Kimbro, Dennis, *Daily Motivations for African-American Success,* New York: Fawcett Columbine, 1993.

FURTHER READING

King, Anita, ed., *Quotations in Black,* Westport, Connecticut: Greenwood Press, 1981.

Low, W. Augustus, and Virgil A. Clift, *Encyclopedia of Black America,* New York: McGraw Hill, 1981.

Marsh, Carole S., *Black Trivia: The African-American Experience, A-to-Z!,* Decatur, Georgia: Gallopade Publishing Group, 1992.

Mullane, Deirdre, ed., *Crossing the Danger Water: Three Hundred Years of African-American Writing,* New York: Doubleday, 1993.

Pelz, Ruth, *Black Heroes of the Wild West,* Seattle: Open Hand Publishing, 1990.

Salley, Columbus, *The Black 100: A Ranking of the Most Influential African-Americans, Past and Present,* New York: Carol Publishing Group, 1993.

Shaw, Arnold, *Black Popular Music in America,* New York: Schirmer Books, 1986.

Thum, Marcella, *Hippocrene U.S.A. Guide to Black America: A Directory of Historic and Cultural Sites Relating to Black America,* New York: Hippocrene Books, 1991.

Westridge Young Writers Workshop, *Kids Explore America's African-American Heritage,* Santa Fe, New Mexico: John Muir Publications, 1992.

INDEX

A

Aaron, Hank 542, 544
Abbott, Robert Sengstacke 128, 474, 566
"ABC" 501
Abdalla, Mohammed Ahmed ibn 44
Abdul-Jabbar, Kareem 546
Abernathy, Ralph 13, 159, 289-291, 293
Abiel Smith School and Museum of Afro-American History 139
Abolition Movement 222, 296, 371
Abraham's Oak 531
Abyssinia 433
Abyssinian Baptist Church 144, 145
Acquired Immune Deficiency Syndrome (AIDS) 24, 329, 345
Act to Prohibit the Importation of Slaves (1807) 81
Act to Suppress the Slave Trade in the District of Columbia 85
Acts of Art Gallery 526
Adams, John Quincy 136
Adams Memorial Museum 179

The Addams Family 466
Adelina, Patti 512
Affirmative action 16, 313
Africa 21-54
Africa Bambaataa 503
Africa World Press 489
African American Museums Association 478
African American National Historic Site 139
African Ceremonial 438
African Civilization Society 249
African Free Schools 350
African Grove Theatre 431
African Lodge No. 459 282
African Meeting House 139
African Methodist Episcopal (AME) Church 134, 269, 282-283, 354, 369, 379, 486
African Methodist Episcopal Zion (AME Zion) Church 370, 380, 486
African National Congress 51
African Orthodox Church 380
African Party for the Independence of Guinea-Bissau and Cape Verde 26, 29

African Protestant Episcopal Church 222
African Union Church 369, 380
African Union First Colored Methodist Protestant Church, Inc. 380
Afrikaner 49, 51
Afro-American Historical and Cultural Museum 150
Afro-American Museum of Detroit 129
Afro-American Music Opportunities Association 515
Afro-American Symphony 513, 515
Afrocentrism 279
Agriculture 319
Aida 437
AIDS (Acquired Immune Deficiency Syndrome) 24, 329, 345
Aiello, Danny 460
Ailey, Alvin 438, 442
Ain't Misbehavin' 441
"Ain't That A Shame" 497
Akim Trading Company 250
Al-Amin, Jamil Abdullah (see H. Rap Brown)

185

INDEX

Albert, Donnie Ray 517
Alcoholism 346
Alcorn College 354
Alcorn State University 354
Aldridge, Ira 431
Alexander, Archie Alphonso 170
Alexander, Cheryl 441
Alexander, Erika 472
Alexander, John H. 561
Alexander, Marcellus 483
Alex Haley House 157
Alhambra Theatre 434
Alice Adams 452
Ali, Muhammad 7, 549, 578
Allen, Debbie 441, 443, 463
Allen, Richard 150, 222, 249, 268-269, 282-283, 366, 369-370, 379-380
Allensworth, Allen 171
Allensworth Colony 171
All God's Chillun' Got Wings 435
All in the Family 467-468
The All-Negro Hour 479
"All She Wants To Do Is Rock" 494
Almond, Edward M. 569
Alvin Ailey American Dance Center 442
Alvin Ailey American Dance Theater 429, 442
Alvin Ailey Repertory Ensemble 442
"Amazing Grace" 368
AME Book Concern 486
Amen 470
American Anti-Slavery Society 223, 284
American Baptist Home Mission Society 355
American Colonization Society 30, 222, 246, 249, 284, 370-371
American Freedmen's Aid Union 352

American Missionary Association 355
American Muslim Mission 384
American National Baptist Convention 384
American Negro Academy 170, 356, 488
American Negro Theater 436
American Revolution 218
The American Society of Free Persons of Color 269
American Urban Radio Network 479
American Visions 478
Ames, Alexander 140
AME Sunday School Union and Publishing House 486
AME Zion Book Concern 486
AME Zion Churches 283
Amin Dada, Idi 46
Amistad Murals 153
Amistad 136
Amos Fortune Grave Site 142
Amos, John 467
Amos 'N' Andy 464
Amsterdam News 145, 475
Anderson, Eddie 451-452
Anderson, James H. 145, 475
Anderson, James, Jr. 578
Anderson, Jo 534
Anderson, Marian 169, 490, 513
Anderson, Thomas 436
Andersonville Prison 161
Angelou, Maya 75, 121-123, 418, 427, 439
Anglican Society for the Propagation of the Gospel 366
Angola 23, 35, 39
Anguilla 56, 64
Anjouan 53
Anna Lucasta 436
Annie Allen 417
Ansel Clark Grave Site 135
Antigua 56, 64

Anti-Slavery Record 223
Apartheid 51-52
Apollo Theater 145-146, 438
Apostolic Overcoming Holy Church of God 380
Appo, William 512
Arceneaux, Andrea 485
Argentina 55
Aristide, Jean-Bertrand 56, 63
Armstrong, Henry 549
Armstrong, Louis 148, 450, 505-507, 511
Aronson, Arnold 289
Art Ensemble of Chicago 511
Arthur, Chester 561
Aruba 57, 64
Asbury, Francis 137, 367
Asbury Methodist Episcopal Church 137
Ashantis 29
Ashe, Arthur 542-543, 552, 555
Associates in Negro Folk Education 355, 488
Association for the Advancement of Creative Musicians 511
Association for the Study of Afro-American History and Literature 488
Association for the Study of Afro-American Life and History 356
Association for the Study of Negro Life and History 167, 356, 488
Atlanta University 161, 354
Atlanta University Press 487
The Atlanta Daily World 476
Atlanta Voice 476
"Atlantic Coastal Line" 498
Attucks, Crispus 3, 4, 140, 557
Augin, Charles 441
Augusta Institute 354
"Aunt Clara" Brown's Chair 173

INDEX

Autobiography of Miss Jane Pittman 469
Avery, Margaret 458
Ayler, Albert 510

B

Back to Africa movement 288, 373
Bahama Islands 58
Bailey, Deford 498
Bailey, Pearl 435
Baker, David 511, 515
Baker, Josephine 434
Bakongo 35, 39
Baldwin, James 145, 425, 427, 439
Baldwin, Maria 141
Baldwin, Ruth Standish 287
Baldwin, William H. 287
Ballard, Hank 496
Ballou, Charles C. 565
Baltimore Afro-American 474-475
Bambara, Toni Cade 463
Bandanna Land 433
Banker's Fire Insurance Company 322
Bannarn, Henry 522
Banneker, Benjamin 76, 137-138, 165, 533, 534
Banneker-Douglass Museum 137
Banneker's Almanac 533
Bannister, Edward Mitchell 520
Bantu 26, 37-39, 44
Baptist Foreign Mission Convention of the U.S.A. 384
Baraka, Imamu Amiri 15, 145, 426, 439, 460
Barbados 55, 58
Barber-Scotia College 354
Barbuda 56, 64
Barkley, Charles 542, 546
Barnett, Neema 463

Barrow, Willie 294, 328
Barry, Marion 291
"Bars Fight" 417
Barthe, Richmond 522, 530-531
Baseball 543
Basie, Count 493, 507
Basketball 546
Basquiat, Jean-Michel 524
Basutoland 49
Bates, Daisy 356, 359
Battle, Hinton 441, 444
Baylor, Elgin 554
A Bayou Legend 517
Beacon Hill 139
"Beale Street Blues" 159
Beale Street Historic District 158
Beard, Andrew 535
Beard, Matthew (Stymie) 449
Bearden, Romare 523, 528, 531
Beatty, Tally 442
Beauford Delaney 527
Bebop 508
Bechet, Sidney 506
Beckwourth, Jim 172, 174, 178, 180
Beckwourth Pass 172
Beckwourth Trail 178
Bedouin, King 40
Belafonte, Harry 436, 453-454
Belasco Theater 438
Belize 68
Bell, Alexander Graham 538
Bell, Thomas 168
Beloved 418, 421
Belton, Sharon Sayles 276
Benedict College 354
Benezet, Anthony 350
Benin 24, 33, 214
Benjamin Banneker Boundary Stone 165
Benjamin Banneker Marker 138
Benjamin, Eli 573
Benjamin, Fred 444
Benny, Jack 451

Benson, Al 495
Berber 32
Bergon, Flora Baston 512
Bermuda 58
"Bernadette" 501
Berry, Chuck 497
Best, Willie "Sleep 'n Eat" 450
Bethel African Methodist Episcopal Church 222, 269, 366
Bethune-Cookman College 159, 169, 354
Bethune, Mary McLeod 9, 160, 167, 169, 274, 354
Bethune Museum and Archives 167
Bethune, Thomas "Blind Tom" Green 430, 511
BET News 485
Betsimisaraka 53
Beulah M. Davis Collection 138
Beverly Hills Cop 445, 458
Beverly Hills Cop II 458
Bickerstaff, Bernie 554
Biddle University 354
Biggers, John 523
Billingsley, Andrew 314, 330
Billops, Camille 528
"Bird on a Wire" 498
Birth of the Blues 452
The Birth of a Nation 448
Birthright 446
Black Power movement 291
Black Aesthetics Movement 425
Black American 476
Black Arts Movement 425
Black Birds 434
Black Cabinet 9, 274
Black Civil War Veterans' Memorial 166
Black Classic Press 489
Black Codes 228
Black Codes of Mississippi (1865) 92
Black Composers Series 515

187

INDEX

Black Enterprise 328, 473, 478
Black Entertainment Television 473, 485
Black Families in White America 334
Black Family 478
"Black Family Summit" 17
Black Faneuil Hall 139
Black Filmmakers Hall of Fame 449
Black Heritage Trail 139
Black History Month 167
Black Is the Color of My TV Tube 481
Black Jews of Harlem 251
Black Leadership Forum 277
Black Magic 429
Black Muslims 7, 11, 13, 37, 252, 377
Black nationalism 8, 10, 245, 375
Black Nativity 440
Black Panther Manifesto 112
Black Panther Party for Self-Defense 11, 13, 14, 112-113, 236, 291-292
Black Patti 512
Black Perspectives on the News 483
Black Regiment Memorial of the Battle of Rhode Island 151
Black Star Line 288
Black Stars 477
Black Swan 512
Black Theology movement 375
Black Women in American Bands and Orchestras 513
Blackbirds of 1928 434
Blackboard Jungle 453
Blackburn, Robert 522
Black Nationalism movement 245-254
The Blacks 439
Blackwell, David H. 533

Blair, Henry 535
Blair, Mary 435
Blake, Eubie 434
Blanche K. Bruce House 167
Bland, James A. 150, 432
Blanshard, Terence 510
Blanton, Jimmy 508
Bledsoe, Jules 435
Bledsoe, Tempestt 472
Blow, Kurtis 503
"Blueberry Hill" 497
Blue Flames 495
Blues 490
Blues for Mr. Charlie 439
The Bluest Eye 420
Bluff City News 479
Bluford, Guion 538
Blyden, E. W. 249-250, 253
Body and Soul 449
Boer Wars 51
Boley Historic District 179
Bolling v. *Sharpe* 359
Bonaire 57, 64
Bond, Julian 232, 291
Bond, Margaret 515
Bonds, Barry 545
Bonet, Lisa 472
Bontemps, Arna 425
Booker T. Washington Monument 154, 170
Booker T. Washington National Monument 167
Boone, John William 512
Bootee, Duke 503
Bootsy's Rubber Band 502
Borde, Percival 438
Bornu 33
Boston Guardian 474
Boston Massacre 140
Botswana 49
Bowe, Riddick 550, 551
Bowers, Thomas 512
Boxer, David 532
Boxing 549

Boyd, Richard Henry 372, 486
Boyle, Robert 318
Boyz N the Hood 448, 461
Brac, Cayman 60
Braddock, Jim 130
Bradford, Alex 440, 441
Bradford, William 141
Bradley, Ed 482, 484
Bradley, Thomas 16
Bragg Smith Grave Site and Memorial 162
Braun, Carol Moseley 17, 19, 243, 267-268, 280-281, 305
Brazil 25, 70, 72
"Brer Rabbit, Brer Fox, and the Tar Baby" 419
Brides of Funkenstein 502
Bridge, Edmund Pettis 153
Bridgewater, Dee Dee 441
Briggs-Hall, Austin 436
Briggs v. *Elliott* 359
British Togoland 29
British Virgin Islands 56, 59
Brockington, Horace 530
Brokaw, Tom 243
Brooke, Edward W. 112, 268
Brooks, Gwendolyn 417, 425
Brooks, William Henry 285
Brotherhood of Sleeping Car Porters and Maids 290, 566
Brown, Ann 434
Brown, "Aunt Clara" 173
Brown, Buster 444
Brown, Charlotte Hawkins 353
Browne, Roscoe Lee 439, 440
Brown, Henry 429, 431
Brown, H. Rap (Jamil Abdullah Al-Amin) 291, 232, 291
Brown, James 426, 495, 499, 501
Brown, Jesse 281
Brown, Jim 548
Brown, John 133, 143-144, 170, 176-177
Brown, Linda 107, 177, 265

INDEX

Brown, Morris 370
Brown, Morris, Jr. 512
Brown, Ronald H. 17, 19, 280
Brown, Roy 494
Brown, Sterling 488
Brown, Tony 473, 483, 484
Brown v. Board of Education of Topeka, Kansas 11, 107, 177, 195, 228, 232, 256-257, 265-266, 274, 286, 350, 356, 359
Brown, William 517
Brown, William Wells 417
Brown, Wilson 156
Bruce, Blanche K. 133, 167, 268
Bruce, John E. 250, 355
Brunson, Dorothy 483
Bryan, Andrew 163, 368
Bryant, Linda 527
Bryant, William Cullen 352
Bubbles, John 435
Buck Benny Rides Again 451
Buffalo Soldiers 560
Buganda 46
Bunche, Ralph J. 9, 131, 149, 267, 488
Bunker Hill Monument 139
Burke, Selma 518
Burke, Solomon 499
Burleigh, Harry T. 149
Burns, Francis 370
Burroughs, Margaret 528
Burroughs, Nannie Helen 353
Burrows, Stephen 526
Burr, Seymour 140
Burruss, K. H. 382
Burton, LeVar 470
Burundi 43
Bush, George 119-120, 261, 565
Business 315-328
Bussey, Charles M. 575
Butler, Jo 527
Butler, Octavia 428
Butterbeans and Susie 438
Butts, Claudia 279

By Any Means Necessary: The Trials and Tribulations of the Making of Malcolm X 447
Bynoe, Peter C. B. 555

C

Cabin in the Sky 435, 452-453
Cabin, Mayhew 177
Cabral, Luis 29
Cadoria, Sherian Grace 557
Cain, Richard 374
Caldwell, James 140
Calloway, Cab 450, 493
Cambridge, Godfrey 439, 444
Cameroon 26
Campbell, Clive 503
Campbell, E. Simms 524
Campbell, Joan Salmon 366
Campbell, Sally 178
Canada 73
Cannon, Katie 375
Capers, Virginia 441
Cape Verde 26, 29
Caribbean 56
Caribbean basin 55
Carmen 442
Carmen Jones 435, 453-454
Carmichael, Stokely 13-14, 232, 236, 291-292
Carney, William H. 140, 560
Carroll, Diahann 458, 464, 466
Carroll, Vinette 440
Carr, Patrick 140
"Carry Me Back to Old Virginny" 150
Carter, Benny 507
Carter G. Woodson House 167
Carter, Jimmy 278
Carter, Nell 441
Carver, George Washington 154, 156, 175, 535, 539
Car Wash 444
Cary, Lott 370

Cary, Mary Ann Shadd 169
The Cascades 157
Casey Jones Railroad Museum 158
Catlett, Elizabeth 528-529
Catlett, Mary 368
Catlett, Sid 507
Cato 3
Cayman Islands 60
Cay, Samana 58
Ceasar, Adolph 440
Cedras, Raoul 63
Center for Black Music Research 516
Center for Training Entrepreneurship (CTE) 323
Central African Republic 36-38
Central City, Colorado 173
Central High School (Little Rock, Arkansas) 108, 154, 155
Chad 36-38
Chamberlain, Wilt 546
Chameleon Street 462
Chance, Cathy 530
Chapelle Administration Building 164
Charismatic movement 374, 376
Charity 430
Charles Alston, Charles 521, 523
Charles H. Mason Theological Seminary 383
Charles, Ray 496, 497
Charles Richard Drew House 165
Charles, Suzette 17
Charlotte Forten Grimké House 168
Charlton, Cornelius H. 575
Chavis, Benjamin 287, 337
Chavis, John 163, 371
Checole, Kassahun 489
Chehalis County Museum 180
Cherry, F. S. 380
Chesnutt, Charles W. 417, 423

189

INDEX

Chicago Defender 128, 474, 476, 479, 564, 566
Chicago South Side Community Art Center 522
Chicago Tribune 476
Childress, Alice 436
Childress, Alvin 436
A Child's Story of Dunbar 488
Chisholm, Shirley 11, 16, 267-269
Chocolate Dandies 434
"Choice of Color" 498
Christ Missionary and Industrial College 382
Christian, Charlie 508
Christian Methodist Episcopal (CME) Church 373, 381
Christophe, Henri 62
Christy Minstrels 432
Chuck, Berry 497
Chuck D 305, 503
Churches of God, Holiness 382
Church of Christ (Holiness) Inc. 381
Church of God and Saints in Christ 380, 486
Church of God in Christ 366, 374, 376, 382
Church of God in Christ Publishing House 486
Cinqué Gallery 528
Cinqué, Joseph 136, 528
City of Richmond v. *Croson* 324
Civil disobedience 13
Civil Rights Act (1866) 93, 228
Civil Rights Act (1875) 227, 257-258
Civil Rights Act (1957) 289
Civil Rights Act (1960) 289
Civil Rights Act (1964) 11, 13, 111-112, 235, 257, 277, 289
Civil Rights Act (1990) 119
Civil Rights Act (1991) 119
Civil Rights Cases 260

Civil Rights Memorial 152
Civil Rights Movement 8, 227-244, 245-254
Civil War 74, 225, 557
The Clansman 448
Clark, Ansel 135
Clark-Atlanta University 161, 354, 441
Clark College 161
Clarke, Kenny 508
Clark, Joe 363
Clark, Mark 236, 292
Clark, William 175, 177, 179
Claude McKay Residence 147
Clay, Henry 246
Cleage, Albert 375
Cleaver, Eldridge 236, 292
Clements, George 376-377
Cleveland Gazette 474
Clifton, Nat "Sweetwater" 546
Climbing Jacob's Ladder 331
Clinton, Bill 19, 121, 243, 280-281, 314, 336, 418
Clinton, George 501
Clorinda: The Origin of the Cakewalk 149, 433
Clotel; or, The President's Daughter 417
CME Publishing House 486
Coachman, Alice 551
Coalition Against Blaxploitation 456
Coates, Paul 489
Coburn, Titus 140
Codrington, Christopher 56
Coffey, Alvin Aaron 172
Cohen, Leonard 498
Coker, Daniel 370
Coker, Gylbert 529
"Cold Sweat" 499
Cole, Bob 432, 433
Cole, Nat "King" 490
Coleman, Ornette 509, 515
Coleridge-Taylor, Samuel 515

Coles, Honi 444
Coles, Kim 472
Collins, Janet 438
Collins, Marva 361
Colombia 72
Colonel Robert Gould Shaw Monument 140
Colorado Pioneers Association 173
Colored Methodist Episcopal Church 372, 486
The Color Purple 458
Coltrane, John 426, 509-511
Columbus, Christopher 1, 2, 56, 58, 65, 67, 70, 72-73, 216
Coming to America 445
Commandment Keepers 380
Committee for the Improvement of Industrial Conditions Among Negroes in New York 287
Committee on Civil Rights 289
Committee on Urban Conditions Among Negroes 287
Commodores 501, 502
Comoros 52
Cone, James 376
Conference of Prince Hall Grand Masters 282
Congo 36-39
Congressional Black Caucus 242, 277, 279, 282
Congress of National Black Churches 376
Congress of Racial Equality (CORE) 232, 288-290
The Conjure Woman 417
Connell, Pat 482
Connelly, Marc 435
Connor, Aaron J. R. 512
Constitution House 152
Constitution of the United States 4, 257
Contemporary Craft Center 528
Conwill, Houston 527

INDEX

Cooke, Sam 495-496
Cookman Institute 354
Cook, Will Marion 149, 433
Cooper, Anna 372
Cooper, Chuck 546
Cooper, Jack L. 478
Cooper v. *Aaron* 266
Coppin, Frances Jackson 372
Cordero, Roque 515
Cornish, Samuel 223, 473, 476
Coronado, Francisco 178
Cortes, Hernán 2
Cortor, Eldzier 528
Cosby, Bill 305, 327, 444, 460, 464-465, 470
The Cosby Show 327, 463-464, 470
Costa Rica 70
Côte d'Ivoire (see Ivory Coast)
Cotton Club 450, 507
Cotton Comes to Harlem 456, 466
Counter, S. Allen 138
Cowper, William 368
Cozy Cove 435
Craig, Walter F. 512
Crawford, George Williamson 488
Credo 515
The Creole Show 432
Crichlow, Ernest 528
Crisis 286, 356, 423-424, 476
Crispus Attucks Monument 140
Crockett, Phyllis 485
Crooklyn 461
Crosby, Mattie 170
Crosswhite, Adam 132
Crosswhite Boulder 132
Crowdy, William 380
Crummell, Alexander 170, 223, 249-250, 270, 356, 488
Cry 442
"Crying in the Chapel" 495
Cry the Beloved Country 453

Cuba 60
Cuffe, Paul 10, 141-142, 246, 249, 284
Cullen, Countee 424
Culp, Robert 465
Cunningham, Randall 549
Curaçao 57, 64

D

da Gama, Vasco 45
"Daddy Rice" 432
Dahomey 24
The Daily Challenge 476
The Daily Drum 481
Daily World 476
Daley, Richard 127
Dance Theater of Harlem 442, 443
Dandridge, Dorothy 453-454
Daniel "Chappie" James Aerospace Center 154
Daniel Hale Williams House 125
Daniel, Payne 354
Daniels, Billy 441
Darnell, D. S. B. 354
Dash, Julie 446, 448, 463
Daughters of the American Revolution 169
Daughters of the Dust 448, 463
David Harum 451
Davis, Alonzo 528
Davis, Benjamin O., Sr. 9, 557, 567
Davis, Dale 528
Davis, Gary 492
Davis, Jefferson 225
Davis, Miles 490, 509
Davis, Ossie 436, 440, 441, 456, 466, 481
Davis, Rodney M. 578
Davis, Sammy, Jr. 440-441
Davis v. *Prince Edward County School Board* 359

Day, Tom 163
Daytona Normal and Industrial Institute for Girls 169, 354
"Deadwood Dick" 179
DeBarge 501
Declaration of Independence 4, 76, 86
Dede, Edmond 512
Deep River 150
Dee, Ruby 436, 437
The Defiant Ones 453
DeFrantz, Anita 552
DeKlerk, F. W. 52
de la Beckwith, Byron 266
Delaney, Benford 523
Delany, Martin R. 10, 249, 270
Delany, Samuel 428
de Lavallade, Carmen 444
DeLoatch, Gary 442
Democratic National Convention (1988) 18
Denmark, James 527
Denmark Vesey Conspiracy 219
Denmark Vesey House 164
de Paur, Leonard 517
DePriest, James 516
DePriest, Oscar 127
Derricks, Cleavant 441
de Saint Georges, Chevalier 515
DeShazor, Jacqueline 322
DeShields, Andre 441
Dessalines, Jean Jacques 62
Detroit News 482
Detroit riots 14
Deuce Coupe 524
Devine, Loretta 441
Dexter Avenue Baptist Church 152
Diary of an African Nun 463
A Different World 463, 472
Diff'rent Strokes 469
Dillard, James 155
Dinkins, David 17, 276
Dixon, Alan 280

191

INDEX

Dixon, Ivan 437
Dixon, Lucille 516
Dixon, Thomas 448
Djibouti 40
Do the Right Thing 459, 503
Dominica 60
Dominican Republic 61, 62
Domino, Antoine "Fats" 497
Dominoes 495
Donaldson, Ray 548
Don't Bother Me, I Can't Cope 441
Doo-wop 495
Dorsey, Thomas A. 490-492
Douglas, Aaron 521-523
Douglas, Buster 550
Douglas, John Thomas 512
Douglass, Frederick 1, 4, 8, 85, 137-138, 149, 168, 216, 223, 250, 268, 270-271, 284, 371, 422, 473
Douglass, Sarah Mapp 223
Douglas, Stephen A. 128
Dove, Ulysses 442
Downbeat 509
Downing, Big Al 498
Dozier, Lamont 501
The Drama of King Shotaway 429, 431
Dream Girls 441
Dred Scott v. *Sandford* 249, 257-258, 271
Drew, Richard Drew 165, 541
Drexler, Clyde 546
Drifters 491
Driskell, David C. 532
Drug use 344, 346
Du Bois, W. E. B. 8, 75, 101, 141, 229-230, 250, 262, 272-273, 284, 331, 356, 358, 424, 476, 487, 522
Dubose Hayward House 164
Dudley, S. H. 433
Dukakis, Michael 17, 117

Duke, Bill 448, 462
Dunbar, Paul Laurence 356, 417, 422, 433
Duncan, Todd 434, 435
Duncanson, Robert 520
Dunham, Katherine 435-437, 442
Durham Business and Professional Chain 323
Durham, North Carolina 321
Durham Realty and Insurance Company 322
Durham Textile Mill 322
Du Sable, Jean Baptiste Pointe 4, 125, 126, 316
Du Sable Museum of African-American History and Art 125, 528
The Dutchman 439
Dutton, Charles 472
Duvall, Cheryl 485
Dvorak, Antonin 149
Dwinddie Colored Quartet 493
Dykes, Eva B. 533

E

Earth, Wind, and Fire 501
East Side, West Side 464
Eatonville, Florida 160
Ebenezer Baptist Church 161, 289
Ebony 327, 476-479
Ebony and Topaz 488
Economic Opportunity Act 277
Economics 305-314, 315-328
The Economic Status of the Negro 487
Ecuador 72
Ecumenism 376
Eddie Murphy Productions 445
Edelman, Marian Wright 343
Edge of the City 453
Edison, Thomas 538

Edmonson, William 524, 531
Education 349-364
Edward Kennedy "Duke" Ellington Birthplace 168
Edward Kennedy "Duke" Ellington Residence 147
Edwards, Stoney 498
Eisenhower, Dwight D. 108, 154
El Morro castle 65
El Pueblo Museum 174
Elaw, Zilpha 371
Elder, Lonnie, III 437
Elders, Joycelyn 17, 281
Eldridge, Roy 506-507
Elijah McCoy Home Site 129
Elise, Sister 516, 517
Eller, Carl 548
Ellington, Edward Kennedy "Duke" 147, 149, 168, 442, 507-508, 510-511
Ellison, Ralph 425-426
Ellis, William 250
Elmer Brown 521
Elmwood Cemetery 166
Emancipation Act 257
Emancipation Proclamation 5, 8, 90-91, 143, 216, 225
Emancipation Statue 168
Embry, Wayne 555
Emerson, John 132, 157, 257
Emlen Tunnel 548
Emmett, Dan 432
The Emperor Jones 136, 435, 437, 451
The Empire Strikes Back 446
Employment 305-314
Encyclopedia Africana 356
Endeavor 540
English, Charlotte Moore 483
Ennis, William P., Jr. 569
Entrepreneurship 315-328
Equatorial Guinea 37
Eritrea 40

INDEX

Eritrean People's Liberation Front 40
Erving, Julius "Dr. J" 546
Espy, Mike 280
Essence 473, 478
Estevanico 1, 2, 74, 178
Ethiopia 22, 40, 41
Ethiopian Minstrels 432
Evans, Estelle 436
"An Evening Thought: Salvation by Christ with Penitential Cries" 417
Evers, Medgar 266
Ewe 34
Ewing, Patrick 546
Ex parte Virginia 165
Executive Order No. 8802 (1941) 106
Executive Order No. 9981 (1948) 106
Executive Order No. 10730 (1957) 108
The Exile 446, 449
Exodus of 1879 228
Exodusters 176, 297
Experience; or How to Give a Northern Man a Backbone 417
Extended families 334
Eyes on the Prize 484

F

Face the Nation 481
Fagan, Garth 444
Fair Housing Act (1968) 289
Faison, George 442
Falana, Lola 441
Famous Flames 499
Fanti 29
Fard, W. D. 7, 252
Farmer, Jackie 484
Farmer, James 288, 290
Farrakhan, Louis 253-254, 378, 384
Faso, Burkina 25
Father Augustine Tolton Grave Site 128
Father Divine 375
Faubus, Orval 108
Faubus, Orville 154
Fauset, Jessie 424
Fear of a Black Planet 503
Federal Theater Project 436
Feldman, Nita 444
Fences 440
Ferris, William 250, 532
Fetchit, Stepin 438, 450-451
Fête Noire 443
Fields, Kim 472
Fields, Mary 177
Fifteenth Amendment 94, 225, 227, 257-258, 318
Fifth Amendment 359
54th Massachusetts Infantry Regiment 140, 150, 161, 559
"Fight the Power" 503
Film 446-463
Fine Art 518-532
Fire Baptized Holiness Church 383
Firebird 443
First African Baptist Church 368, 369
First Baptist Church 374
First Black School 180
First Church of Christ 136
First Colored Methodist Protestant Church 380
First Parish Church 137
Fishburne, Laurence 440
Fisher, John 172
Fisk Jubilee Singers 491
Fisk University 159, 354
Fisk University Press 487
Fiske, Pomp 140
The Fist 130
Fitzgerald, Ella 506
Five Blind Boys from Mississippi 493
Five Guys Named Moe 441
The Five Heartbeats 462
Five Royales 495
Fletcher, Dusty 438
The Flip Wilson Show 467
Flipper, Henry Ossian 561
Floyed, Alpha 517
Food Stamp Program 312
Football 547
Foote, Julia A. J. 372
For Colored Girls Who Have Considered Suicide/When the Rainbow Is Enuf 440
Ford, Barney 173
Ford, Carl 440
Forrest, Edwin 432
Forster, James 318
Fort Buford State Historic Site 178
Fort Clatsop National Memorial 179
Fort Des Moines Provisional Army Officer Training School 128
Fort Douglas Military Museum 180
Forten, Charlotte 223
Forten, James 151, 246
Fort Gadsen 160
Fort Manuel Marker 177
Fort Snelling 157
Fort Snelling State Historical Park 132
Fortune, Amos 142
Fortune, T. Thomas 143, 474
Fort Union National Historic Site 178
Fort Washakie Blockhouse 181
48 Hours 445, 457
Foster, Gloria 439
Foster, William 446
Fourteenth Amendment 93, 97, 225, 227-229, 257-259, 266, 318, 357, 359

INDEX

Four Tops 130, 501
Foxx, Redd 438, 444, 466
Frances Ellen Watkins Harper House 150
Franklin and Armfield Office 164
Franklin, Aretha 498-499
Franks, Gary 279
Franzel, Carlotta 435
Fraunces, Samuel 147
Fraunces Tavern 147
Frazier, E. Franklin 331, 355, 487
Frazier, Joe 549
Frederick Douglass House 168
Frederick Douglass Institute 529
Frederick Douglass Monument 138, 149
Free African Societies 248
Free African Society 150, 222, 227, 268, 282-283, 366
Free Haven 143
The Free Negro Family 487
Freedmen's Bureau 350, 352
Freedom National Bank 145, 324
Freedom's Journal 223, 249, 270, 473, 476
Freeman 479
Freeman, Al, Jr. 439
Freeman, Morgan 458
Freeman, Paul 515
Freire, Helena 515
Frémont, John C. 558
French Guiana 72
The Fresh Prince of Bel-Air 472
Friendly Society 246
Friends of Johnny Mathis 282
Front for Liberation of Mozambique (FRELIMO) 47
Frost, Robert 121
Fugitive Slave Act (1850) 249
Fuller, Charles 439
Fuller, Meta Warrick 520, 521
Fuller Products Company 327-328
Fuller, S. B. 327
Funkadelic 501
Furious Five 503
Futch, Eddie 551
Fye, Samba 158

G

Gable, Clark 452
Gabon 36-38
Gaines, Lloyd 263-264, 357
Gaither, Barry 532
Gaither, Edmond Barry 528
Gambia 28
Gandhi, Mohandas K. 7, 289
Gangs 337
Gantt-Blackwell Fort 174
Garnet, Henry Highland 10, 223, 249, 270, 371
Garrison Marker and Bennington Museum 152
Garrison, William Lloyd 151, 152, 223, 352
Garrison, Zina 552
Garvey, Amy Jacques 489
Garvey, Marcus 8, 10, 102, 245, 250-251, 253, 287-288, 375, 380, 385
Gates, Henry Louis, Jr. 305, 313, 418-419, 532
Gaye, Marvin 130, 501
Gebhart v. *Belton* 359
General Hag's Skeezag 439
Genet, Jean 439
George, David 368
George, R. S. 322
George, U. M. 322
George Washington Carver Birthplace and National Monument 156
George Washington Carver Foundation 154
George Washington Carver Homestead 175
George Washington Carver Museum 154
George Washington Park 180
Gershwin, George 164, 434
Ghana 21, 22, 28, 32, 35, 213
Ghent, Henri 530
Ghost 458
Gibbs, Marla 468, 470
Gibson, Althea 542, 551, 552
Gibson, Truman K., Jr. 570
Gillespie, Dizzy 508
Gilpin, Charles 435
Giovanni, Nikki 417, 427
"The Girl Can't Help It" 497
Giselle 443
Giuliani, Rudolph 276
Glanville, Maxwell 436
Glory 161, 559
Glover, Danny 458
"Go Down Moses" 491
Go Tell It on the Mountain 425
"God's Gonna Cut You Down" 491
God's Step Children 449
Goines, Donald 428
Goldberg, Whoopi 305, 458
Gold Coast 29, 35
Golden Boy 441
Gold Mining Camp 172
Gone with the Wind 11, 446, 452
"Good Golly Miss Molly" 497
"Good Rocking Tonight" 494
Good Times 467-468
Goode, Mal 481-483
Goode, Sarah E. 533
Gooding, Henry 161
Goodin, Prince 135
Goodman, Benny 507, 508
Goodwyn, Morgan 350
Gordone, Charles 439
Gordy, Berry, Jr. 130, 328, 499, 501
Gore, Al 281
Gorleigh, Rex 528

INDEX

Gospel 490
Gospel Starlighters 495
Gossett, Louis, Jr. 436, 437, 439, 441, 458, 470
Graham, Gordon 485
Graham, Larry 501
Graham, Robert 130
Granary Burying Ground 141
Grand Cayman 60
Grand Comore 53
Grand Ole Opry 498
Grandmaster Flash and The Three MCs 503
Granger, Lester B. 287
Granny Maumee 433
Grant, Cecil 494
Grant, Jacquellyn 375
Grant, Micki 441
Grant, Ulysses S. 4
Gravely, Samuel R. 573
Graves, Earl G. 328, 478
Gray, Samuel 140
Great Plains Black Museum 177
Great Society 312, 338
The Great White Hope 439
Greenburgh, Jack 290
Green, Chuck 444
Green, Dennis 549, 555
Greene, "Mean" Joe 548
Greene, Nathanael 151
Greenfield, Elizabeth Taylor 512
Green Pastures 436
Green, Paul 435
Greenwood, L. C. 548
Gregory, Dick 444
Gregory, Frederick 538
Grenada 62
Grenadines 66
Grier, Rosey 548
Griffith, D. W. 448
Griggs v. *Duke Power Company* 266
Grosvenor, Vertamae 485
Guadeloupe 62

The Guardian 142
Guatemala 70
Guess Who's Coming to Dinner? 454
Guillaume, Robert 441
Guinea 22, 29
Guinea-Bissau 29
Gumbel, Bryant 484
Gunn, Moses 439, 440
Guy, Edna 437
Guy, Jasmine 472
Guyana 72
Guzman, Jessie Parkhurst 487

H

Hagar in the Wilderness 520
Hagler, Marvin 550
Haile Selassie I 40-41, 385
Haines Normal and Industrial Institute 353
Haiti 61, 62
Hale, Edward Everett 352
Haley, Alex 16, 158, 428, 469
Hallam, Lewis 431
Hall, Arsenio 445, 464
Hall, Charles B. 567
Hallelujah 450
Hallelujah Baby 441
Hall, Juanita 435
Hall, Prince 10, 140, 282, 283
Hall v. *DeCuir* 318
Hamblin, Ken 480
Hamilton, Ed 130
Hamlet 431
Hammon, Jupiter 417, 421
Hammons, David 527, 530
Hampton, Eleanor 444
Hampton, Fred 236, 292
Hampton, Henry 485
Hampton Institute Press 487
Hampton, Lionel 507
Hampton University 165
Hancock, John 141

Handy, Dorothy Antoinette 513
Handy, W. C. 152, 159, 432, 490, 493
Hansberry, Lorraine 436, 441
Hardney, Florence 530
Hare, Maude Cuney 488
Haring, Keith 524
Harlan, John Marshall 97, 260
Harlem Art Center 522
"The Harlem Dancer" 423
Harlem, New York 145
Harlem Renaissance 145, 146, 423-424
Harlem Riot (1964) 14, 237
Harlequin 431
Harmon Foundation 526
Harmon, Leonard 573
Harmon, William E. 521
Harper, Frances Ellen Watkins 150, 421
Harpers Ferry, Virginia 133
Harpers Ferry National Historic Park 170-171
Harriet Beecher Stowe House 133
Harriet Tubman House 143
Harris, Barbara 366, 378
Harris, James 548
Harris, Joel Chandler 419
Harris, Leon 485
Harris, Margaret 517
Harris, Neil 439
Harrison, Donald 510
Harrison, Richard B. 436
Harris, Wynonie 494
Harry, Jackee 472
Harry T. Burleigh Birthplace 149
Hartford Inquirer 476
Hartford 156
Hartigan, Linda Roscoe 532
Hastie, William 9, 68, 274
Hatch-Billops Studio 528
Hatch, Jim 528
Hatcher, Richard 15, 242, 277

195

INDEX

Hausa 33
Hawkins, Coleman 506
Hawkins, June 435
Hayden, Palmer 521, 527
Hayden, Robert 425
Hayes, Elvin 546
Hayes, Rutherford 227
Haynes, Daniel 450
Haynes, George Edmond 287
Haynes, Lemuel 149, 152
Hayward, Dubose 164
Hayward, William 564
Hazel 488
H-D-H 501
Health 344-348
Hearns, Thomas 550
Hearts in Dixie 450, 451
Height, Bob 432
Heights, Dorothy 120
Hemsley, Sherman 468-470
Henderson, Cassandra 485
Henderson, Fletcher 506, 507
Henderson, Gordon 526
Henderson, Julia L. 488
Henderson, Ricky 544
Hendrix, Jimi 497, 501-502
Henry, Andrew 177
Henry, Herbert 436
Henry O. Tanner House 150
Henson, Josiah 139, 224
Henson, Matthew 137-138, 148
Hepburn, Katharine 454
Herc, Cool 503
Here's Lucy 466
Hermenway, James 512
Herrings, James V. 518
Hewlet, James 431
Hickman, Fred 485
Highway No. 1 USA 516
Hill, Abram 436
Hill, Anita 261-262
Hill, Robert 288
Hill, Robert B. 336
Hill, T. Arnold 287, 488

Hinds, Ester 517
Hines, Gregory 441, 444
Hines, Maurice 444
Hinkson, Mary 444
Hinton, William A. 541
His Honor the Barber 433
Hispaniola 61, 62
The History of the Negro 481
Hogan, Ernest 432, 433
Holder, Geoffrey 438, 444
Holiday, Billie 496
Holiday, Jennifer 441
Holland, Brian 501
Holland, Eddie 501
Holley Knoll (Robert R. Moton) House 165
Holly, James T. 370
Hollywood Shuffle 447
Holman, Kwame 484
Holmes, Larry 550
Holmes, Oliver Wendell 263
Holsey, Lucius 374
Holyfield, Evander 550
Home Modernization and Supply Company 322
The Homesteader 449
Hood Theological Seminary 380
Hooks, Benjamin 120, 242, 287, 484
Hooks, Matthew Bones 180
Hooks, Robert 439, 441
Hoover, Herbert 274
Hoover, J. Edgar 14
Horne, Lena 450, 452-453
Horny Horns 502
Horton, Austin Asadata Dafore 437
Horton, George Moses 421
Hoskins, Allen Clayton (Farina) 449
Hot Chocolates 434
Hotel Theresa 146
Hot Fives 507
Hot Sevens 507

Houghton, Katherine 454
House, Colonel Charles Young 134
House Committee on Education and Labor 277
House of Flowers 438
House Party 2 462-463
Houston Hall, Lincoln University 157
Houston Opera Company 517
Howard, Oliver Otis 168, 350, 352
Howard University 169, 354
Howard University Press 488
Howe, Cato 140
Howells, William Dean 133
Hudlin, Warrington 463
Hudson, Cheryl Willis 489
Hudson, Wade 489
Hughes, Langston 145, 423-424, 429, 436, 440
Hughes, Sarah Ann 372
Hulsinger, George 521
Hunter, Clementine 524
Hunter-Gault, Charlayne 476, 484
Hurston, Zora Neale 104, 160, 419, 424, 427
Hustler's Convention 502
Hutu 45
Hyers, Emma Louise 512
Hyman, Earl 436

I

"I Can't Stop Loving You" 498
Ida B. Wells-Barnett House 126
"If We Must Die" 423
"If You See My Savior Tell Him You Saw Me" 492
"I Got a Woman" 496
"I Have a Dream" Speech 11, 13, 109, 162, 169, 228, 232
I Know Why the Caged Bird Sings 121
"I'll Be There." 501

INDEX

"I'll Overcome Someday" 491
Imam of Oman 44
Imani Temple African-American Catholic Congregation 383
"I'm Black and I'm Proud" 499
Imbokodvo National Movement 52
"I'm Moving On" 497
"I'm Walkin" 497
In Abraham's Bosom 435
Income 305-314, 315-328, 334
Indianapolis World 474
Indian Campaigns 560
In Dohomey 433
Industrial Work of Tuskegee Graduates and Former Students D 487
Infant mortality 344
Ingram, Rex 435, 436
Ingrams, Zell 521
Inkspots 495
In Living Color 471-472
Innis, Roy 289
Interdenominational Theological Center 380-381, 383
Inter-Ocean Hotel 173
Interracial Marriage 342, 343
In the Heat of the Night 454
Invisible Man 425
In White America 439
Ishaw, John W. 432
Isiah Thornton Montgomery House 156
Islam 377, 384
Island in the Sun 453
Isley Brothers 501
I Spy 464-465
It Takes A Nation of Millions to Hold Us Back 503
Ivax Corporation 328
"I've Been Loving You Too Long" 499
Ivory Coast 27
"I Wonder" 494

J

Jackman, Oliver 488
Jack, Sam 432
Jackson, Andrew 172, 246
Jackson, Augustus 533, 535
The Jackson Five 130, 501
Jackson, Janet 460, 462
Jackson, Jesse 1, 17-19, 117, 159, 242-243, 254, 267-268, 278-279, 290, 292-293, 545, 552
Jackson, Joseph H. 375
Jackson, Mahalia 493
Jackson, Michael 490, 501
Jackson, Nigel 526
Jackson, Rebecca Cox 372
Jackson Ward Historic District 166
Jacob, John E. 287
Jaffrey Public Library 143
Jamaica 55, 60, 63, 68
James A. Bland Grave Site 150
James, Daniel "Chappie" 154, 575
James H. Dillard House 155
James, Kay 279
James, King 385
Jamestown, North Carolina 166, 214, 295
James Weldon Johnson House 159
James Weldon Johnson Residence 147
Jamieson, Samuel 512
Jamison, Judith 442
Jan Ernst Matzeliger Statue 142
Jasper, John 166
Jawara, Dauda 27
Jay, Bill 439
Jazz 490
The Jazz Singer 450
Jean Baptiste Pointe Du Sable Homesite 126
Jeff Liberty Grave Site 136

The Jeffersons 464, 467, 470
Jefferson, Thomas 2, 76, 81
Jelly's Last Jam 441
Jemison, Mae C. 540-541
Jet 327, 477, 478
Jewell, K. Sue 338
Jewison, Norman 460
Jim Crow segregation 9, 10, 228, 372, 432
Joel, Lawrence 578
Joe Louis Memorials 130
John Brown House and Grave Site 144
John Brown Memorial State Park 176
John Brown Monument 132
John Brown's Caves 177
John Chavis Memorial Park 163
John Lawson 156
John Mercer Langston House 133
"Johnny B. Goode" 497
John Rankin House and Museum 133
John Roosevelt "Jackie" Robinson House 148
Johnson, Andrew 8, 174
Johnson, Anna 489
Johnson, Anthony 316
Johnson, Benjamin G. 562
Johnson C. Smith University 354
Johnson, Charles Spurgeon 279, 287, 331, 424, 487, 489
Johnson, Dwight H. 578
Johnson, Earvin "Magic" 546-547, 555
Johnson, Francis 512
Johnson, George 327, 328
Johnson, Hazel 557, 575
Johnson, Henry 564
Johnson, James Weldon 21, 101, 147, 159, 287, 433
Johnson, J. Rosamond 101, 159, 433, 435

INDEX

Johnson, Joan B. 328
Johnson, John H. 315, 326-327, 330, 335, 476
Johnson, Larry 526
Johnson, Louis 442, 444
Johnson, Lyndon B. 11, 111, 112, 235, 239, 256, 274, 277
Johnson, Malvin Gray 521, 522
Johnson Products Company 315, 328
Johnson Publishing Company 327-328
Johnson, Richard 216
Johnson, Robert L. 485
Johnson, Virginia 443
Johnston, Joshua 518, 520
John Swain Grave Site 170
Jones, Absalom 150, 222, 268, 282-283, 366
Jones, Alpheus 560
Jones, Casey 158
Jones, Charles Price 381
Jones, Clarence B. 476
Jones, C. P. 382
Jones, David "Deacon" 548
Jones, Elayne 513, 516
Jones, Eugene Kinckle 287
Jones, Gayl 427, 428
Jones, James Earl 439, 440, 446, 458, 470
Jones, LeRoi (see Imamu Amiri Baraka)
Jones, Lois Mailou 527
Jones, Matilda Sisieretta 512
Jones, Quincy 305, 501, 504
Jones, Robert 512
Joplin, Scott 157, 504, 513, 517
Jordan, Louis 441, 493-494
Jordan, Michael 305, 460, 546, 547
Jordan, Vernon E., Jr. 287, 470
Joseph H. Rainey House 164
Journal of Negro History 167, 356

Joyner, Florence Griffith 551-552, 555
Joyner-Kersee, Jackie 305, 551-552, 554, 555
Jubilee 517
Judaism 380
Judith Rutherford Marechal 439
The Juggler of Our Lady 517
Julia 464, 466
Julian, Percy Lavon 541
Jungle Fever 462
Just Above Midtown/Downtown Alternative Art Center 527
Just Us Books, Inc. 489

K

Kansas Exodus 249
Kay, Ulysses 515, 517
Keep Shuffling 434
Kennedy, John F. 11, 111, 121, 277
Kenny, John 487
Kenya 22, 44-45
Kenya African National Union 45
Kenyatta, Jomo 45
Kenyatta, Kwame 362
Kerner Commission 239, 483
Kerner Commission Report 239
Kersands, Billy 432
Kersee, Bob 555
Keyes, Alan 480
Kid Creole 503
Kincaid, Jamaica 427
King, Ben E. 491
King, Coretta Scott 290
King, Don 551, 553
King, Emeline 526
King, Mabel 441
King, Martin Luther, Jr. 1, 8, 11-12, 17, 19, 75, 109, 115, 118, 137, 152, 153, 159, 161-162, 169, 228, 232, 240-241, 243, 245, 267, 277, 279, 289-290, 293, 366, 375, 384, 426, 455, 470, 481, 578
King-Reeves, Hattie 436
King, Rodney 17, 20, 237, 243, 376
Kingsley Plantation 160
Kingsley, Zephaniah 160
Kinshasha Holman Conwill 527
Kongo 37
Kool and the Gang 502
Korean War 573-574
Kountz, Samuel L. 541
Krone, Gerald 439
Ku Klux Klan 5
Ku Klux Klan Act (1871) 94
Kykunkor 437

L

L'Enfant, Pierre-Charles 138
La Guiablesse 437
Lady Sings the Blues 444
Lane, William Henry 432
Laney, Lucy 353
Langston, John Mercer 133
Lanier, Willie 548
Lankfor, John Anderson 164
Lankford, John A. 525
Larsen, Nella 424
The Late Show 445
Lawnside, New Jersey 143
Lawrence, Jacob 523, 532
Lawrence, Robert H. 538
Lawson, James 376
Lawson, Jennifer 464, 484
Laying Down the Law: Joe Clark's Strategy for Saving Our Schools 363
The Lazarus Syndrome 470
Leadership Conference on Civil Rights 289
Lead Story 485
Lean on Me 363
The Learning Tree 456

INDEX

Lear, Norman 466
LeBeauf, Sabrina 472
Ledger 479
Lee, Bertram 547, 555
Lee, Canada 436
Lee, Don L. 426
Lee, Everett 517
Lee, Jarena 371
Lee, Robert E. 4, 558
Lee-Smith, Hughie 521, 523
Lee, Spike 305, 447, 448, 459-460, 503
Lee, Tom 159
Leeward Islands 64
Leidesdorff Street 173
Leidesdorff, William Alexander 173, 315
Leigh, Vivien 452
Leland, John 367
Lemuel Haynes House 149
Leonard, Matthew 578
Leonard, Sugar Ray 550
Leone, Sierra 34
Leopold, King 39
Lesotho 50
Lester Bowie's Brass Fantasy 511
Lethal Weapon 458
Levi Coffin House 128
Lewaro, Villa 144
Lewis and Clark Expedition 179
Lewis, Delano Eugene 476
Lewis, Edmonia 518, 520
Lewis, James 139
Lewis, John 232, 290-291
Lewis, Meriwether 175
Lewis, Norman 523, 528
Lewis, Reggie 555
Lewis, Reginald F. 324-325, 327
Lewis, Samella 523, 528
The Liberator 151, 152, 223
Liberia 21, 22, 30, 222
Liberty, Jeff 136
Liele, George 368
Life 476

Life expectancy 346
"Lift Every Voice and Sing" 100, 148, 159
Like It Is 483
Lilies of the Field 453
Lincoln, Abraham 8, 90, 135, 143, 150, 168, 216, 224
Lincoln Center Jazz Orchestra 510
Lincoln Hall (Berea College) 154
Lincoln Institute 354
Lincoln Memorial 169, 228
Lincoln Picture Co. 449
Lincoln University 156, 354
Lisa, Manuel 177
Liscome Bay 175
Lisle, George 163
Listen Chicago 479
Literature 417-428
Little Cayman 60
Little Ham 436
Little Richard (see Little Richard Penniman)
The Little Colonel 450
The Littlest Rebel 450
Live at the Apollo 499
Livin' Large 462
Living Single 472
Livingston, David 47
Livingstone College 380
Locke, Alain 355, 424, 488, 518, 522
Long, Donald R. 578
Long, Herman 487
"Long Tall Sally" 497
Lorraine Hotel 159
Los Angeles riots 14, 17, 20, 376
Lothery, Eugene 483
Louis Armstrong House 148
Louis, Joe 11, 130, 479, 549
Louis Jordan and the Tympany Five 494
Loury, Glen 279
Love, Nat 179-180

Love Thy Neighbor 451
Lowery, Joseph E. 289
Lucas, Sam 446
The Lucy Show 466
Lunceford, Jimmie 507
Lundy, Lamar 548
Lyles, Aubrey 434
Lynching 100, 228, 487
Lynching by States, 1882-1958 487

M

Mabley, Jackie "Moms" 438, 443-444
Madagascar 53, 54
Madah Hyers, Anna 512
Madhubuti, Haki R. 426, 489
The Mad Miss Manton 452
Mae C. Jemison Academy 540
Magazines (see Media)
Maggie Lena Walker House 166, 167
Majors and Minors 133
Makeba, Miriam 291
Malagasy Republic 53
Malawi 46, 48
Malcolm X 7, 10, 11, 13, 145, 148, 235, 245, 252, 288, 375, 426, 455, 460, 503, 578
Malcolm X 459, 461
Malcolm X Academy 362
Malcolm X Residence 148
Mali 21, 28, 30, 34, 213
Malinke 29, 30
Malone, Moses 546
Man about Town 451
Mandela, Nelson 52, 293
Manelik II 40
Manumission Society 350
"Maple Leaf Rag" 157
Marbury, Donald L. 484
March on Washington 12-13, 169, 232, 243, 290

199

INDEX

Maria Baldwin House 141
Mariam, Mengistu Haile 41
Mariel boatlift 55, 300
Markham, Pigmeat 502
Markings 515
Marley, Bob 385
Maroons 3, 34
Marsalis, Branford 510
Marsalis, Wynton 510
Marshal, Jim 548
Marshall, George C. 567
Marshall, Thurgood 11, 107, 112, 255-256, 261, 263, 359
Martel, Linda 498
Martha and the Vandellas 130, 501
Martin 472
Martin Beck Theater 441
Martin, Dewey "Pigmeat" 432
Martin, Helen 436, 439, 441
Martinique 64, 66
Martin Luther King Day 17, 243
Martin Luther King, Jr. Center for Nonviolent Social Change 162, 290
Martin Luther King, Jr. National Historic Site 162
Martin, Nan 439
Martin, Sallie 493
Marvellettes 500
Mary Ann Shadd Cary House 169
Mary Church Terrell House 169
Mary McLeod Bethune Memorial 169
Mary Tyler Moore Show 467
Mason, Charles H. 382
"Master Juba" 432
Matney, William C., Jr. 481-482
Matthew Henson Memorial 137
Matthew Henson Residence 148
Matthews, Benjamin 517
Matzeliger, Jan 142, 533, 535
Maude 467

Mau Mau rebellion 45
Maurice, Prince 54
Mauritania 32
Mauritius 54
Maverick, Samuel 140
"Maybelline" 497
Mayfield, Curtis 498, 501
Mayflower 2, 216
Mayhew, Allen B. 177
Maynard, Robert 473
Mayotte 53
Mays, Willie 544
Mbuti 39
McAdoo, Bob 546
McAlpin, Harry 476
McBride, William, Jr. 528
McCall's Pattern Company 325
McCannon, Dinga 527
McClendon, Rose 435, 436
McClenny, Cheryl 530
McClinton, O. B. 498
McCormick, Cyrus 534
McCoy, Elijah 327, 533, 535
McCullers, Carson 436
McDaniel, Hattie 11, 446, 452
McDuffie, Arthur 16, 20, 242
McElroy, Guy C. 531
McGovern, George 293
McGuire, George Alexander 380
McKay, Claude 147, 423-424
McKayle, Donald 442, 444
McKee, Clarence 483
Mckenna, Maureen A. 532
McKenney, Morris 436
McKenzie, Vashti 378
McKenzie, Vinson 525
McKinney, Nina Mae 450
McKissick, Floyd 289
McLaurin, G. W. 264
McLaurin v. *Oklahoma State Regents for Higher Education* 264
McMillan, Terry 427
McNair, Lesley James 571

McNair, Ronald 538
McNamara, Robert 577
McNeil, Claudia 437
McPhatter, Clyde 495
McQueen, Armelia 441
McQueen, Butterfly 436, 452
McShine, Kynastan 529
McTell, Blind Willie 492
The Meanest Man in the World 452
Media 473-489
Medicaid 312, 348
Medicare 312
Meharry Medical College 539
Meharry Medical School 159
Mel, Melle 503
Meltzer, Milton 429
Member of the Wedding 436
Memoria 442
Memphis Blues 490
Memphis Free Speech 476
Menellik, King 41
Merina 53
Metronome 509
Mexican-American War 221
Mexico 55, 74
Mfume, Kweisi 281
Miami riots (1980) 16, 242
Micheaux, Oscar 446, 448-449
Michigan Chronicle 482
Midnighters 496
"Midnight Hour" 499
Mighty Clouds of Joy 493
Miles, George L., Jr. 484
Military 556-579
Miles, William H. 381
Miller, Dorie 174, 570, 572
Miller, Flournoy 434
Mills, Florence 434, 437
Mills, Stephanie 441
Milton House and Museum 135
Milton, John 141
Milton L. Olive Park 127
Mingus, Charles 510

200

INDEX

Minton's Playhouse 508
Missouri Compromise 221, 271
Missouri ex rel. Lloyd Gaines v. *Canada* 263, 357
Mitchell, Abbie 435
Mitchell, Arthur 438, 443
Mitchell, Nellie Brown 512
Modeliste, Ziggy 501
Modern Sounds in Country Music 497
Modern Sounds in Country Music Volume 2 498
Moheli 53
Momeyer, William M. 567
Moms Mabley at the Geneva Conference 444
Moms Mabley at the UN 444
Monagas, Lionel 481
Mondale, Walter 112, 279-280
Monk, Thelonius 490, 508
Monroe, James 30, 222
Monroe, Marilyn 453
Monrovia 30, 222
Montgomery, Barbara 440
Montgomery Bus Boycott 11
Montgomery Improvement Association 11, 289
Montgomery, Isiah Thornton 156
Montserrat 64
Moon, Warren 549
Moore, Charles 444
Moore, Gatemouth 492
Moore, Kermit 516
Moore, Melba 441
Moore, Tim 438
Moorish Science Temple 251
Moorland-Spingarn Collection 169
Morehead, Scipio 519
Morehouse College 161, 354
Moreland, Mantan 450
Morgan, Garrett 533
Morris Brown College 161
Morrison, Toni 305, 417-421, 427, 463

Morton, Joe 441
Mosell, Sadie T. 533
Mosely, Robert 517
Moshoeshoe I 50
Moskowitz, Henry 284, 285
Mossi 25
Mother Bethel African Methodist Episcopal Church 150
Motley, Archibald 521, 522
Moton, Robert R. 165
Motown Museum 130
Motown Record Corporation 130, 328, 499, 501
Mott, Lucretia Coffin 223
Mount Pisgah African Methodist Episcopal Church 143
Movement for the Liberation of São Tomé and Príncipe 38
Mowry, Tamera 472
Mowry, Tia 472
Moynihan, Daniel Patrick 338
Mozambique 47
Mr. Ed 466
Mr. Lord of Koal 433
Mswati 52
Muhammad, Clara 360
Muhammad, Elijah 7, 11, 13, 251-252, 254, 360, 375, 378, 384, 566
Muhammad, Sister Clara 360
Muhammad, Wallace Fard 252
Muhammad, Warith D. 384
Muhammad's Temple No. 2 Publications Department 486
Mulatto 429, 436
Mules and Men 419
Multicultural teaching 364
Murphy, Eddie 444, 445, 457-458
Murphy, John Henry 475
Murray, Ellen 164
Murray, Joan 476
Murray, Oliver E. 573
Muscle Shoals Sounds 500

Museum of African Art 528
Museveni, Yoweri 46
Music 490-517
Muslim Mosque, Inc. 13
Mutual Black Network 479
Mutual Building and Loan Association 322
Muzorewa, Bishop 49
Myers, Milton 442
Myers, Pauline 436
"My Jesus Is All the World to Me" 496

N

NAACP Legal Defense and Educational Fund, Inc. 288, 359
NAACP v. *Alabama* 286
Nairobi Day School 360
Namibia 24, 50
Narrative of the Life of Frederick Douglass 422
Natchez National Cemetery 156
National Aeronautics and Space Administration (NASA) 540
National Afro-American Museum 134
National Association for the Advancement of Colored People (NAACP) 8, 101, 228, 231-232, 242-243, 255, 273, 283, 284, 288, 290, 314, 356, 476, 488
National Association of Colored Women 169, 284
National Association of Colored Women's Clubs 168
National Baptist Convention 366
National Baptist Convention of America, Unincorporated 383
National Baptist Convention of the U.S.A., Inc. 375, 383-384
National Baptist Educational Convention of the U.S.A. 384

201

INDEX

National Baptist Publishing Board 486
National Black Caucus of State Legislators 277
National Black Network 479
National Black Political Convention 15
National Center of Afro-American Artists 528
National Conference of Black Mayors 277
National Conference on a Black Agenda for the Eighties 277
National Council of Churches 376
National Council of Negro Women 277
National Endowment for the Arts 518
National Freedmen's Relief Association 352
National Institute Against Prejudice and Violence 243
National League for the Protection of Colored Women 287
National League on Urban Conditions Among Negroes 287
National Medical Association 284
National Museum of African Art 169
National Museum of the Tuskegee Airmen 131
National Negro Business League 273, 284, 305, 318
National Negro Committee 284
National Negro Finance Corporation 322
National Negro Newspaper Publishers Association 474
National Primitive Baptist Convention of America 384
National Rainbow Coalition 293
National Training School for Women and Girls 353

National Union for the Total Independence of Angola (UNITA) 35
National Urban League 231, 232, 243, 283, 287, 290, 314, 488
Nation of Islam 7, 13, 148, 251, 254, 279, 360, 378, 384, 486, 503
Native Son 418, 425
Naylor, Gloria 427
Negritude 521
Negro American Labor Council 232
The Negro and Economic Reconstruction 488
The Negro and His Song 487
Negro Digest 327, 476, 477
Negro Ensemble Company 439, 440
The Negroes in Medicine 487
Negro Membership in Labor Unions 489
Negro Poetry and Drama 488
Negro Society for Historical Research 355
Negro Soldiers Monument 151
"The Negro Speaks of Rivers" 423
The Negro World 250, 489
The Negro Yearbook 487
Negro Yearbook Publishing Company 487
Nell, William C. 141
Netherlands Antilles 57, 64
Nevis 56, 64, 66
New Bedford Whaling Museum 142
New Concept Development Center 360
New England Anti-Slavery Society 284
New England Freedmen's Aid Society 352
New Jack City 448, 462

New Jersey-based Education, Training and Enterprise Center 323
New York Manumission Society 222
New York African Free School 350, 351
New York Age 143, 474
National Foundation for Teaching Entrepreneurship 323
Newman, Rock 551
The New Negro, 424
Newspaper Boy 520
Newspapers (see Media)
Newton, Huey P. 14, 15, 113, 236, 291
Newton, John 368
Nez Percé National Historical Park 175
Nguema, Francisco Macias 38
Niagara Movement 230, 284
Nicaragua 70
Nicephore Soglo 25
Nichols, Denise 439
Nicodemus Colony 176
Nicodemus, Kansas 297
Niger 32
Nigeria 32
Nilotic 44
Niño, Pedro Alonzo 1, 2, 216
9th Cavalry Regiment 180-181, 560
Nixon, L. A. 262
Nixon v. *Condon* 263
Nixon v. *Herndon* 262
Nkrumah, Kwame 28
Nobel Peace Prize 51
Noble, Gil 473, 482, 483
Nonviolent philosophy 235
Norris Wright Cuney 488
North Carolina Mutual Life Insurance Company 163, 322
Northern Star 223
North Star 149, 270, 473

INDEX

Northrup, Solomon 88
Northwest Ordinance 221
Norton, Eleanor Holmes 267
No Way Out 453
Ntozake Shange 440
Nyasaland 47

O

Oak and Ivy 133
Oak Hill Cemetery 172
Oakland Memorial Chapel and Alcorn State University 156
Oberlin College 133
Obote, Milton 46
The Octoroon 432
Odets, Clifford 441
An Officer and a Gentleman 458
Officer Training School 557, 564
Of Mice and Men 452
"Oh Freedom" 491
Ohio Players 502
Oklahoma movement 249
Old Courthouse 157, 178
Oldsmobile Achieva SC 526
O'Leary, Hazel R. 281
Olive, Milton 578
Oliver, Joe "King" 485, 506
Oliver Otis Howard House 168
O'Neal, Frederick 436
O'Neal, Shaquille 305, 546
O'Neill, Eugene 435
One More Spring 451
On the Pulse of Morning 121
101 Ranch 179
Onesimus 539
Open Hand Publishing Inc. 489
Opera Ebony 517
Opera/South 516
Operation Breadbasket 293
Operation PUSH (People United to Save Humanity) 242, 292-293
Opportunity 423, 424

O'Ree, Willie 542
Organization of African Unity (OAU) 24
Organization of Afro-American Unity 13
Oriental America 432
The Original Colored American Opera Troupe 512
Original Dixieland Jazz Band 506
Orioles 495
Orozco, Jose Clemente 523
Oscar Micheaux Corp. 449
Oscar Staton DePriest House 127
Othello 431
Ottolenghi, Joseph 350
Our Gang 449
"Out of Sight" 499
Ovington, Mary White 284, 285, 488
Owens, Jesse 542-543
Oyo 33
Oyster Man 433

P

The Padlock 431
Page, Allan 548
Page, Clarence 476
Page, Ken 441
Page, Ruth 437
Paige, Satchel 470
Palmer, Henry 125
Palmer Memorial Institute 353
Panama 70, 72
Panama Hattie 453
"Papa's Got a Brand New Bag" 499
Paradise Lost 141
Paris 470
Parker, Charlie "Bird" 508-511
Park, Robert E. 487
Parks, Gordon, Sr. 476, 478, 456, 528

Parks, Rosa 1, 11, 118, 228, 231-232, 289
Parliment 501
Parliment-Funkadelic 502
Partners in Ecumenism 376
Party of the Hutu Emancipation Movement (PARMEHUTU) 45
Paul Cuffe Farm and Memorial 142
Paul Cuffe Memorial 141
Paul Laurence Dunbar House 133
Paul Robeson Residence 135, 148
Paul, Willard S. 571
Payne, Daniel A. 354, 366, 371
Payne, Les 473
Payne Theological Seminary 379
Payton, Walter 548
Peace Corps 540
Pearl Harbor, Hawaii 174
Pearl Primus Dance Language Institute 438
Peary-McMillan Arctic Museum 137
Peary, Robert E. 137, 148
Pecanha, Nilo 72
Peebles, Melvin Van 456
Pendleton, Clarence M., Jr. 16
Penniman, Little Richard 497
Penn School Historic District 164
Pennsylvania Society for Promoting the Abolition of Slavery 222
Pentecostalism 366, 374
"People Get Ready" 498
People's Building and Loan Association 322
People versus Property 487
Pepper Jelly Lady 523
Pepsi Bethel 444
Performing Arts 429-445
Perry, Julia 515
Perry, Regina 530, 532

203

INDEX

Pershing, John J. 564
Persian Gulf War 577-579
Person to Person 481
Peters, Clark 452
Peterson, Louis 436
Peterson, Oscar 506
Philadelphia Female Anti-Slavery Society 223
Philadelphia Tribune 474
Philander-Smith College 154
Philip, Randolph, A. 10, 290
Phillips, Channing E. 268
Phillips School of Theology 381
Phillis Wheatley Folio 141
The Philosophy and Opinions of Marcus Garvey 489
Pickett, Bill 179
Pickett, Wilson 499
Pierce, Delilah 523
Pilgrim Baptist Church 492
Pinchback, P. B. S. 268
Pindell, Howardena 527, 529
Pinklon, Thomas 553
Pinkney, Jerry 526
Pinkney, William 574
Pinto da Costa, Manuel 39
Pioneers' Home 170
Pippin, Horace 524
Pittsburgh Courier 479, 481, 566
Pitts, Riley L. 578
Pittsylvania County Courthouse 165
The Plantation Revue 434
Planter 558
"Please Mister Postman" 500
Plessy, Homer Adolph 228, 260
Plessy v. Ferguson 96, *107, 228, 229, 232, 257, 260, 318, 356*
A Poetic Equation: Conversations between Nikki Giovanni and Margaret Walker 488
Poetic Justice 462
Poitier, Sidney 436-437, 446, 453-455, 457

The Policy Players 433
Pollock, Jackson 523
Ponce de León, Juan 2, 65
Poole, Elijah 252
"Poor People's Campaign" 290
Poor People's March on Washington 481
Poor, Salem 140, 557
The Poor Soldier, Obi 431
Pope, Alexander 419
Pop music 501
Popular Movement for the Liberation of Angola (MPLA) 35
Population 295-304
Porgy and Bess 164, 434, 453
Positively Black 473
Poverty 309, 341
Powell, Adam Clayton, Jr. 145, 268, 275-276, 577
Powell, Adam Clayton, Sr. 145
Powell, Adam Clayton, III 485
Powell, Clilan B. 476
Powell, Colin L. 17, 556, 557, 576-577, 579
Power of the Ballot: A Handbook for Black Political Participation 489
Precipice 442
Presbyterian Church, U.S.A. 366
Price, Florence 514, 515
Price, Leontyne 514
"Pride and Joy" 501
Pride, Charley 498
Primus-Borde School of Primal Dance 438
Primus, Pearl 437, 442
Prince 305, 460
Prince Goodin Homestead 135
Prince Hall and His Followers 488
Príncipe 38
Progressive National Baptist Convention, Inc. 366, 375, 384
Project Headstart 312

Prosser, Gabriel 247
Provident Hospital 125, 533
Provident Hospital and Training School 127
Provincetown Theatre 435
Pryor, Richard 444, 457
Public Enemy 503
Publishing (see Media)
Pueblo, Hawikuh 178
Puerto Rico 64
Pulliam, Keshia Knight 472
Purlie Victorious 441
Purviance, Florence 522
Purvis, William 535
PUSH-EXCEL 293
Pygmies 26

Q

Quarles, Norma 482, 485
Queen Latifah 305, 472, 503
Quintet 442
Quitman, Cleo 440

R

Rabah 37
"Rabbi Matthew" 380
Race, Fear and Housing in a Typical American Community 489
Racism 242
Radio (see Media)
A Rage in Harlem 448, 462
Ragtime 504
The Railroad Porter 446
Rainbow Coalition 19
Rainey, Gertrude "Ma" 432
Rainey, Joseph Hayne 164
Raisin 441
Raisin in the Sun 437, 441
Ralph Bunche House 149
Ranch, E. J. "Lucky" Baldwin 172
Randolph, A. Philip 10, 262, 267, 275, 289-290, 566

INDEX

Rangel, Charles 288, 579
Rang Tang 434
Rankin, John 133
Ransom, Reverdy 295, 304, 375
"Rapper's Delight" 503
Rashad, Phylicia 472
Raspberry, William 473
Rastafarians 385
Ray, Marcus H. 570
"Reach Out I'll Be There" 501
Reagan, Ronald 16-17, 243, 280
Reconstruction 8, 9, 227, 249
Recorder 479
The Redd Foxx Comedy Hour 467
The Redd Foxx Show 467
Redding, Otis 499
Redd, Veronica 439
Redman, Don 506, 507
Red Sea Press 489
Reed, Ishmael 426
Reed, Napoleon 435
Reed, Willis 546, 555
Reflections in D 442
Regal Theater 438
Reid, Tim 472
Religion 365-385
Réunion 54
Revelations 442
Revels, Hiram R. 6, 8, 164, 268, 271-272, 372
Reverend George Lisle Memorial 163
Revolutionary War 556
Reynolds, Joshua 519
Rhode Island Black Heritage Society 151
Rhodesia 47, 49
Rhythmetron 443
Rice, Jerry 548
Rice, Thomas Dartmouth 432
Richard Pryor—Live in Concert 457
Richard III 431

Richie, Lionel 501
Rich, Matty 448
The Rider of Dreams 433
Riggs, Marlon 485
Riley, Clayton 480
Ringgold, Faith 527
Riots 14, 237
"Rip It Up" 497
Rivera, Diego 523
The River Niger 439
Rivers, Ruben 571
Roach, Hal 449
Roach, Max 506
Robert S. Abbott House 128
Robert Smalls House 163
Robertson, Don 527
Robeson, Paul 129, 135, 148, 435, 449, 451
Robinson, Bill "Bojangles" 166, 434, 437, 450
Robinson Crusoe 431
Robinson, Frank 16, 544, 545
Robinson, Jackie 146, 148, 481, 542-544
Robinson, Lavaughn 444
Robinson, Max 482
Robinson, Randall 293-294
Robinson, Smokey 130
Robinson, Sugar Ray 549
Roc 472
Rodgers, Jonathan 483
Rodgers, Moses 172
Rogers, Joel Augustus 250
Rogers, Rod 444
Rogers, Timmie 464
Rohan, Shelia 443
Roker, Roxie 439
Rolle, Esther 439, 467-468
Rollins, Sonny 510
Roman Catholic Church 376, 383
Romare, Eleo 442-443
Romney, George 519
Roosevelt, Franklin D. 8, 106, 160, 274, 518, 566, 572

Roosevelt, Theodore 149
Roots 16, 121, 158, 428, 464, 467, 469, 470
Roots: The Next Generation 470
Rose, Edward 177
Rosenwald Fund 518
Ross, Diana 501
Ross, Ted 441
Rotardier, Kelvin 442
Roundtree, Richard 456, 470
Rowan, Carl T. 473, 573
Rowland and Mitchell 322
The Royal Family 467
Royal Knights Savings and Loan Association 322
Royal Sons 495
Roy Wilkins House 149
Rozelle, Robert V. 532
Rudolph, Wilma 470, 542, 551
Rufus Rastus 433
Runnin' Wild 434
Rush, Christopher 371
Russell, Bill 546, 547
Russell, Jane 453
Russwurm, John B. 223, 249, 270, 473, 476
Rustin, Bayard 289, 290
Rwanda 44, 45

S

Sackler, William 439
Saddler, Joseph 503
Saint Christopher 56, 66
Saint Croix 68
Saint-Gaudens, Augustus 140
Saint John 68
Saint Kitts 64, 66
Saint Lucia 66
Saint Thomas 68
Saint Vincent 66
Sakalava 53
Salem, Peter 140, 557
Sallee, Charles 521

INDEX

Salt-N-Pepa 503
Sam, Alfred C. 250
Sanchez, Sonia 427
Sanders, Wayne 517
Sands, Diana 437, 439
Sanford and Son 444, 466
Sanford, Isabel 468-469
San Salvador Island 58
Santa Anita Race Track 172
Santería 366
Santo Domingo 62
Santomee, Lucas 533, 539
Sao Tomé 38
Saratoga 452
Sargent, Ruppert L. 578
Sasser, Clarence E. 578
Saturday Night Live 445, 457
Saunders, Wallace 158
Savage, Augusta 521
Savory, P. M. H. 476
Savoy Ballroom 507
Saw the House in Half, a Novel 488
Saxon, Luther 435
Sayers, Gayle 548
Scarborough, William Sanders 356
Scheherazade 443
Schindler's List 458
Schmeling, Max 130, 549
Schmoke, Kurt 276
Schomburg, Arthur A. 146, 355, 528
Schomburg Center for Research in Black Culture 146, 527
School Daze 459
Schuller, Gunther 511
Science 533-541
Scotia Seminary 354
Scott, Charlotte 168
Scott, Dred 132, 157, 257-258
Scott, Emmett J. 487
Scott, Hazel Dorothy 464
Scott Joplin House 157

Scottsboro Boys 11, 104, 105
Scott, Tasha 472
Scott, William Edouard 521
Seale, Bobby 14, 113, 236, 291-292
Search for Missing Persons 479
Segregation 228
Selida, Marie 512
Selway, Robert R. 567
Selznick, David O. 452
Senegal 32, 34
Senga Nengudi 527
Senghor, Leopold Sedar 34
Sensational Nightingales 493
Separate but equal doctrine 229
704 Hauser 467
"Seven Rooms of Gloom" 501
Seychelles 54
Shaft 456
Shaka 51
Shakesnider, Wilma 517
Shakespeare, William 431
Shaw, Bernard 485
Shaw, Robert Gould 140, 161
Shaw University 354
Sheba, Queen of 41, 385
Shell, Art 549, 555
Sheridan Broadcasting Corporation 479
She's Gotta Have It 447, 459
The Shoo-Fly Regiment 433
Shook, Karel 443
Show Boat 136, 451, 452
Shrine of the Black Madonna 375
Shuffle Along 434
Sickle Cell Anemia 345
Silver Bluff Baptist Church 366, 367
Silver Streak 457
Simms, Hilda 436
Simon the Cyrenian 433
Simpson, Carole 484
Simpson, Georgiana Rose 533

Sims, Lowery 530, 531
Singleton, John 446, 448, 462
Sipuel, Ada Lois 263
Sipuel v. *Board of Regents of the University of Oklahoma* 263
Siqueiros, David Alfero 523
Sissle, Noble 434
Sister, Sister 472
Sitting Bull 178
Six Degrees of Separation 472
The Six Million Dollar Man 467
60 Minutes 482
Skies of America 515
Sklarek, Norma Merrick 525
Slave trade 22, 368
Slavery 213-226
Sloane, Paul 449
Sly and the Family Stone 501
Small Business Administration 324
Small, Mary J. 372
Smalls, Robert 163, 558
Smith, Abiel 139
Smith, Bessie 432, 495
Smith, Bragg 162
Smith, Freeman M. 322
Smith, Gerritt 143, 144
Smith, Ian 49
Smith, James McCune 539
Smith, Lowell 443
Smithsonian Institution 169
Smithsonian Jazz Masterpiece Ensemble 510
Smith v. *Allwright*.) 256
Smith, Will 472
Smith, Willi 525-526
Smith, William E. 521
"Snakes Crawl at Night" 498
Snelling, Josiah 132
Snow, Hank 497
Sobhuza II 52
Social Gospel Movement 375
Society for the Propagation of the Gospel in Foreign Parts 350

INDEX

Society of California Pioneers 172
Sojourner Truth Grave Site 129
The Soldier's Play 439
Solomon, King 385
Somalia 23, 41
Sonata for Piano and String Quartet 515
Song of Solomon 420
Songhai 21, 28, 213
So Nice, They Named It Twice 439
Sons of Ham 433
Soul Train 328, 464
Sounder 456
South Africa 22, 51-52, 294
South Central 472
Southern Christian Leadership Conference (SCLC) 13, 232, 283, 289-290, 292
The Southerners 433
The Southern Workman 487
South View Cemetery 162
South West Africa People's Organization (SWAPO) 50
Southwest Atlanta Youth Business Organization (SWAYBO) 323
Sowell, Thomas 16, 279, 312, 314
Soyinka, Wole 418
Spanish-American War 180, 561
Spelman College 161
Spencer, Peter 369, 380
Spielberg, Steven 458
Spingarn, Joel E. 287
Spingarn Medal 287
Spinks, Leon 550
Sports 542-554
Spriggs, Edward 527
Spruill, James 439
S.S. *Liberia* 250
Stabat Mater 515
Stallings, George A., Jr. 377, 383

"Stand by Me" 491
St. Andrew's African Methodist Episcopal Church 172
Stand Up and Cheer 451
Stanley, W. Jerome 555
Stans, Jacob 512
Stanton, Elizabeth Cady 223
Star Trek: The Next Generation 470
Star Wars 446
Stars of Faith 440
The State of Black America 489
Stax Records 500
Steele, Shelby 16, 279
Steinberg, Benjamin 516
Stephenson, Dwight 548
Stevenson, Mickey 500
Stevens, Thaddeus 150, 271
Steward, Susan McKinney 533
Stewart, Maria 247, 371
St. George's Church 366
St. George's Episcopal Church 149
Still, William Grant 143, 513, 515, 517
Stimpson, Henry L. 570
Stir Crazy 444, 457
St. Jacques, Raymond 439
"St. Louis Blues" 152
St. Louis Woman 435
St. Luke Penny Savings Bank 167
St. Luke's Episcopal Church 170
St. Mark's Theater 439
Stokes, Carl 277
Stono River Slave Rebellion Historic Site 164
Stormy Weather 453
Stowe, Calvin 137
Stowe, Harriet Beecher 4, 133, 134, 137, 139, 446
Stowe House 137
Stowers, Freddie 565
Straight out of Brooklyn 448, 462

Strait, George 484
Strange Incident 452
Strictly Business 462
Strode, Woodrow 548
St. Thomas's Protestant Episcopal Church 366
Student National Coordinating Committee (SNCC) 290
Student Non-Violent Coordinating Committee (SNCC) 13, 290-291, 232
Studio Museum in Harlem 527
Suber, Jay 485
Sudan 43
Sugar Hill 146
Sugar Hill Gang 503
Sugar Hill Times 464
Suicide 347
Sula 420
Sumner, Charles 174, 271
Sumner Elementary School 177
Sunday School Publishing Board 486
Super Fly 456
The Supremes 130, 500, 501
Suriname 73
Survival of the Black Family: The Institutional Impact of U.S. Social Policy 338
Sutton, Percy 293, 476, 480
Swain, John 171
Swan Lake 443
Swazi 52
Swaziland 52
Sweatt, Herman Marion 264, 358
Sweatt v. Painter 256, 264
Sweet Auburn Historic District 162
Sweet Charity 441
Sweet Daddy Grace 375
Sweet Sweetback's Baadasssss Song 456
Swing High 451
Symphonic Concertante 515

207

INDEX

Symphony in E Minor 514, 515
Symphony of the New World 516

T

Take a Giant Step 436
"Take the A Train" 147
"Take These Chains from My Heart" 498
Talladega College 354
Talladega College and Swayne Hall 153
Tallman Restorations 134
Tallman, William M. 134
Tan 477
Tandy, Vertner Woodson 144
Taney, Roger Brook 157, 258
Tanganyika 46
Tanksley, Ann 527
Tanner, Henry Ossawa 150, 153, 518, 520, 531-532
Tanzania 45
Tar Baby 419, 420
Tate, Larenz 472
Tatum, Art 507
Taureg 32
Taylor, Cecil 510
Taylor, Robert 525
Taylor, Susan 478
Teenage pregnancy 310, 343
Television 446, 464-472
Tell My Horse 419
Temple, Lewis 142
Temple, Shirley 450
The Temptations 130
10th Cavalry 181, 560
Terrell, Mary Church 169, 284
Terry, Lucy 417
Tex, Joe 499
Thaddeus Stevens Grave Site 150
Tharp, Twyla 524
That's My Mama 468
Thea 472

Theater Four 439
Theodore Drury Colored Opera Company 512
Third World Press 489
Thirteenth Amendment 92, 225, 227, 257-259
Thirty Years of Lynching in the United States, 1889-1918 488
Thomas Baily & Sons 322
Thomas, C. Edward 515
Thomas, Clarence 17, 257, 261-262
Thomas, Debi 552
Thomas, Edna 436
Thomas, William Henry (Buckwheat) 449
Thompson, Bob 527
Thompson, Clive 440, 442
Thompson, Robert Ferris 532
Thompson, William 575
Thrash, Dox 522
Threadgill, Robert 527
Three Black Kings 442
Three Years in Europe 417
Thriller 490
Tidal Basin Bridge 170
"Tight Like That" 492
Tilden, Samuel 227
Timbuktu 213
Tindley, Charles Albert 491
TLC Beatrice International Holdings Inc. 315, 325, 327
Tobago 67
Togo 33, 34
The Toilet/The Slave 439
Tolson, Melvin B. 425
Tolton, Augustine 128
Tom and Jerry 431
Tombalbaye, François 37
Tom Lee Memorial 159
Tones 443
Tongues Untied 485
Tony Brown's Journal 473, 484
Toomer, Jean 424

Toomes, Lloyd 527
Torrence, Ridgely 433
To Sir with Love 454
Tougaloo College 354
Toure, Kwame (see Stokely Carmichael)
Toure, Samory 29, 32
Toussaint L'Ouverture 62, 247
Towne, Laura 164
Townsend, Robert 447-448
Townsend, Ronald 484
T. P. Parham and Associates 322
Tracy, Spencer 454
Trading Places 457
Trail, William 128
TransAfrica 294
Travis, Dempsey 489
Travis, Jack 525
Treemonisha 513, 517
Trinidad 67
Trip to Coontown 429, 432
The Triumph of Love 431
Trotter, William Monroe 142, 284
Troubled Island 436
Troy Game 443
Truman, Harry S 10, 106, 160, 228, 289, 574
Truth, Sojourner 129, 223, 271, 371
T. Thomas Fortune House 143
Tubman, Harriet 4, 143, 224, 270-271, 284, 470
Tucker, Lem 482
Tucker, William 1, 2, 216
Turks and Caicos Islands 68
Turnbull, Walter 517
Turner, Big Joe 494
Turner, Henry McNeal 250, 372
Turner, Nat 82, 163, 248, 371
Turner, Ted 485
Turner Theological Seminary 379
Tuskegee Airmen 154, 568

INDEX

Tuskegee Institute Press 487
Tuskegee Normal and Industrial Institute 8, 153, 156, 165, 229, 273, 353, 487, 525, 539
Tutsi 45
"Tutti Frutti" 497
Twelve Years a Slave 88
24th Infantry Regiment 172, 180, 560
25th Infantry Regiment 560
Twilight, Alexander Lucius 268
Two Trains Running 440
227 470
Tyson, Cicely 439, 456, 458, 464, 469-470
Tyson, Mike 550, 553

U

Uganda 46
Uggams, Leslie 441, 470
"Uncle Jack" 371
Uncle Remus: His Songs and His Sayings 419
Uncle Tom's Cabin 4, 133, 134, 137, 139, 446
Underground Railroad 4, 7, 15, 74, 135, 143, 177, 224
Underground Railroad Marker 132
Unemployment 306
Union Church of Africans 380
Union Insurance and Realty Company 322
United Negro Improvement Association 380
United States Colored Troops 559
United States Commission for the Relief of the National Freedm 352
United States Constitution 218
Universal Negro Improvement Association (UNIA) 102, 245, 250, 287, 489

University of Islam 360
Unseld, Wes 546
Up against the Wall 462
Upper Volta 25
Up Tight 455
Uptown Saturday Night 457
Urban Research Press 489
Uridin, Jalal 502
U.S. Episcopal Church 366
U.S.S. *Arizona* 573
U.S.S. *Arizona* Memorial 174
U.S.S. *Enterprise* 574
U.S.S. *George Washington Carver* 574
U.S.S. *Intrepid* 573
U.S.S. *Iowa* 563
U.S.S. *Jesse L. Brown* 574
U.S.S. *Liscome Bay* 573
U.S.S. *Maine* 561
U.S.S. *Miller* 574
U.S.S. *San Francisco* 574

V

Van Buren, Martin 136
Vanderhorst, Richard 381
Van Der Zee, James 527
Vann, Robert 566
Van Peebles, Mario 448
Varick, James 369, 380
Vaughn, Lyn 485
Venezuela 72, 73
Vereen, Ben 444, 470
Vesey, Denmark 164, 247, 370
Victoria, Queen 50
Victory Monument 128
Vidale, Thea 472
Vidor, King 450
Vietnam War 574-575
Vincent, Eddie "Cleanhead" 494
Violence 336, 337
Virginia Union University 354
Virgin Islands 68
Voodoo 366

Voter Education Project 277
Voting Rights Act (1965) 235, 241, 257, 277, 289

W

Walcott, Derek 418
Walk Hard 436
Walker, Alice 160, 427, 428, 458, 463
Walker, David 223, 247
Walker, George 433, 437, 438, 515
Walker, Jimmie 467-468
Walker, Madame C. J. 144, 315, 319-320
Walker, Maggie Lena 166, 167
Walker, Rachel 512
Walker, T-Bone 494, 497
Wallace, George 153
Waller, Thomas "Fats" 441
Walling, William English 284, 285
Walters, Alexander 285
Warbourg, Eugene 519
Ward, Billy 495
Ward, Douglas Turner 437, 439
Ward, Francis 242
Ward, Theodore 430
Wardlaw, Alia J. 532
Waring, Laura Wheeler 521
Warmoth, H. C. 268
Warner, Malcolm-Jamal 472
War on Poverty 235, 277
Warren, Earl 107
Washington Bee 474
Washington, Booker T. 6, 8, 95, 153, 156, 165, 167, 229, 262, 273, 284, 305, 318-319, 353, 474, 487, 539
Washington, Denzel 440, 461
Washington, George 79, 147, 557
Washington 136

209

INDEX

The Washington Post 481
Water Boy 521
Waters, Ethel 435, 436
Waters, Maxine 237
Waters, Muddy 497
Watson, Clifford 362
Watson, Johnny "Guitar" 501
Watts Riot (1965) 14, 238-239
Wayans, Damon 472
Wayans, Keenan Ivory 472
Wayans, Kim 472
Wayans, Shawn 472
"We Are the World" 501
W. E. B. Du Bois Homesite 141
Weaver, Faith 530
Weaver, Robert 9
Weaver, Robert C. 268
The Weekly Anglo-African 249
Welburn, Edward T. 526
Wells-Barnett, Ida B. 100, 126, 228-229, 476
Wells, Mary 130, 501
"We're a Winner" 498
"We Shall Overcome" 491
Wesley, John 367
Western World Reporter 479
West Indies 62
Westside Preparatory School 361
Wharton, Clifton R., Jr. 281
"What I'd Say" 496
What's Happening 468-469
Wheatley, Phillis 133, 141, 417, 419, 422, 519
Whitaker, Hudson "Tampa Red" 492
White, Bill 545, 554-555
White, Charles 521, 523, 528
White, Dwight 548
White, Effie Melody 441
Whitefield, George 367
White, Maurice 501
White, Michael 276
White, Slappy 438, 444
White, Walter 287

Whitman, Walt 150
Whitney, Eli 8, 216, 218
Whitney Foundation 518
"Whole Lotta Loving" 497
Wilberforce University 354, 379
Wilberforce, William 354
Wilder, Gene 457
Wilder, L. Douglas 17, 268
Wilkins, Roy 149, 287, 289, 290
Wilks, Gertrude 360
William C. Nell House 141
William Christopher Handy Birthplace 152
William Christopher Handy Park 159
William Monroe Trotter House 142
Williams, Armstrong 480
Williams, Bert 432, 433, 437-438
Williams, Billy Dee 458
Williams, Daniel Hale 125, 127, 533, 539
Williams, Delores 375
Williams, Doug 548
Williams, George Washington 355
Williams, Hank 498
Williams, Marion 440
Williams, Marshall 439
Williamson, Richard 280
Williams, Paul R. 525
Williams, Peter 249
Williams, Randy 527, 530
Williams, Vanessa 17
Williams, Walter 16, 314
Williams, Walter E. 279
Willis, Ben 548
Will Marion Cook Residence 149
Wilson, Arthur Dooley 436
Wilson, August 440
Wilson, Billy 442
Wilson, Brenda 485

Wilson, Dooley 435
Wilson, Dudley 442
Wilson, Flip 444
Wilson, Margaret Bush 286-287
Wilson, Teddy 507
Wimberly, Frank 527
Winchester, Jesse 498
Winfield, Hemsley 437
Winfield, Paul 456
Winfrey, Oprah 17, 305, 458, 460, 473, 476, 484
Winslow, Vernon 495
Winter, Marian Hannah 432
Wisconsin Historical Society 135
Within Our Gates 448
The Wiz 429, 441
The Wizard of Oz 441
Woman Resting 529
Women in Sports 551
The Women of Brewster Place 458
Wonder, Stevie 130
Woodard, Charlene 441
Wood, Donna 442
Woodruff, Hale 153, 521, 522, 527
Woods, Granville T. 535
Woods, Love B. 146
Woodson, Carter G. 167, 356, 488
Woodson, Robert L. 279, 305
Woodson, Robert, Sr. 16
Woodward, Sidney 512
Wordlaw, Gary 484
Work, John W. 487
Work, Monroe N. 487
Works Project Administration 518
"Work with Me Annie" 496
World Community of Al-Islam in the West 384
World Saxophone Quartet 511
A World View of Race 488
World War I 562-564

210

INDEX

World War II 565
Wright, Dolores 530
Wright, Elizabeth 279
Wright, Richard 418, 425
Wright, Will 484

Y

Yaraborough, Sara 442
The Yellow Tavern 163
Yordan, Philip 436
York 175, 179
Yorkin, Bud 466
"You Beat Me to the Punch" 501
"You Don't Know Me" 498
Young, Charles 134
Young, Charles A. 561
Young, Graylian 485
Young, Lester 507
Young, Whitney M., Jr. 287, 290
"Your Cheating Heart" 498
"You're on My Mind" 498
"You Send Me" 496
Youth Unemployment 310
Yucca Plantation 155

Z

Zaire 39, 45
Zambia 47, 48
Zanzibar 46
Zenobia 451
Ziegfield Follies 433
Zimbabwe 48, 49
Zora Neale Hurston Grave Site 160
Zora Neale Hurston Memorial 160
Zulu 51, 52

SEP - 9 1994
21.00

SOUTH HUNTINGTON PL
0652 9100 053 754 8

474131

JR   Estell, Kenneth
973   The African-American
      Almanac (Volume 1)

Reference Children Dept.

South Huntington Public Library
Huntington Station, New York
11746

005

For Reference

Not to be taken from this room

DISCARDED